MULTICULTURALISM

Multiculturalism

Roots and Realities

Edited by C. James Trotman

INDIANA
University Press

Bloomington & Indianapolis

This book is a publication of
Indiana University Press
601 North Morton Street
Bloomington, IN 47404-3797 USA

http://iupress.indiana.edu

Telephone orders 800-842-6796
Fax orders 812-855-7931
Orders by e-mail iuporder@indiana.edu

© 2002 by Indiana University Press

The paper used in this publication meets the minimum requirements of American National Standard for Information Sciences—Permanence of Paper for Printed Library Materials, ANSI Z39.48-1984.

Manufactured in the United States of America

Library of Congress Cataloging-in-Publication Data

Multiculturalism : roots and realities / edited by C. James Trotman.
p. cm.
Includes bibliographical references and index.
ISBN 0-253-34002-0 (cloth : alk. paper) — ISBN 0-253-21487-4 (pbk. : alk. paper)
1. African Americans—Social conditions—19th century. 2. African Americans—Intellectual life—19th century. 3. African Americans—Race identity. 4. Pluralism (Social sciences)—United States—History—19th century. 5. United States—Race relations. 6. African Americans in literature. 7. Pluralism (Social sciences) in literature. 8. Race relations in literature. 9. American literature—African American authors—History and criticism. 10. American literature—19th century—History and criticism. I. Trotman, C. James, date
E185.86 .M946 2002
305.896'073'009034—dc21

2001004274

1 2 3 4 5   07 06 05 04 03 02

Acknowledgments

Different settings and many different persons are a major part of this book's history. The stories behind them are rich and much more deserving than these few words can offer.

There is my own dining room table where the possibilities of an academic program using Frederick Douglass were outlined with my colleagues Patricia Grasty Gaines and Jerry Williams early in the 1990s. There was the telephone call to Seattle, Washington that brought Jacob and Gwen Lawrence to grace our campus in 1994 to help us celebrate the Douglass centennial. There has been the exceptional support of the scholars who patiently supported this project until it could find its place in the capable and sensitive editorial direction of Indiana University Press.

None of these developments would have taken place without the discovery by West Chester University students of the unique relationship between the very courageous and prolific Frederick Douglass and the campus that tries to do justice to its newly found educational legacy.

Chris Kwame Awuyah, Geetha Ramanathan, Kim Browne, Frank Helms, and Frank Faragasso of the National Park Service have been more than just colleagues during the process that has completed this phase of the Douglass Institute. Their advice and wisdom have been invaluable.

Finally, with praise to the God of justice and peace, I thank Him for bringing the life of Frederick Douglass before me, and always for the love and support I receive from Anita, Thane, and Braeden.

C. James Trotman
West Chester University
October 17, 2001

Contents

Contents

Introduction

Multiculturalism: Roots and Realities

C. James Trotman

As one of today's most important and intensely debated terms, *multiculturalism* has become a conceptual flash point inviting some of the most stimulating and acrimonious discussions within and outside of the academic community. To some it is an idea about diversity. If we see the world from the perspective of many cultures and histories, we are in a better position to understand the past and the world today. To others the term represents the end of European dominance, a balkanization of heritage and legacy at the expense of time-honored western traditions. However, in its simplest, most basic context, multiculturalism is the name for an approach that shows us another way of using knowledge to understand ideas and events. Most often a multicultural approach uses several disciplines to highlight neglected aspects of our social history, particularly the histories of women and minorities. Concepts of race, class, culture, gender, and ethnicity are the driving themes of a multicultural approach, which also promotes respect for the dignity of the lives and voices of the forgotten. By closing gaps, by raising consciousness about the past, multiculturalism tries to restore a sense of wholeness in a postmodern era that fragments human life and thought. Whether community is always attained or not is difficult to say because multiculturalism is still evolving.

The most meaningful support for multiculturalism has come from intellectuals, such as those represented in this book, who have discovered greater meaning in our American past by incorporating these conceptual themes into their thought and work. The essays presented here move along the spectrum of the controversy surrounding multiculturalism. They engage the word and its meanings, as varied as they are, in an effort to expand the dialog around this increasingly vital concept. However, instead of encountering a debate, readers will immediately discover that each essay generally uses multiculturalism as a way of examining history and social themes, while providing a broader and perhaps deeper view of nineteenth-century American life and thought. I hope, however, that this book will encourage other scholars to pursue its mission. This mission, which belongs to all of us, is to recognize excellence through extending scholarship, usually but not exclusively found in the cultures of the historically neglected, claim excellence where it is found, and position it so as to contribute to a fuller understanding of the human condition.

Ronald Takaki, for example, a renowned multiculturalist, describes multiculturalism in subjective terms as a reference point for examining history. "Where am I?" he implicitly asks. "Where are my culture and my contributions to this nation?" (Takaki, 2). Takaki's concerns are not purely rhetorical. Rather, they are framed by a familiar awareness expressed by the historically marginalized. As an American of Japanese ancestry, Professor Takaki traces his family's American roots to the 1880s, but except for the most stereotyped experiences he is unable to identify his group's collective role in American life. This experience creates unnecessary levels of frustration that lead quite frequently to themes of alienation, which are found often in multicultural writings. The poet Langston Hughes reflected upon diversity and our nation's struggle with it in one of his most famous poems, "I, Too."

> I, too, sing America.
> I am the darker brother.
> They send me to eat in the kitchen
> When company comes,
> But I laugh,
> And eat well,
> And grow strong.
> Tomorrow,
> I'll be at the table
> When company comes.
> Nobody'll dare
> Say to me,
> "Eat in the kitchen,"
> Then.
> Besides,

Introduction

They'll see how beautiful I am
And be ashamed—
I, too, am America.

For Hughes and Takaki, multiculturalism is a dynamic concept that can energize the individual into searching for an authentic depiction of self and group life.

The essays in this book made their public debut as conference papers delivered at "Voices of the Nineteenth Century: Roots and Realities of Multiculturalism" on the campus of West Chester University of Pennsylvania, October 12–13, 1994. The conference inaugurated a yearlong national commemoration of the centennial of the death of Frederick Douglass (1818–1895), the famous black abolitionist who was a major voice in nearly every significant nineteenth-century American movement. The celebration included far more than this one conference. The Smithsonian's National Portrait Gallery drew thousands with its exhibit "Majestic in His Wrath: The Life of Frederick Douglass." The Library of Congress and the National Park Service co-sponsored a symposium on Douglass. Most important, a new generation started reading the 1845 story that brought him fame, *The Narrative of the Life of Frederick Douglass, An American Slave, Written by Himself.*

The presence of Frederick Douglass in this book commemorates an extraordinary life, the life of a man who celebrated the themes driving multiculturalism even before the word was part of our national conversation. Douglass, as we shall see, is an anchor and an exemplary figure for having had meaningful discussions on race, class, culture, gender, and ethnicity, the themes driving multiculturalism. As a fugitive slave, orator, abolitionist, autobiographer, journalist, diplomat, and consummate public servant, Douglass stands indomitably in his time as an eloquent symbol for freedom. In our time, however, and in the context of this book, Douglass provides us with a glimpse of the potential of multiculturalism to sharpen our methods of scholarly investigation and to be more culturally diverse while doing so. The experience of one campus with Frederick Douglass may serve to illustrate that valuable discoveries can come from many sources.

In 1993, students in my African-American literature course, on an assignment to research Douglass, were the first to discover that the great abolitionist gave his last public lecture on February 1, 1895, at West Chester University in West Chester, Pennsylvania. More searches uncovered the lecture's title ("Against Lynch Law") and content from a report published in the local newspaper the next day. The archives of the West Chester University library contained little-known letters exchanged between Douglass and his hosts before his visit, including a letter from his second wife, Helen Pitts Douglass, confirming that this was his last formal public lecture. And the West Chester campus, which is about twenty-five miles southwest of Philadelphia, Pennsylvania, in the historic Brandywine River area, celebrated this discovery of its Douglass legacy by holding an academic conference in his honor. What exactly is Douglass's legacy in American history and how does it embody multiculturalism today?

The abolitionists of the nineteenth century knew Frederick Douglass as the representative voice declaring the chattel slave's desire and human right to be free. In an age of oratory, the self-taught Douglass added to his speaking brilliance by writing the tension-filled 1845 *Narrative*, which is now viewed as an American classic. He followed the autobiography by founding *The North Star*, a newspaper, in 1847, and this entry into journalism further widened his influence and authority. The suffrage movement knew him as the only male public figure to support the Declaration of Sentiments and women's right to vote at the Seneca Falls Convention of 1848. American presidents from Abraham Lincoln through Grover Cleveland knew Douglass as an advisor and consultant on many public issues. The international community knew him as a commissioner to the Dominican Republic in 1871 and as ambassador to Haiti in 1889.

Today's scholarship has strengthened Douglass's place in American history and has positioned his life and work as a standard for a variety of uses in historical and cultural studies. Nathan Huggins's *Slave and Citizen* (1980) and David Blight's *Frederick Douglass' Civil War* (1989) framed Douglass's politics, as their titles suggest, around the great themes and events of the republic. Historian William McFeely published a celebrated biography titled *Frederick Douglass* in 1991, one of many studies of Douglass's life that have appeared in the last century. Political and intellectual themes were explored in Robert S. Levine's *Martin Delany, Frederick Douglass, and the Politics of Representative Identity* (1997). For Gregory Lampe, the historical record was enriched by a study of the early influences on the orator's skill as a speaker, and in 1998 he published *Frederick Douglass: Freedom's Voice, 1818–1845*. In 1999, the cultural historian Maria Diedrich informed readers about Douglass's controversial relationship with the German-born Ottilie Assing in *Love across Color Lines*.

By the time of his death in 1895, Douglass, then known as the Sage of Anacostia, was an American social and political icon whose passionate and articulate denunciations of slavery had made him famous. For the sons and daughters of slaves, Douglass was the image of freedom in the flesh; for many others, his demand that freedom be the right of all Americans was a reminder of the irreducible standard in a democracy. Is there any wonder, therefore, that when revisionists and advocates for multiculturalism look for a standard-bearer from our past to lean on for support, the courageous, talented, and prolific Frederick Douglass is a strong and useful figure?

In this book's opening essay, based on his keynote lecture at the "Voices of the Nineteenth Century" conference, Henry Louis Gates, Jr., writes that a rigorous multiculturalism promotes an inclusiveness that is committed to closing conceptual gaps and that also offers fresh images of human excellence. A major voice shaping the concept of multiculturalism, Professor Gates discusses Douglass, diversity, and the impact of multiculturalism on the academic community and public policy. Gates reminds us of the intellectual role that Frederick Douglass played in bringing to the surface various problems in American life, many of which, particularly in the area of social equity, still exist. Gates also calls attention to a particular quality of multicultural scholarship: it can not only examine a period more closely, though that is always valuable and desirable, but also identify new relationships between the subject at hand and its historical context. The first part of this book, "Frederick Douglass and Slave Narratives," considers those relationships. It begins with essays that study Douglass and the literary and social significance of the slave narrative, which he influenced, of course, with his own 1845 *Narrative*.

Julie Husband opens the section by examining Douglass's rhetorical strategies. She sees the gifted orator as using public speech and journalism as instruments for abolishing slavery and, at the same time, as part of his search for political common ground in America. Her focus on Douglass's rhetoric and his vision of America leads Husband to establish an unusual association between Douglass and Dr. Martin Luther King, Jr. The relationship between the famous fugitive slave and the famous preacher who called himself a "drum major for justice" links two of our best-known freedom fighters in two centuries: men of one nation, but a nation without a history of racial peace and harmony.

Jeannine DeLombard, in an essay that reaches beyond national borders, argues for specific cultural ties between Harriet Jacobs's well-known autobiographical narrative, *Incidents in the Life of a Slave Girl*, and accounts that have come from Jewish holocaust testimonial literature and from Latin American women. It is a multicultural, multinational record written against the background of several women's experiences in bondage. Richard Hardack ends the first section with his work on the travel motif in the slave narrative. This motif has gained more attention recently because more questions are being asked about the life of the individual chattel slave. No longer perceived as being numbed by the slave experience, slaves who traveled are now seen to have provided a trail of freedom ways, documenting degradation and their desire to be free. Hardack uses Douglass symbolically to consider the meaning of travel in the 1845 *Narrative* as a ritual that explains the ways that Douglass and other slaves found to survive.

"Race and Slavery" is the focus of the second section of the book. The title epitomizes two of the major conflicts and contradictions in American life. As an experiment in political freedom, America has always been its own best hermeneutic, its own instrument for determining progress toward our becoming "one nation, indivisible." Nevertheless, in pursuing freedom, the republic denied freedom to some and thus handicapped all. Are we colonists or conquerors, venerable democrats or racist despots in disguise? Frederick Douglass's response to this question was expressed in terms that are certainly appreciated by multiculturalists today. He registered this response in a speech titled "The Claims of the Negro Ethnologically Considered," which he gave on July 12, 1852, before the faculty and graduating class of Western Reserve College in Ohio. In it Douglass named specific authors, their works, and their contributions to the racist rhetoric of the day. His point was to emphasize the ethical error of any field of knowledge whose scientific results denigrated a culture and excluded our common humanity. Ultimately, Douglass asserted, scholars were making race a divisive element by ignoring the distinctive social and historical features of African cultures. The consequence, as Douglass saw it, was not just neglect but actions that created opportunities, almost a license, for human bondage.

"Race and Slavery," the second section of the book, brings together discussions of nineteenth-century historical figures and the impact of race and slavery on them, beginning with essays by Julie Winch and Verner D. Mitchell. Each scholar argues for a re-examination of these largely neglected themes, which enhance our picture of nineteenth-century America, but for entirely different reasons. Winch describes the life of the wealthy James Forten and his influence in Philadelphia, and explores his influence within the evolving social class conventions of Philadelphia's "black elite." For Mitchell, the realities of race, religion and relationships, the three Rs of much of cultural studies, have the strongest implications in his treatment of the apocalyptic vision of the fiery David Walker.

Barbara J. Ballard writes about the Chicago World's Fair of 1893. Es-

Introduction

tablished by an act of Congress and intended to celebrate Columbus's expedition, the Fair displayed the wealth and sophistication of the western world, and particularly the United States, but deliberately avoided any representation of African-American contributions to American life. This omission outraged many in the black community, including Frederick Douglass and the journalist Ida B. Wells, both of whom decided to do something about it. As Ballard relates it, this episode establishes an often-neglected link between black culture in North America and in the Afro-Caribbean culture of Haiti, this hemisphere's second oldest democracy. Haiti's pavilion at the Fair became a place for black Americans to protest the much-debated nineteenth-century racist notion that civilization and Africa had little or nothing to do with each other. "Race and Slavery" ends with Christine Palumbo-DeSimone writing about the double burden of racial and sexual identity as it specifically relates to a category of black womanhood, the mulatta. While African-American literature and social history concerning black women have been popular, this article describes and examines the complex history of power relations between social conventions and those who are physically branded by the scarlet letter of "mixed-race" labeling. The essay leads to a broader consideration of women and their voices, which is the subject of the next section, "Images of Women."

"Images of Women" begins with an essay by Susan Alves, whose subject is working-class white women in New England. Their voices, compelling in tone and content, are rarely heard in the traditional canon of American literature. Alves demonstrates how the language of slavery, its metaphors of bondage and subservience, became part of the rhetoric of activism among white female mill workers in the North. At the same time, the essay offers additional insight into the way feminism and sexuality interact to construct a white racial identity. Next, Juniper Ellis examines the famous twentieth-century writer Zora Neale Hurston and compares her work with that of the nineteenth-century folklorist Joel Chandler Harris. Ellis puts them on common ground as ethnographers of Southern black culture. This comparison leads to some fresh insights into the preservation of oral cultures that are part of a multicultural base in literature and ethnography. The final essay in "Images of Women" assesses the contribution of a woman often forgotten but now being reintroduced to today's readers. Richard E. Greene discusses the life and the historical importance of Abby Kelley Foster, a Quaker whose voice contributed to both the feminist and the abolitionist movements.

"Exploring the Canon" is the final section of this anthology. This group of essays reinforces a major premise in multicultural scholarship.

Multiculturalism's principle of intentionally including the historically marginalized also serves to stimulate re-examinations of familiar personalities and ideas in social history.

Janet Harrison Shannon returns the historical focus to antebellum America and considers the neglected stories of children. Her essay documents the mistreatment of children, mostly black, who were indentured servants to the wealthy in Philadelphia. While Shannon's essay brings out the sordid lives of these children, the familiarity of the social stereotype in the adult world allows us to look at our history more closely and more analytically. Matthew Wilson contributes to our understanding of Sambo and the plantation darky, two of the most provocative racist images in our history. Wilson's work shows the correlation between literature and its historical context by discussing the stories of Charles W. Chesnutt and Stephen Crane, two well-respected nineteenth-century American writers.

The essays by Gillian Johns and Joe B. Fulton call attention to scholarship inspired by the discourse on multiculturalism. Johns's review of work on William Wells Brown reveals that existing scholarship has neglected major parts of Wells's work, thus giving only a partial picture of an escaped slave whose life is strikingly similar to Frederick Douglass's. Lastly, Fulton builds on an influential thesis about the uses of black voices in Twain's work. The efforts of both scholars are a harbinger of multiculturalism's ability to refine and extend existing scholarship.

Multiculturalism: Roots and Realities engages an American society already divided over what it is and what it wants to be. The new century finds most Americans publicly rejecting the behavior of a racist cultural past, if they acknowledge it at all, without ever having looked at its causes and consequences except through the filtered lens of what is known and safe. *Multiculturalism: Roots and Realities* does not take a safe path for either scholars or readers. The revisions and reclamations of our history will continue, of course. The ultimate contribution of these essays will be to raise standards and move us closer to a deeper human understanding of nineteenth-century America and its multicultural society.

Perhaps Frederick Douglass's own words about his career ably summarize the mission. Multiculturalism is an important contribution to "a sort of rounding up of the arch to the point where the keystone may be inserted, the scaffolding removed, and the work, with all its perfections or faults, left to speak for itself" (Douglass, 844). Hopefully, these essays will move us closer to the keystone.

References

Douglass, Frederick. *Autobiographies.* New York: The Library of America, 1996.

Gordon, Avery F., and Christopher Newfield. *Mapping Multiculturalism.* Minneapolis: University of Minnesota Press, 1996.

Henderson, Mae, ed. *Borders, Boundaries, and Frames: Cultural Criticism and Cultural Studies.* New York: Routledge, 1995.

Hughes, Langston. *The Collected Poems of Langston Hughes.* Edited by Arnold Rampersad. New York: Knopf, 1994.

Levine, Lawrence W. *The Opening of the American Mind: Canon, Culture, and History.* Boston: Beacon Press, 1996.

McClintock, Anne, Aamir Mufti, and Ella Shohat. *Dangerous Liaisons: Gender, Nation, and Postcolonial Perspectives.* Minneapolis: University of Minnesota Press, 1997.

Takaki, Ronald. *A Different Mirror: A History of Multicultural America.* Boston: Little, Brown, 1993.

MULTICULTURALISM

One

"The Lives Grown Out of His Life"

Frederick Douglass, Multiculturalism, and Diversity

Henry Louis Gates, Jr.

When it is finally ours, this freedom, this liberty, this beautiful
and terrible thing, needful to man as air,
usable as earth; when it belongs at last to all,
when it is truly instinct, brain matter, diastole, systole,
reflex action; when it is finally won; when it is more
than the gaudy mumbo jumbo of politicians:
this man, this Douglass, this former slave, this Negro
beaten to his knees, exiled, visioning a world
where none is lonely, none hunted, alien,
this man, superb in love and logic, this man
shall be remembered. Oh, not with statues' rhetoric,
not with legends and poems and wreaths of bronze alone,
but with the lives grown out of his life, the lives
fleshing his dream of the beautiful, needful thing.
    —Robert Hayden, "Frederick Douglass"

A friend of mine, who happens to be a woman and black and a film-maker, was invited recently by a Hollywood production company to pitch a few ideas for features that would be based upon the African-American literary tradition: how far we have come. First, my friend suggested Zora Neale Hurston's 1937 novel, *Their Eyes Were Watching God,* but she was told it had been optioned already to Oprah Winfrey and Quincy Jones. "So how about *Beloved*" (1987), she said, "by Toni Morrison, of course?" "Oprah," was the reply. Ralph Ellison's *Invisible Man* (1952)—Quincy Jones had already optioned that. Next my friend told a story of Harriet Jacobs's harassment by the evil Dr. Flint and her seven years of hiding in her grandmother's attic, from *Incidents in the Life of a Slave Girl* (1861). No one would believe it, the executive responded. Frustrated, angry, wondering why she had bothered with this fruitless enterprise, my friend told the well-known anecdote reported by Profes-

1

sor Peter Walker in his stellar essays on Frederick Douglass collected in his book *Moral Choices*.

By the end of 1894, Frederick Douglass had begun to prepare for his death. Unbowed and energetic even till the last, Douglass had, however, apparently reconciled himself to live and rejoice, as he put it in his autobiography in 1881: "to occupy with dignity and gravity the peculiar role conferred upon [him] by friend and foe alike." To his black countrymen and white, contemporaries and disciples, he was the representative colored man of the United States. But despite the unassailable respect that he commanded throughout the country, one bit of ordinary knowledge had never been Douglass's to possess and, as Peter Walker movingly recounts, the final entry in his diary suggests that it haunted him to his death.

On a March evening in 1894, just less than a year before he died, Frederick Douglass left his home at Anacostia and boarded a train for the brief ride from Washington to Baltimore. At Baltimore, Douglass went directly to the home of the physician Thomas Edward Sears. After a carefully calculated but leisurely conversation, during which Douglass put to Dr. Sears a series of specifically formulated questions, Douglass returned by train to Washington and then by coach to Anacostia Heights. Early the next day he went to his study, took out his diary, and wrote as that day's entry an account of this trip to Baltimore. Now this was to be the final entry in Douglass's diary. In the months remaining to him, no event moved Douglass sufficiently to record another. Indeed, no other event had moved Douglass to make an entry since he had made an apparently hurried note in the diary when he was in London six years earlier.

Douglass's visit with Dr. Sears can be called, without hyperbole, a mission. It was not that these two men had so much in common, nor that through their visit they sought to cement a friendship about to end. Rather, Sears, the descendant of Douglass's old master, would be the last contact Douglass was to have with the family that had once owned him. But more important, Sears had some information about his slave past that Frederick Douglass wanted. Throughout his self-conscious life, Douglass had pursued passionately all concrete information about his lost or hidden past.

What sort of information about his past was Douglass seeking from Dr. Sears that day in March of 1894? What sort of private compelling quest could have prevailed upon such a great statesman, so honored, so praised, to make such an odd pilgrimage so near to his own death? Surely it was not to reminisce with Sears about the good old days back in slavery. In Dr. Thomas Edward Sears, Douglass so painfully knew, resided his last opportunity to ascertain once and for all that crucial piece of data about his own origins, which had systematically been denied to Douglass and to the largest part of all black slaves, the absence of which marked the terrible terrain that separated the free person from the slave, and without which even a slave of Douglass's bearing could not recapture and master his own elusive past. Douglass, it turns out, had been in search of his birth date, his lack of certainty about which he called in his diary entry "a most serious trouble."

A slave's deprivation of his birth date has such subtle, yet poignant, impact that Douglass draws upon it at the outset of the first of his three autobiographies as the very first evidence of his personal status as a slave. The skeletal facts of Douglass's journal entry suggest the pathos of the unconsummated quest: "I called yesterday while in Baltimore upon Dr. Thomas Edward Sears, the grandson of Thomas and Lucretia Auld, and I learned the following facts: Captain Thomas Auld was born in 1795, Amanda Auld, his daughter was born in January 28, 1826; Thomas, son of Hugh and Sophia Auld, was born January 1824, and Captain Aaron Anthony died November 14, 1823." The death of Aaron Anthony, Douglass concluded, "makes me fix the year in which I was sent to live with Mr. Hugh Auld in Baltimore as 1825."

At last, with the date of his master's death, Douglass could deduce when he was sent to Baltimore as a boy, the key signpost on his road to freedom. Perhaps emboldened by the specificity of Aaron Anthony's date of death, Douglass concluded this curious diary entry by being even more specific about when in 1825 he had come to Baltimore, even if, like the slaves, he once more dated the passage of time by the movements of the animals and the seasons. But still, even to his death Douglass was haunted by his inability to ascertain his birth date.

"We'll do it!" the Hollywood executive exploded breathlessly, "we'll shoot it with Denzel Washington as the young Frederick Douglass and Morgan Freeman as the old man." It is a mirror, he concluded, of our times. And they are doing it.

Now, among the works in the black tradition written by African-American men, few if any are more widely taught than is the *Narrative of the Life of Frederick Douglass*. Almost 150 years after it was published in Boston, Douglass's slender volume remains invitingly readable, accommodating its rhetorical antitheses to a remarkable range of critical approaches. In two recently published essay collections, for example, one edited by Eric Sundquist and the other by William Andrews, we can see clearly the narrative's wide readability. One essay addresses the masculine ideal in Douglass's "The Heroic Slave," and is counterbalanced by Douglass and the construction of the feminine; a Marxian meditation on Douglass's seizure of the dialectic counters a deconstructive reading of Douglass's language use in slavery.

I could go on reading the ninety-nine titles yielded by my most recent Nexus search. Douglass's texts, particularly the *Narrative* of 1845 and to a lesser extent *My Bondage and My Freedom* (1855), have lent themselves readily to a multiplicity of critical approaches, ranging from feminist and afrocentric to new-historical and deconstructive, psychoanalytic and Marxian. Indeed, when my friend's Hollywood interlocutor responded that the story of Douglass's search for his birth date was a mirror of our times, he was echoing, doubtless unwittingly, the focus of an essay on Douglass by Princeton historian James McPherson, published in 1968, in which he called Douglass's life a "key" to our times.

Douglass's insistence on freedom, McPherson says, has now found its parallel in the civil rights movement. Eighty-five years ago Douglass asserted that agitation about the race problem would go on until blacks were free. "This psychological insight," McPherson continues, "helps to explain the peculiar sense of exhilaration and release exhibited by urban Negro rioters in the 1960s. For them as for Douglass, retaliatory violence against the white man had a cleansing, lifting effect on the spirit and seemed to bring about a psychological, if not physical, emancipation from the intolerable tensions of submission" (xi).

Many texts, of course, can be read in this way, but Douglass's capacity to mirror has an extraordinarily long history starting in 1845, the year of the publication of the *Narrative*. And as I have written elsewhere, that was the year that Frederick Douglass replaced the seemingly unassailable Phillis Wheatley as *the* black invisible sign of reason within abolitionist discourse, beginning what we would later call the "one Negro syndrome."

In his 1941 introduction to Douglass's third autobiography, *The Life and Times of Frederick Douglass*, Alain Locke, the great philosopher, the dean of the Harlem Renaissance, professor at Howard University, identifies this phenomenon as Douglass's capacity to embody what he calls the epical. "In the lightening perspective of the Negro's history in America, the career and character of Frederick Douglass take on more and more the stature and significance of the epical. For in terms of the race experience, his was beyond doubt the symbolic career, typical, on the one hand, of the common lot, but on the other inspiringly representative of outstanding achievement" (xv). Its basic pattern, he says, is that of chattel slave–become-free-man, with the heroic addition of self-emancipation and successful participation in the struggle for group freedom. Superimposed is the dramatic design of a personal history of achievement against great odds, in the course of which the hero becomes both an acknowledged minority leader and spokesman and a general American publicist and statesman.

"Both chance and history conspired toward this," Alain Locke writes, "as [Douglass] himself acknowledges modestly enough in his autobiography. But no one can come away from the reading of it except with the conviction that in mind and character he was in large part, author of his own destiny" (xv). His heroic cast makes the story of Frederick Douglass an imperishable part of the Negro epic and should make his life and times the classic work of American Negro biography. From Harriet Beecher Stowe in 1868 through Charles Chesnutt and Booker T. Washington at the turn of the century, to William Pickens, Arna Bontemps, and Benjamin Quarles in the '40s, Philip Foner, John Blassingame, and Nathan Huggins in the '60s, '70s, and '80s, and David Blight, Waldo Martin, and William McFeely more recently, the life of Frederick Douglass continues to inspire scholars and creative writers to retell it. At least three historical novels figure Frederick Douglass as their protagonist. Douglass's narratives and indeed Frederick Douglass himself have become an ur-text of the African-American tradition, and we can illustrate this rhetoric by even a cursory glance at his biographers.

For Booker T. Washington, Frederick Douglass was a John the Baptist who roamed the deserts of antebellum and Reconstruction America, clearing the way for the great deliverer, Booker T. Washington himself. For Charles Chesnutt, Frederick Douglass was the black man's most cogent response to American pseudo-scientific Social Darwinism at the end of the century. In Benjamin Quarles's biography, Douglass is a black Ragged Dick; indeed, Quarles presents Douglass as the black incarnation of Andrew Carnegie's rise to wealth. For Philip Foner, Douglass is the first great black general in the Marxian warfare between social classes, a war in which Douglass enlisted first to free the Negro masses from chattel slavery, then after emancipation to free them from an oppressive capitalism. And finally for Nathan Huggins, whose title *Slave and Citizen: The Life of Frederick Douglass* echoes both Frank Tannenbaum's *Slave and Citizen* and Ralph Korngold's *Citizen Toussaint,* the life of Frederick Douglass is that of the questing man of color and consciousness in the public arena. This above all else is Huggins's Douglass—the pragmatic black nationalist fighting consistently for full American citizenship between 1841 and 1895.

Now these readings of Douglass, various and contradictory as they are, attest to what Eric Sundquist rightly calls the protean character of his life and writings, as well as his commanding presence in the history of African-American thought. My own uses of Frederick Douglass's work fit this pattern very well. In 1977, for example, I turned to his

1845 narrative to find the site in which to undertake a poststructural reading of the critique of binary oppositions. Four years later, I turned to the anecdote about his poignant search for his birth date—the story that my friend pitched in Hollywood—as an allegory for our generation's quest to reconstruct the African-American canon and concomitantly to revise the larger American canon in that very process.

Here I want to turn to an essay that Frederick Douglass published in 1854, because I find in it an opportunity to consider Douglass within the context of our recent debates about multiculturalism and cultural diversity generally, and the future of African-American studies more specifically. I have another reason, as well. I thought of this essay as I was preparing a short response to the racist implications of Charles Murray and Richard J. Herrnstein's spurious claims in *The Bell Curve: Intelligence and Class in American Life* (1994) that blacks score lower on IQ tests because of unalterable, natural genetic differences. It is natural to turn to Frederick Douglass when thinking about the sordid history of attempts by western pseudoscientists to describe, ostensibly objectively, a set of observable differences—differences of custom, differences of culture, differences of so-called intelligence as measured on an IQ test—and then to ascribe to these differences the fixity and unalterability of nature itself.

Frederick Douglass, of course, confronted this argument squarely in the first chapter of his 1845 *Narrative,* by charting what we might think of as the world the master made through a series of extensively fixed and unalterable binary oppositions, and then critiquing, or exploding, these oppositions by revealing them to be both arbitrary and conventional, socially constructed, and not a part of a natural, divinely ordained order. He returned to this theme and this great task nine years later in an address that he delivered at Western Reserve College on July 12, 1854. The address was titled "The Claims of the Negro Ethnologically Considered."

Douglass begins by stating the urgency of the matter, insisting upon the apparently moral nature of sound scholarship and stating that "the relation subsisting between the white and black people of this country is the vital question of the age. In the solution of this question the scholars of America will have to take an important and controlling part. This is the moral battlefield to which their country and their God now call them. In the eyes of both, the neutral scholar is an ignoble man. Here a man must be hot, or be accounted cold or, perchance something worse than hot or cold. The lukewarm and the cowardly will be rejected" (Douglass 500). Douglass then sets out to establish, first, that "the Ne-

gro is a man"; second, that human beings of all sorts of shapes constitute one unified species, a unified human community; and third, that
the ancient Egyptians, "the grandest of all the nations of antiquity, the
builders of the pyramids," as Douglass puts it, underscoring his words
there, had what he calls a direct relationship to the Negro race. And,
finally, that the people of Africa are probably one people (517).

Now, I do not have space to do full justice to Frederick Douglass's
carefully crafted refutation of the claim that, as he puts it, the African
is not only an inferior race but a distinct species "naturally and originally different from the rest of mankind, . . . placing him nearer to the
brute than to man" (520). Douglass confesses to his audience early on
that he feels himself on trial, attesting to the urgency that scholarship
and the refutation of racist claims about nature, such as those to be
found in Murray and Herrnstein's book, have had for African-American
scholars since the very origin of our discipline in the nineteenth century. Indeed, I believe that Douglass's 1854 address is one of the foun-
dational gestures in the field of what we now call African-American
studies, because it identifies the pivotal areas into which so many of our
scholarly efforts have tended to fall, wittingly or unwittingly, in the
century and a half since. What are these areas?

The first is the demonstration that persons of African descent are
indeed human beings, because we possess reason and have mastered
its two prime vehicles or conduits: speech and writing. The second, as
I have said, is that despite apparent differences of tradition and culture the human community is fundamentally united. Of this, Douglass
argues,

It is somewhat remarkable that at a time when knowledge is so generally diffuse, when the geography of the world is so well understood, when time and space and the intercourse of nations are almost annihilated, when oceans have become bridges, the earth a
magnificent ball, the hollow sky a dome under which a common
humanity can meet in a friendly calm place, when nationalities are
being swallowed up and the ends of the earth brought together, I
say it is remarkable and it is strange that there is a rise of men
speaking in the name of *science* to forbid the magnificent reunion
of mankind in one brotherhood.

A mortifying proof is here given that the moral growth of a nation, or an age, does not always keep pace with the increase of
knowledge and suggests the necessity of means to increase *human
love with human learning.* (504)

Douglass's third point is that differences in performance (such as the results of an IQ test) that are traceable to environmental causes are imputed through racist reasoning to natural causes. He says,

> The temptation, therefore, to rid the Negro out of the human family is exceedingly strong, and may account somewhat for the repeated attempts on the part of Southern pretenders to science, to cast a doubt over the Scriptural account of the origin of mankind. If the origin and motives of most works opposing the doctrine of a unity of the human race could be ascertained, it may be doubted whether *one* such work could boast an honest parentage.
>
> Pride and selfishness, combined with mental power, never want for a theory to justify them, and when men oppress their fellow men, oppressor ever finds, in the character of the oppressed, a full justification for that oppression. Ignorance and depravity, and the inability to rise from degradation to civilization and respectability, are the most usual allegations against the oppressed.

Furthermore,

> The evils most fostered by slavery and oppression are precisely those which slave holders and oppressors would transfer from their system to the inherent character of their victims. Thus the very crimes of slavery become slavery's best defense. By making the enslaved a character fit only for slavery, they excuse themselves for refusing to make the slave a freeman. A wholesale method of accomplishing this result is to overthrow the instinctive consciousness of the common brotherhood of man. For, let it be once granted that the human race are of multitudinous origin, naturally different in their moral, physical and intellectual capacity, and at once you make plausible a demand for classes, grades, and conditions for different methods of culture, different moral, political and religious institutions, and a chance is left for slavery as a necessary institution.

It is crucial for the scholar, Douglass continues, to chart and find in splendid detail all that accounts for the specificity of all the world's great civilizations: their differences, "their methods of culture, different moral, political, and religious institutions" (507). Their moral, physical, and intellectual capacities, in short: the sort of work that has become a central component of what today can be commonly called multiculturalism. Douglass anticipates the so-called balkanization arguments of scholars such as Arthur Schlesinger and William Bennett (and I use the term "scholar" loosely in the case of the latter) by arguing that we must do so, not to stake a claim for the existence of natural differences, but to argue for "the instinctive consciousness of the common brotherhood of man."

Accordingly, while scholarship, Douglass predicts, will eventually reveal the underlying commonality of black African cultures, it will do so in order to demonstrate African cultures' contribution to the store of the world's great civilizations. Rather than leading to the conclusion that African culture is a thing apart, fissured from the rest, a body of knowledge only to be approached by other Africans, such work will show "that the people of Africa have an African character, as general, as well defined, and as distinct, as half the people of Europe, or the people of Asia; the exceptional differences among them afford no ground for supposing their difference of race. But on the contrary it will be inferred that the people of Africa constitute one great branch of the human family, whose origin may be properly referred to the families of Noah, as can be any other branch of the human family from whom they differ. [This will provide the] ultimate proof of both the intellectual potential of the African and the central role that black African culture has played in the shaping of western civilization itself," Douglass argues. "It is not in my power, in a discourse of this sort, to adduce more than a very small part of the testimony in support of a near relationship between the present enslaved and degraded Negroes and the ancient highly civilized and wonderfully endowed Egyptians." But not only do the humanities as we know them, as they have evolved in the west, turn out to have a black African foundation, Douglass argues; America does as well (517).

American culture is a mosaic, he writes prophetically, using a metaphor that would become central to our cultural wars a century and half later. Dr. James McCune Smith, "himself a colored man, a gentleman and a scholar, alleges—and not without excellent reason," Douglass writes, "that this, our own great nation so distinguished for industry and enterprise, is largely indebted to its composite character." Even England, Douglass said, "that most terrible nation which now threatens the peace of the world to make its will the law of Europe is a grand piece of Mosaic work, in which almost every nation has its most characteristic feature from the wild Tartar to the refined Pole."

Douglass ends by challenging the scholars of the country, as he puts it,

to accept the burden of their roles if not exactly as social engineers, then as those whose work is central in the shaping of public policy in this country, policy that has enormous moral implications. Now whether this population shall by *freedom, industry, virtue and intelligence* be made a blessing to the country and the world or whether their multiplied work shall kindle the vengeance of an offended God will depend upon the conduct of no class so much as upon the Scholars of this country.

"Born, as I was, in obscurity, a stranger to the halls of learning, environed by ignorance, degradation and their concomitants from birth to manhood, I do not feel at liberty to mark out with any degree of confidence or dogmaticism what is the precise vocation of the Scholar," Douglass said modestly. "Yet this I can say as a denizen of the world, and a citizen of a country rolling in the sin and shame of Slavery, the most flagrant and scandalous that ever saw the sun, 'Whatsoever things are true, whatsoever things are honest, whatsoever things are just, whatsoever things are pure, whatsoever things are lovely, whatsoever things are in good report, if there be any virtue and if there be any praise, think on these things.'"

Douglass's challenge confronts us today, when statistics reveal the black community to be fissured by economic differentials of the grossest sort, with 44.8 percent of all black children living at or beneath the poverty line. In 1990, 2,200,080 black men and boys were jailed or imprisoned while 23,000 earned a college degree: a ratio of 99 to 1 compared to a ratio 6 to 1 for white Americans. In 1993, 53 percent of black males between the ages of 25 and 34 were jobless or underemployed, earning wages, as Roger Wilkins reported in *The New York Times* on Oct. 12, 1994, too low to raise a family of four out of poverty. In this context two scholars, Professors Murray and Herrnstein, fabricate a theory of natural intelligence and argue strongly against environmental deficiencies as a cause for black impoverishment. In doing so, they argue against the efficacy of compensatory education programs, against entitlements, and against affirmative action: the affirmative action programs that led so many of us, including me, into the academy and into related professions.

The implications of Frederick Douglass's address for the debates about multiculturalism and cultural diversity and the relation of African-American studies to these debates seem to me to be clear. For Frederick Douglass, if I may extrapolate, a rigorous multiculturalism does not entail when–in–Rome relativism; it forbids it. For relativism is finding a way of not taking other cultures seriously. A rigorous multiculturalism does not entail the elevation of difference over commonality; it rejects it. For such a multiculturalism seems to promote the constricted vistas of ethnic absolutism. And finally a rigorous multiculturalism does not entail the proliferation of vulgar identity politics, for an honest account of ethnic dynamism gives full weight to the forces of assimilationism and convergence as well as those of differentiation and divergence.

Once we manage to sort things out, we might be able to retrieve a viable vision of multiculturalism as an antidote to the ever alluring perils of ethnocentrism and cultural chauvinism. After all, we haven't just entrusted to schools the task of reproducing the democratic polity; we've asked that they improve it, too. We want our schools to teach—as they increasingly do—the story of America as a plural nation with people from different lands who had different and shared experiences, and not simply as a fantasy of Pilgrim triumphalism. But we also want elementary schools to inculcate civic virtues: we want them to discourage youngsters from smoking, from accepting candy from strangers, and from hating brown-skinned people. We do not call for distortion in the name of celebration. The truth will serve very well, thank you.

Cathy Davidson, former president of the American Studies Association, in her inaugural address, spoke about multicultural representation, gender equity, and diversity: just give her good history. Whether social or literary history, the idea of a single American story is a far more dangerous proposition. As Davidson notes, this continent was inhabited by various American cultures long before the Puritans ever made their way to the shore. Slaves and immigrants built much of the country, a country that extends far beyond New England. Roughly half the population has always been female, not all of it was ever heterosexual, and relatively little of it in any gender, racial, or immigrant group has been rich. With this kind of history, in short, who needs special pleading? It may well be that such special pleading is not the province of multiculturalism but the denial of multiculturalism, and that's because Americans have been multiculturalists all along. We've only denied that we've been multiculturalists all along.

We cannot even imagine a culture, if we're honest, that is not multiple in its roots and multiple in its branches. Within African-American studies specifically, Douglass's address would seem to argue that we must insist upon the soundness of scholarly reconsiderations of the relations of sub-Saharan black Africa to Nubia and Egypt and ultimately to the Greeks. We must continue to establish a canon of knowledge and texts about the black world in all its particularity. We do this not to claim for it a status as a species apart, but rather to see it as a part of what we might think of as the rough magic of the cultural mix.

We establish the black particular, Douglass argues, so as to redefine the shape, contours, and colors of the larger indissoluble whole. Neither we nor any other people will ever be respected until we respect our-

selves, Douglass once wrote, and we will never respect ourselves until we have the means to live respectably (168). And this attention to
the redistribution of wealth, to shifting the bell curve of class within
the black community from a preponderance of the impoverished to a
fairer and more equitable distribution of opportunity and wealth—the
claims of the Negro, to paraphrase Frederick Douglass, economically
considered—it seems to me is the ultimate moral challenge confronting
African-American studies in the final decade of the 20th century. To
address it, to quote Frederick Douglass one final time, is to insist upon
the necessity of means *to increase human love with human learning.*

Works Cited

Andrews, William. *The Oxford Frederick Douglass Reader.* New York: Oxford
University Press, 1996.

Blight, David W. *Frederick Douglass's Civil War: Keeping Faith in Jubilee.* Baton
Rouge: Louisiana State University Press, 1989.

Bontemps, Arna. *Frederick Douglass: Slave, Fighter, Freeman.* New York: Knopf,
1959.

Chesnutt, Charles W. *Frederick Douglass.* Boston, 1899.

Davidson, Cathy N. "'Loose Change': Presidential Address to the American
Studies Association, November 4, 1993." *American Quarterly* 46, no. 2 (June
1994): 123–138.

Douglass, Frederick. *The Frederick Douglass Papers: Speeches, Debates, and Interviews.* Series 1, vol. 2. Edited by John W. Blassingame et al. New Haven:
Yale University Press, 1979.

Foner, Philip, ed. *The Life and Writings of Frederick Douglass.* New York: International Publishers, 1995.

Huggins, Nathan I. *Slave and Citizen: The Life of Frederick Douglass.* New
York: Harper Collins, 1980.

Locke, Alain. Introduction to *The Life and Times of Frederick Douglass, Written
by Himself,* by Frederick Douglass. New York: Pathway Press, 1941.

Martin, Waldo E. *The Mind of Frederick Douglass.* Chapel Hill: University of
North Carolina Press, 1985.

McFeely, William S. *Frederick Douglass.* New York: W. W. Norton, 1991.

McPherson, James M. Preface to *Frederick Douglass,* by Benjamin Quarles.
New York, Atheneum Press, 1968.

Murray, Charles, and Richard J. Herrnstein. *The Bell Curve: Intelligence and
Class Structure in American Life.* New York: Free Press, 1994.

Pickens, William. *Bursting Bonds: The Heir of Slaves: The Autobiography of a
"New Negro."* Edited by William L. Andrews. Bloomington: Indiana University Press, 1991.

Quarles, Benjamin. *Frederick Douglass.* With a preface by James M. McPherson. New York: Atheneum Press, 1968.

Sundquist, Eric J., ed. *Frederick Douglass: New Literary and Historical Essays.* Cambridge: Cambridge University Press, 1990.

Walker, Peter F. *Moral Choices: Memory, Desire, and the Imagination in Nineteenth-Century American Abolition.* Baton Rouge: Louisiana State University Press, 1978.

Washington, Booker T. *Frederick Douglass.* Philadelphia: G. W. Jacobs, 1907.

PART I
FREDERICK DOUGLASS AND SLAVE
NARRATIVES

Linecut from an 1880s issue of *Harper's Weekly*
on which George Morris Philips, the school's first
principal, made his notation.

Two

Frederick Douglass's American "We"

Julie Husband

[A]n American wherever met with is simply a bundle of
contradictions, incongruities and absurdities. . . . The attempt to reconcile slavery and freedom has given three
tongues to all our politicians, a tongue for the north and a
tongue for the south, and a double tongue for the nation.
—Frederick Douglass, "America before the Global
Tribunal," June 30, 1861

Multiculturalism, the non–hierarchical celebration of cultural diversity,
is a difficult concept to translate into nineteenth-century American race
relations. When we look for cultural difference, we find persecution—of
Mormons in the west, Irish immigrants in eastern cities, and especially
African Americans and abolitionists throughout the nation. Defenders
of slavery claimed that substantial differences of intelligence and tem-
perament among races made slavery "natural" and even beneficial to
African Americans. In the face of this use of difference, Frederick
Douglass emphasized the common goals and ideals of democratic America in contrast to those of the anti-democratic slaveholding states. For
Douglass, sectional diversity rather than racial diversity characterized
the nation. The most memorable appeals for the value of diversity came
from states' rights advocates who defended the South's "peculiar institution" against any national policy hostile to slavery. Douglass argued
that the attempt to "reconcile slavery and freedom" in a multicultural
(read sectional) nation led to a national forked tongue, an inscrutable
American character in an impossibly contradictory national narrative.
Douglass's task was to develop an American "we," a national character
shaped by the "global tribunal" and dedicated to a narrative of liberty
and progress. Whatever Douglass's personal feelings about the unique

Portions of this chapter appeared in *Proteus: A Journal of Ideas* (Spring 1995). Copyright
1995 by Shippensburg University. Reprinted with permission.

contributions and vitality of African-American culture, he pursued an integrationist political strategy, calculated to encourage white liberals to identify with the emancipatory aspirations of African Americans.[1]

Not all African-American leaders agreed with Douglass's integrationist strategy. Martin Delany, Douglass's one-time business partner and later political opponent, explicitly defined himself against Douglass as a separatist. Initially, the two worked together to generate support for Douglass's newspaper, *The North Star*, in the late 1840s. The two grew apart during the 1850s when Delany increasingly devoted his energies to fostering a separate community outside the United States for escaped slaves and free African Americans. Delany's commitment to various colonization plans ebbed and flowed over the years with the nation's political climate. He served as the first African-American military officer during the Civil War and as a part of South Carolina's freedmen's bureau during Reconstruction. But with the collapse of Reconstruction, Delany renewed his emigration plans and pan-African views. Even if African Americans had widely supported Delany's model of black nationalism and emigration, only a small proportion could have been transported to Africa, because resources were limited. The presence of Martin Delany—a militant figure asserting the superiority of African-based accomplishment and culture—in the movement for emigration may have had the effect of popularizing its integrationist political opponents.

Douglass's strategy, however, involved more than integration, more than an extension of citizenship; he made African Americans the test case of America's democratic experiment. Douglass placed the history of African Americans at the very center of the American Enlightenment narrative. Not only did Douglass frequently cite the Declaration of Independence to assert the natural equality of all people, an Enlightenment construct, but he also applied an Enlightenment conception of national narrative. Douglass may not have read Immanuel Kant or Georg Hegel, but he was clearly aware of the German philosophers' widely disseminated ideas. In particular, Douglass used a trope commonly associated with the German Enlightenment: world history pictured as "a court of judgement" (Hegel 216).[2] Part of what made the German philosophers distinctly modern was their sense that the guiding force of history was a "world mind," the accumulated though partial views of historical actors, rather than divine judgment. Following the German philosophers, Douglass replaced the image of a critical and interventionist God evaluating the American "errand into the wilderness" with the vision of a court of public opinion judging America on the basis of its democratic experiment.[3] Douglass replaced the Puritan conception of "providential history" with a modern historian's concern for public opinion. He articulated an ideal America and narrativized the actual America as a character moving toward the realization of its single, noble concept. Douglass read culture politically; the nation was divided between free-labor and slaveholding cultures. The worst enemy to free labor was the forked-tongued politician ostensibly promoting both.

Frederick Douglass developed the predominant rhetorical positions later integrationists adopted toward American creeds and icons. For Douglass, "we" invariably included black and white Americans who shared a multiracial vision of the republic, and "America" remained their unrealized vision. Douglass, like other Enlightenment historiographers, believed in history's progressive trajectory toward human liberation and rationality. As David Blight argues in his study of the latter half of Douglass's career, the Civil War became a touchstone in Douglass's rhetoric.[4] It became a means through which Douglass could reinsert black accomplishments into "America's cultural memory" (Blight 236). For Douglass, the Civil War was the second half of the American Revolution, in which America would finally realize the ideals of liberty and equality stated in the Declaration of Independence. When Radical Reconstruction gave way to a rapprochement between Northern and Southern whites, Douglass retaliated by reminding his audiences of the black soldiers' patriotism. He encouraged Americans to remain loyal to Union veterans, black and white, by supporting black civil and political rights. To disavow black civil rights was to betray Union veterans.

If the Civil War created a space in Douglass's rhetoric for alternative alignments, the figure of Abraham Lincoln appealed to the unrealized goals for which the martyred president died. Lincoln's position within America's Enlightenment narrative is central. He challenged the American public's commitment to the Enlightenment experiment upon which the nation was founded—not upon a particular nation's customs, but upon a social contract guaranteeing fundamental freedoms defined against social or religious custom. Douglass incorporated Lincoln's rhetoric—often referring to "the stern logic of events"—to signal the progressive tendency of history. Later integrationists, especially Martin Luther King, Jr., have continued to deploy Lincoln as the founder of a more complete social contract, an American contract extending Constitutional rights to black Americans.

Douglass did not, however, always treat Lincoln so reverently. Prior to Lincoln's assassination, Douglass frequently and vehemently criticized him because of his policies on slavery, his disregard for black soldiers, and his plans for freed slaves. Douglass's speeches and articles between August 1862 and Lincoln's second inauguration tell a much different story than his revisionary treatment of the same period in the twelfth chapter of his 1892 autobiography, *Life and Times of Frederick Douglass*. His treatment of Lincoln in this chapter, significantly titled "Hope for the Nation," establishes the progressive trajectory Douglass insisted upon in his historical writings. Even during the discouraging final decades of the nineteenth century, Douglass subscribed to an Enlightenment conception of history as a teleology tending toward human liberation and truth. Moreover, in Douglass's historiography, and later in King's, the telling of a progressive tale encouraged such a historical tendency.

Just prior to the September 22, 1862, preliminary Emancipation Proclamation, Douglass devoted two issues of the *Douglass Monthly* to scathing attacks on Lincoln and his policies. In the August 1862 issue, he wrote,

> In the conflict between these two elements [liberty and slavery], [Lincoln] arrayed himself on the side of freedom, and was elected with a view to the ascendancy of free principles. . . . Whatever may have been his intentions, the action of President Lincoln has been calculated in a marked and decided way to shield and protect slavery from the very blows which its horrible crimes have loudly and persistently invited. (Douglass, *Life and Writings*, 256)

Douglass accused Lincoln of violating his presidential mandate by supporting pro-slavery measures, refusing to arm slaves, returning fugitive slaves, promoting pro-slavery generals, and failing to emancipate slaves.

In the next issue of the *Douglass Monthly*, Douglass made a more personal attack upon Lincoln, whom he described as "unusually garrulous, characteristically foggy, remarkably illogical and untimely in his utterances" (Douglass, *Life and Writings*, 266). Lincoln had proposed that freedmen should voluntarily leave the United States to colonize an unknown section of Central America, suggesting that the presence of African Americans in the United States was the primary cause of the war. Douglass held Lincoln personally responsible for his speeches and policies, with none of the ambiguity that characterized his later discussions of Lincoln's administration:

> Illogical and unfair as Mr. Lincoln's statements are, they are nevertheless quite in keeping with his whole course from the beginning of his administration up to this day, and confirm the painful conviction that though elected as an anti-slavery man by Republican and Abolition voters, Mr. Lincoln is quite a genuine representative of American prejudice and Negro hatred and far

more concerned for the preservation of slavery, and the favor of the Border Slave States, than for any sentiment of magnanimity or principle of justice and humanity. (268)

Deeply disappointed by Lincoln's apparent betrayal, Douglass separated the significance of the Emancipation Proclamation from its author. Though the proclamation was to Douglass "the most important of any to which the President of the United States has ever signed his name," he felt its author was guilty of "slothful deliberation" and motivated only by the imperatives of war (274).

Compare this 1862 condemnation of Lincoln to Douglass's summary of the events leading to the Emancipation Proclamation as he constructed them in his 1892 autobiography. In the first paragraph of the twelfth chapter, "Hope for the Nation," Lincoln is virtually absent. The "federal arm" was responsible for the nearly identical list of grievances Lincoln was personally blamed for in the August 1862 *Douglass Monthly:* overturning the emancipation policy of Governor John Fremont in Missouri, returning fugitive slaves, and refusing to support slave insurrections. According to the 1892 autobiography, Secretary of War William Seward, not Lincoln, advocated a return to the union as it was prior to the Civil War. General George McClellan, not Lincoln, "had been trying to put down the rebellion without hurting the rebels, certainly without hurting slavery" (Douglass, *Life and Times,* 351). The government and "we" also worked against emancipation, but President Lincoln has no role in this narrative, other than that he was "besought" in vain to adopt another policy. Even in this single allusion, Lincoln is the object and not the subject of action.

Whereas the "federal arm" was responsible for pro-slavery measures in the period prior to emancipation, Douglass now credited Lincoln with progressive measures during that period. He commended Grant for cooperating "with President Lincoln in his policy of employing colored troops" and treating them with "due respect" (357). After deflecting responsibility for policies unfavorable to African Americans away from Lincoln, Douglass was careful to recuperate him as an active, even prophetic, force in history.

At this point the chapter becomes a more direct tribute to Lincoln, as he is referred to as "thoughtful," "sagacious," and "not only a great President but a great man" (358, 359). Douglass had briefly explained his grievances regarding the treatment of colored soldiers in the previous chapter, thereby fostering an impression that this was part of Lincoln's pre-emancipation phase, in which he was more concerned with negotiating a compromise between Copperheads and radical Republicans. However, it was in August 1863, after the Emancipation Proclamation, that Douglass had briefly ceased to recruit for the colored regiments because of their treatment. In an article ironically titled "The Commander-In-Chief and His Black Soldiers," Douglass explicitly repudiated Lincoln as a leader of black soldiers, who were given the most menial and dangerous assignments in the Union army and were routinely executed or enslaved when captured by the Confederate army (Douglass, *Life and Writings,* 371). In the autobiography there is no mention of friction between Lincoln and black soldiers. On the contrary, the autobiography tied the Great Emancipator to his loyal black soldiers, urging the veneration of both.

Further enhancing the effectiveness of his revisionary narrative, Douglass left out his support of a competitor for the 1864 presidential election. Fearful at the time that Lincoln would end the war under pro-slavery terms or send African Americans to a colony after the war, Douglass supported Missouri governor John Fremont for the presidency. Only when McClellan seemed capable of winning the election on a decidedly pro-slavery basis did Douglass again support Lincoln's second term. On this point, Douglass's 1892 autobiography most markedly departed from his earlier views.

> When we were thus asked to exchange Abraham Lincoln for George B. McClellan—a successful Union president for an unsuccessful Union general—a party earnestly endeavoring to save the Union, torn and rent by a gigantic rebellion—I thought with Mr. Lincoln that it was not wise to "swap horses while crossing a stream." (Douglass, *Life and Times,* 361)

However, as Douglass's 1864 writings show, he was willing to "swap horses" if Fremont could have been saddled up as a viable presidential candidate.

Douglass concluded the twelfth chapter of his autobiography by saying of Lincoln,

> His accusers, in whose opinion he was always too fast or too slow, too weak or too strong, too conciliatory or too aggressive, would soon be his admirers; it was soon to be seen that he had conducted the affairs of the nation with singular wisdom, and with absolute fidelity to the great trust confided in him. (370, 371)

Undoubtedly, Douglass included himself among the converted; certainly, he became one of Lincoln's admirers. Lincoln must have seemed all the more admirable in comparison to his successor Andrew Johnson, who was unreceptive to Douglass and the views of African-American leaders. By tapping into the martyred president's legend, Douglass could lend added credibility to the ongoing battle for racial equality. He could develop a usable history for African Americans by revealing Lincoln's "true" philosophy as it was in accordance with his own. By separating Lincoln's discriminatory policies from his more progressive ones and positioning the discriminatory policies in the preceding chapter, out of an otherwise chronological order, Douglass also created a progressive trajectory. Lincoln, he seemed to suggest, led the nation not only through the Civil War but through a process of gradual enlightenment.

Was an older, more discouraged Douglass nostalgic for a period that seemed to hold such promise, to nearly offer full citizenship to African Americans? Was he swayed by Lincoln's powerful iconic status as the martyred president? Lincoln spoke of himself in the last two years of the war as a "tool of destiny," a part of God's divine plan. Was Douglass, like so many others, persuaded by Lincoln's own sense of providential history? Or was Douglass deliberately manipulating the memory of a popular president for political ends? I think one key to that question lies in his 1876 speech at the unveiling of the Freedmen's Monument. Speaking before a largely African-American audience on the eleventh anniversary of Lincoln's assassination, Douglass unveiled more than Lincoln's statue; he unveiled the role Lincoln played in Douglass's own historiography. Douglass opened by forecasting the historical reception of the very event in which he and the audience were participating.

> Wise and thoughtful men of our race who shall come after us and study the lesson of our history in the United States, who shall survey the long and dreary space over which we have traveled, and who shall count the links in the great chain of events by which we have reached our present position, will make a note of this occasion. They will think of it and speak of it with a sense of manly pride and complacency. (*Life and Times*, 481)

For Douglass, history was more than the telling of an oft-told tale; it was the plotting of a future course, an ordering of the past that led to an enlightened future. He continued, "That we are here in peace today is a compliment and a credit to American civilization and a prophecy of still greater national enlightenment and progress in the future" (482).

It is perhaps odd, then, that Douglass should have chosen this opportunity to expose his own deliberate construction of a useful African-American history of Lincoln. He was well aware of the import of the moment; President Grant unveiled the Freedmen's Monument, and members of Grant's cabinet, of Congress, and of the Supreme Court, as well as a large African-American constituency, congregated for the occasion. Imagine the tension in the audience when Douglass turned to his subject, the martyred president, and said,

> It must be admitted—truth compels me to admit—even here in the presence of the monument we have erected to his memory, that Abraham Lincoln was not, in the fullest sense of the word, either our man or our model. In his interests, in his associations, in his habits of thought and in his prejudices, he was a white man. (484)

Douglass then addressed the white members of his audience in what was, for him, an unusually exclusive manner. "You are the children of Abraham Lincoln. We are at best only his step-children" (485). Douglass seldom used "we" to designate African Americans; "we" usually referred to Americans of all races, Northerners, or anti-slavery patriots. Douglass proceeded to list Lincoln's unjust policies concerning African Americans.

Then Douglass began his rehabilitation, not of Lincoln, but of Lincoln's place in history. It was these very injustices, he argued, that enabled Lincoln to gather the popular support necessary for the Civil War, then the limited Emancipation Proclamation, and then the extension of emancipation to slaves in border and free states. "Viewed from the genuine abolition ground, Mr. Lincoln seemed tardy, cold, dull, and indifferent; but measuring him by the sentiment of his country, a sentiment he was bound as a statesman to consult, he was swift, zealous, radical and determined" (489). As an abolitionist, Douglass joined in the condemnation of Lincoln's conservative tendencies, and that condemnation pushed Lincoln toward more radical policies. But it was Lincoln's hesitancy that made him ultimately successful in emancipating the slaves. African Americans, Douglass asserted, understood his position in history.

> We saw him, measured him, and estimated him, not by stray utterances to injudicious and tedious delegations, who often tried his patience—not by isolated facts torn from their connection—not by any partial and imperfect glimpses, caught at inopportune moments—but by a broad survey, in the light of the stern logic of great events, and in view of that "divinity which shapes our ends, rough hew them how we will." (486).

Subscribing to a Hegelian notion of world history unfolding according to a rational logic toward human liberation, Douglass positioned Lincoln as a world-historical actor, gifted with a superior understanding of the "stern logic of great events." Though both phrases—"the stern logic of great events" and the "divinity which shapes our ends, rough hew them how we will"—were frequently used by Lincoln, Douglass distances himself from the second, with its reference to divinity, by placing only this one in quotation marks in his publication of the speech in his *Life and Times*. Lincoln is more a superior historian than a divinely inspired prophet. He understands the rational "logic" by which history unfolds. Douglass continued, "He knew the American people better than they knew themselves and his truth was based upon this knowledge" (492).

Douglass developed a tension between this Lincoln, the leader of free America, and the Lincoln embedded in his "habits of thought" and his "prejudices." The former was useful for Douglass's history. The history that guided the nation was constructed by orators like Douglass using icons like Lincoln. The history of great figures, of messianic leaders, commanded admiration and fidelity. The visionary Lincoln was the Lincoln of Douglass's history; the prejudiced, historically embedded Lincoln was the Lincoln against whom Douglass struggled prior to and during the Civil War. Douglass understood historical relativism too well to doubt the truth of both of these versions. Lincoln could and should be constructed for the event at hand. Douglass acknowledged that "any man can say things that are true of Abraham Lincoln, but no man can say anything that is new of Abraham Lincoln" (488). His object as a public intellectual was not to uncover the truth about Lincoln but to deploy the most useful truth. Lincoln the Great Emancipator was one vehicle through which Douglass made the emancipation of African Americans central to American history and a symbol of the progress of a single, multiracial American culture.

Subsequent integrationist African-American leaders have taken up Douglass's use of Lincoln as a prophet of a future post-racial America. The most well-known example is Martin Luther King, Jr., in his 1963 speech at the culmination of the March on Washington. King had hoped to have President Kennedy commemorate the anniversary of the Emancipation Proclamation with a Second Emancipation Proclamation that would acknowledge not only the incompleteness of the American Revolution, but the incompleteness of its second half, the Civil War.[5] Kennedy ignored King's draft of the Second Emancipation Proclamation, but King nevertheless pointed to the original at the opening of his speech as an unfulfilled promise. With the giant Lincoln Memorial looming behind him, King wove together Lincoln's Gettysburg Address and Douglass's distinction between an ideal America, embodied by the Great Emancipator, and the real, racially divided United States. King opened with an acknowledgment of the occasion's historic import, much as Douglass had opened his 1876 speech: "I am happy to join with you today in what will go down in history as the greatest demonstration for freedom in the history of our nation" (Davis 261).

Like Douglass, King began by describing the vast difference between mythic America and the debtor nation whose promise is yet unfulfilled.

> When the architects of our Republic wrote the magnificent words of the Constitution and the Declaration of Independence, they were signing a promissory note to which every American was to fall heir. This note was a promise that all men—yes, black men as well as white men—would be guaranteed the unalienable rights of life, liberty and the pursuit of happiness. It is obvious today that America has defaulted on this promissory note insofar as her citizens of color are concerned. Instead of honoring this sacred obligation, America has given the Negro people a bad check, a check which has come back marked "insufficient funds." (261)

This is America at its low point, the bad debtor, the father who disavows and disinherits his children. Lincoln's stepchildren become the nation's disinherited in the transition from Douglass to King. The logical extension of this line could be a separatist policy, but just as Douglass recuperated Lincoln after a series of qualifications, King recuperated the nation. "But we refuse to believe that the bank of justice is bankrupt. We refuse to believe that there are insufficient funds in the great vaults of opportunity of this nation" (261). En route to a goal of integration, a disassembling of the color line, the integrationist leaders must reinvest their discourse in the ideal of America.

Martin Luther King, Jr., had intended to end only halfway through what we have come to know as the "I Have A Dream" speech. He planned to conclude with the disappointing line, "And so today, let us go back to our communities as members of the international association for the advancement of creative dissatisfaction" (Branch 882). Instead, he responded to the crowd's enthusiasm, skipped this line with its final emphasis on an unsatisfactory present, and described his vision of a glorious future. He encouraged the crowd to return to their struggles at home and then added the most famous part of his speech, his dream of limitless progress, "deeply rooted in the American Dream" (Davis 263).

In the extemporaneous portion of his famous speech, King used the *if . . . then* formulation typical of Douglass's rhetoric.

This will be the day when all of God's children will be able to sing with new meaning, "My country, 'tis of thee, sweet land of liberty, of thee I sing. Land where my fathers died, land of the pilgrim's pride, from every mountain side, let freedom ring." And if America is to be a great nation, this must become true. (263)

Again, the struggle of African Americans is the test case of the American Enlightenment narrative, the democratic experiment. Repeating "now . . . now . . . now . . . now," King urged marchers to continue their struggles. By projecting the marchers' actions into the future, King developed the progressive trajectory so characteristic of Douglass's national narrative.

America's founding texts are infused with an Enlightenment confidence in the progressive tendency of history toward greater human liberation and rationality. African-American "integrationists" have drawn from this tradition to encourage individual commitment to "world-historical ends," always with a view to the "global tribunal's" future judgment on the American democratic experiment. They have worked within this Enlightenment narrative to make African-American liberation the central sign of America's fidelity to the democratic experiment.

Frederick Douglass established a template for later integrationists, constructing a "we" both multiracial and unicultural, a "we" that pursued a single national ideal. Rarely did Douglass speak of an African-American "we." However, discouraged by the series of setbacks dealt African Americans following Radical Reconstruction, Douglass would defensively address a white public on behalf of an African-American "we." One can hear the exhaustion in his voice as he opens his final autobiography, *Life and Times of Frederick Douglass*, with this reformulation of the "global tribunal":

> I find myself summoned again by the popular voice, and by what is called the Negro problem, to come a second time upon the witness stand and give evidence upon disputed points concerning myself and my emancipated brothers and sisters. (Douglass, *Life and Times*, 512)

But always, this exclusionary reference indicates America's failure, America's unfulfilled ideal of democratic inclusion. Douglass did not create the national discourse in which difference was hierarchized, in which diversity was divisiveness, but he did have to speak within that discourse. For Douglass, the so-called Negro problem was an American problem, and the witness stand upon which he wished to speak was not the white American stage, but the world stage. Imagining a multicultural America may not have been beyond Douglass's powers, but it was beyond the limits of a useful nineteenth-century racial politics.

Notes

1. Douglass did occasionally grant value to aspects of slave culture, but often by connecting them with European customs. For example, he compared the stirring slave songs on the Lloyd plantation to the "mournful" music of the Irish during the Great Famine (Douglass, *Life and Times,* 54). Again, during his trip to Europe, he notes, "I have seen it alleged that the habit of carrying the burdens on the head is a mark of inferiority peculiar to the Negro. It was not necessary that I should go to Europe to be able to refute this allegation, yet I was glad to see, both in Italy and the south of France, that this custom is about as common there as it is among the dusky daughters of the Nile. . . . In any case it may be welcomed as a proof of a common brotherhood" (562–563). For Douglass, these sporadic "multicultural" references are defensive refutations of racist claims.

2. While Douglass used the Enlightenment concept of national ideas and the trope of a world tribunal judging the successes and failures of particular nations, he did not adopt Hegel's naturalization of national ideas. Hegel mapped national ideas onto biologically restricted populations and then theorized that the "natural" progress of "world ideas" would result in the elimination of outdated ideas and the people who embodied them. In the latter part of his career, Douglass was at pains to counter social Darwinism, the application of Darwin's theory of "survival of the fittest" to ethnic groups and social classes. Through a more directly racial than national division of peoples, social Darwinists arrived at conclusions similar to Hegel's, especially that "superior" groups would supersede "inferior" ones for the improvement of the species. See Douglass's discussion of European and North African peoples in chapter 9 of *Life and Times.*

3. David Howard-Pitney frames his analysis of major African-American leaders in terms of the "Afro-American jeremiad." While he and I reach similar conclusions, and his extensive analyses of Martin Luther King, Jr., and Jesse Jackson, in particular, have crucial contemporary implications, I find "jeremiad" a somewhat misleading term for Douglass's rhetoric. Though "jeremiad" accurately encompasses King's evangelical Christianity, it glosses over Douglass's renunciation of an Old Testament conception of a vengeful, interventionist God. He refused to thank God for the passage of the Fifteenth Amendment, and, as a consequence, he was censured by the black Philadelphia ministry as an infidel. As Donald Gibson demonstrates, Douglass believed that only the autonomous individual, an Enlightenment construct, effected change.

4. "Slavery, the war's deepest cause, and black freedom, the war's most fundamental result, remain the most conspicuous missing elements in the American literature inspired by the Civil War. This black invisibility in America's cultural memory is precisely what Douglass struggled against during the last two decades of his life" (Blight 236).

5. When King proposed a Second Emancipation Proclamation, Kennedy encouraged him to draft one. As King paraphrased it, the draft asked that Kennedy "proclaim all segregation statutes of all southern states to be contrary to the Constitution, and that the full power of his office be employed to avoid their enforcement" (Branch 589–590). Kennedy never responded to the draft.

Works Cited

Blight, David W. *Frederick Douglass' Civil War: Keeping Faith in Jubilee.* Baton Rouge: Louisiana State University Press, 1989.

Branch, Taylor. *Parting the Waters: America in the King Years, 1954–63.* New York: Simon and Schuster, 1988.

Davis, Lenwood G. *I Have a Dream: The Life and Times of Martin Luther King, Jr.* Westport, Conn.: Negro Universities Press, 1973.

Douglass, Frederick. *The Frederick Douglass Papers: Speeches, Debates, and Interviews.* Series 1, vol. 3. Edited by John W. Blassingame. New Haven: Yale University Press, 1985.

Douglass, Frederick. *Life and Times of Frederick Douglass.* 1892. Reprint, New York: Collier Books, Macmillan Publishing Company, 1962.

——. *The Life and Writings of Frederick Douglass.* Vol. 3. Edited by Philip S. Foner. New York: International Publishers, 1952.

Gibson, Donald. "Christianity and Individualism: (Re-)Creation and Reality in Frederick Douglass's Representation of Self." *African American Review* 26 (winter 1992): 591–603.

Hegel, Georg Wilhelm Friedrich. *Philosophy of Right.* Translated by T. M. Knox. London: Oxford University Press, 1952.

Howard-Pitney, David. *The Afro-American Jeremiad: Appeals for Justice in America.* Philadelphia: Temple University Press, 1990.

Three

Adding Her Testimony
Harriet Jacobs's Incidents as Testimonial Literature

Jeannine DeLombard

In *My Bondage and My Freedom* (1855), Frederick Douglass explains that he has decided to publish a second account of his life in slavery because "the system is now at the bar of public opinion . . . for judgment. Its friends have made for it the usual plea—'not guilty;' the case must, therefore, proceed. Any facts, either from slaves, slaveholders, or by-standers, calculated to enlighten the public mind . . . are in order, and can scarcely be innocently withheld" (106). Douglass was not alone in drawing on a juridical metaphor to structure his contribution to the national debate over slavery: throughout the antebellum period black and white abolitionists consistently figured slavery as a crime, slaveholders as perpetrators and defendants, slaves as victims and eyewitnesses, abolitionists as advocates for the slave, and the American reading public as judge and jury. Thus, the immensely popular 1837 abolitionist fact-book compiled by Theodore Dwight Weld and Sarah and Angelina Grimké, *American Slavery As It Is: Testimony of a Thousand Witnesses,* begins, "READER, you are empannelled as a juror to try a plain case and bring in an honest verdict" (Weld 7). In this discursive climate, African-American authors of slave narratives repeatedly figured themselves, as Douglass does in the *Narrative of the Life of Frederick Douglass, an American Slave,* as "eye-witness[es] to the cruelty" of slavery (Douglass, *Narrative,* 80), and their narratives, as Harriet Jacobs does in *Incidents in the Life of a Slave Girl,* as "testimony to . . . what Slavery really is" (Jacobs 1–2).

At a time when African Americans, both enslaved and free, were denied the right to institute a suit or to testify against whites in most

American courtrooms, North and South, the widespread deployment of the juridical metaphor in abolitionist discourse enabled a privileged few to gain a hearing at "the bar of public opinion." White Northerners also used the metaphor to authorize their anti-slavery speech, casting themselves as, in Theodore Dwight Weld's words, "*advocates* arguing upon the evidence and . . . *examiners* cross questioning and sifting counter testimony" (Barnes and Dumond 1:389). The juridical metaphor thus gave former slaves and their white sympathizers clearly defined positions from which to speak and be heard in the national debate over slavery. But, as the work of African-American literary abolitionists like Douglass and Jacobs indicates, former slaves often found the witness stand a constrictive space from which to address the court of public opinion. In a famous passage in *My Bondage and My Freedom*, Frederick Douglass acknowledges and rejects the rigid distinction between black testimony and white advocacy when he critiques his white Garrisonian colleagues' command, "Give us the facts . . . we will take care of the philosophy" (Douglass, *My Bondage,* 367). The "rhetorical division of labor between descriptive and interpretive tasks" (Garvey 234) that Douglass found so galling was only one of the difficulties that the juridical metaphor posed to African-American abolitionist speech. For a formerly enslaved woman like Harriet Jacobs, the juridical metaphor posed unique complications: How was she to take the witness stand to relate the "far more terrible" experience of the sexually exploited female slave without having her testimony misread as a confession (Jacobs 77)? How was she to ensure that slavery and its lascivious perpetrators, rather than the "prematurely knowing" slave girl (28, 54), would be brought to "the bar of public opinion . . . for judgment"?

We can begin to answer these questions—and to consider the discursive stakes of the slave narrative's testimonial rhetoric—if we permit ourselves to move beyond the immediate historical and cultural context of the antebellum United States and to situate the slave narrative in a larger testimonial literary tradition that includes twentieth-century documentary first-person narratives from Latin America and post-Holocaust Europe. Adopting such a multicultural critical perspective enables us not only to appreciate more fully what it meant for former slaves to deploy the juridical metaphor in their abolitionist texts, but also to broaden the definition of testimonial literature, a field which has often implicitly (and sometimes explicitly) excluded the slave narrative (see Beverley, "Margin," 113 n. 31).

In this essay, therefore, I want to draw on both African-American literary scholarship and the theory and criticism of Holocaust and Latin American testimonial writing in order to read key testimonial encounters in Jacobs's narrative, *Incidents in the Life of a Slave Girl*. These encounters, in which Linda Brent narrates her personal and sexual history to a variety of auditors, have been read as rehearsals of the scene of *Incidents*'s own difficult production and as models on the basis of which Jacobs instructs her projected readers to respond appropriately to her text by encouraging them to adopt a sympathetic as opposed to a censorious stance (Garfield; Gunning; Nelson). Emphasizing the testimonial aspect of these encounters, I argue that, over the course of the narrative, Jacobs rejects a confessional posture in favor of a testimonial one: adopting the stance of a witness and testifying *against* the crime of slavery and *to* the trauma of sexual exploitation it entails for the female slave, Jacobs not only indicts slavery and its perpetrators in the American court of public opinion but also subpoenas her readers as witnesses in her abolitionist, feminist political project. Here the question of audience is crucial. Thus, after briefly sketching the generic contours of testimonial literature, I will turn to critical assessments of the role of the audience in both testimonial and African-American literature in order to establish a conceptual framework for the remainder of the essay, which provides close readings of six key testimonial encounters in *Incidents*. My reading of these scenes, and particularly my understanding of the political dimensions of readerly sympathy, both benefits from and contributes to the considerable scholarship on what has come to be known as the antebellum culture of sentiment (see Samuels; Tompkins; Fisher).

Much of the work on testimonial literature has focused on the documentary first-person narratives that have emerged in response to the Holocaust in Europe or to the oppressive neo-colonial regimes in Latin America. The narratives of Elie Wiesel, Simon Wiesenthal, and Anne Frank, along with the film *Shoah*, are probably the best-known examples of Holocaust testimonies, and *I, Rigoberta Menchu*, Domatila Barrios de Chungara's *Let Me Speak!* and Alicia Partnoy's *The Little School* are perhaps the most widely read Latin American *testimonios*. Like the slave narrative, testimonial literature arises under conditions of oppression, situates the author or speaker within the larger, struggling collective, incorporates oral culture into the written text, presents itself as an alternative or corrective to official historical accounts, claims to tell the truth, and seeks to effect social and political change (see Yúdice 17). The conditions governing the production and circulation of the slave narrative also resemble the circumstances under which Latin American *testimonios* are written and published. Like the *testimonio*, the slave narrative is "a mediated narrative" that is "told by a speaker from a subaltern . . . social class or group to an interlocutor who is an intellectual or professional writer from the middle or upper class" and "who then edits and textualizes the account, making it available as a printed book or pamphlet to a similarly positioned national and international reading public" (Beverley, "Through," 128). This model reflects the relationship that structured the production of the vast majority of slave narratives, which were usually transcribed or "edited" by white authors and intellectuals for "a similarly positioned national and international reading public" in the Northern United States and Great Britain (see Sekora; Stepto, "I Rose"; Starling; Andrews).

Jacobs targets that reading public on the title page of *Incidents* with a quotation from Isaiah 32:9: "Rise up, ye women that are at ease! Hear my voice, ye careless daughters! Give ear unto my speech" (xxxv). This biblical citation, combined with Jacobs's preface, Lydia Maria Child's introduction, and the frequent apostrophes to the reader in the text itself, clearly identifies Jacobs's target readership as the same white, bourgeois, Northern women who formed the backbone of the antebellum abolitionist movement. In this passage Jacobs also begins instructing her projected readership—before they have read a single word of her narrative—in the appropriate mode of response to her text: namely, political action. As Garfield notes in her insightful discussion of this passage, "the imperatives in *Isaiah*—'Rise up' and 'Give ear unto my speech'—are suggestively reversed, for one is to 'Give ear' and then, herself, 'Rise up' to speak of slavery's violations. The reader is asked to exchange the insulating prerogatives of womanly indifference for the polemical force of abolitionism" (Garfield 122).

It is precisely a desire to elicit from its audience this kind of sympathetic, activist response that distinguishes testimony from confession; for if, in confessional discourse, the auditor or reader "intervenes in order to judge, punish, forgive, console, and reconcile" (Foucault 61), in testimonial discourse the listener is "a party to the creation of knowledge" produced by the autobiographical narrative (Felman and Laub 57). Indeed, based on his experience collecting oral histories of Holocaust survivors for the Yale University Video Archive for Holocaust Testimonies, clinical psychiatrist Dori Laub has found that "[k]nowledge in the testimony is . . . not simply a factual given that is reproduced and replicated by the testifier, but a genuine advent, an event in its own right" (62). As a result, "the listener to trauma comes to be a participant and a co-owner of the traumatic event: through his very listening, he comes to partially experience trauma in himself" (57). Jacobs's determination to produce this kind of response in her readers is evident in her preface to *Incidents:* she justifies the publication of her narrative by insisting that "[o]nly by experience can any one realize how deep, dark, and foul" slavery is (Jacobs 2). By presenting her testimony to her white Northern female readers, Jacobs places them in a position to witness vicariously, and therefore to experience at a remove, the traumatic events described therein.

One of the goals of testimonial discourse, as the epigraph from Isaiah suggests, is to generate further testimony by inspiring political speech in response to outrages "witnessed" in the text through the act of reading or listening. Holocaust scholar James E. Young cites Leviticus 5:1 to illustrate the transitive nature of witnessing: "And he is a witness whether he has seen or known of it; if he does not utter it, then he shall bear his iniquity." As Young notes, "implicit in the testimonial act seems to be the possibility for making more witnesses by informing others of events" (Young 18). If testimony not only communicates but creates knowledge, it also creates more witnesses whose responsibility it is to testify to their newfound knowledge. Doris Sommer has explored how, in the case of Latin American women's *testimonios,* the presence of an intermediary from the dominant culture allows the speaking subject to direct her narrative appeal for justice to the larger audience such an intermediary represents: addressing her interlocutor in the second person, the narrator also "interpellates us as readers who identify with [her] project and, by extension, with the political community to which she belongs" (Sommer 118). Of course, if the audience refuses to accept what Felman and Laub call its "response-ability" (Felman and Laub 200)—the political duty that arises from the vicarious witness's ability to respond to the traumatic events described in the text—that audience's embrace of the role of vicarious witness can promote complacency rather than activism. As John Beverley observes in his discussion of Latin American testimonial literature, "Testimonios are in a sense made for people like us, in that they allow us to participate as academics and yuppies, without leaving our studies and classrooms, in the concreteness and relativity of actual social struggles" (Beverley, "Through," 127). Translating Beverley's observations into the antebellum context, we might say that slave narratives potentially allowed their bourgeois Northern white audiences the sense of participating in abolitionism without leaving their parlors.

Given the highly charged political climate in which slave narratives were produced and circulated, Jacobs could not be sure that her audience's sympathy would survive a reading of *Incidents.* The recurrent figure of the unreliable reader, and the unreliable white reader in particular, has led Robert Stepto to characterize African-American literature as a "discourse of distrust" (Stepto, "Distrust," 304). Traditionally, critics have focused on white audiences' distrust of African-American authors and narrators—a distrust whose origins are usually traced to the antebellum slave narrative's status as abolitionist propaganda (Starling 221–248). Stepto argues that throughout African-American literary history this distrust has been, in fact, mutual, and that "distrust of the American reader and of American acts of reading" is "a primary motivation for African-American writing" (Stepto, "Distrust," 303, 305). African-American authors express this distrust by repeatedly constructing scenes in which characters serve as "tellers and hearers," in an attempt to instruct their readers in appropriate modes of response to their texts. Nothing guarantees, however, that readers will pick up on these textual cues or, if they do, that they will respond to them in the manner prescribed by the narrative. The danger for the African-American slave narrative, as for the oral testimony spoken by the Holocaust survivor, is that the audience's indifferent, judgmental, or dismissive response will effectively "annihilate" the text (Felman and Laub 68; see also Stepto, "Distrust," 308). This is why Felman and Laub insist that for "the testimonial process to take place, there needs to be a bonding, the intimate and total presence of an *other*" who is both sympathetic and "*unobtrusively present*" (70–71). For Stepto, a central issue in African-American literature is therefore "whether the reader is to pursue such self-transformations in accord with or at variance with the model of the listener found within the narrative itself," or, in other words, "how much he will or can submit to the model of listening which almost always is the dominating meta-plot of the tale" (Stepto, "Distrust," 312). Critics have identified precisely this kind of "meta-plot" in *Incidents*, which rehearses the scene of its own production by portraying the female slave's attempts to find a suitable audience to which she can relate her experience of sexual exploitation.[1] Indeed, *Incidents* portrays Linda Brent's search for a sympathetic, unobtrusive listener with whom to share her story of sexual exploitation as a part of her larger quest for freedom. Jacobs presents her readers with a wide range of possible responses on which to pattern their own reception of *Incidents*: guilty silence, cathartic appropriation, contemptuous outrage, condescending pity, polite disapprobrium, and politically inflected sympathy. Reading these scenes as testimonial encounters enables us to see how Jacobs arranges these model responses progressively, in order to guide the reader's transformation into a sympathetic witness who will join her in testifying against the crime of slavery in the court of public opinion.

The first model Jacobs presents to her reader is one in which the act of witnessing is followed not by testimony, but by silence. In this passage Jacobs implies that Dr. Flint's harassment of Linda is exacerbated by the pervasive silence that accompanies it:

I cannot tell how much I suffered in the presence of these wrongs, nor how I am still pained by the retrospect. . . . The other slaves in my master's house noticed the change. Ma[n]y of them pitied me; but none dared to ask the cause. They had no need to inquire. They knew too well the guilty practices under that roof; and they were aware that to speak of them was an offense that never went unpunished.

I longed for someone to confide in. . . . But Dr. Flint swore he would kill me, if I was not silent as the grave. (Jacobs 28)

Acknowledging the powerlessness of Linda's fellow slaves, Jacobs does not deplore their failure to act on Linda's behalf; instead, she laments their refusal to provide Linda with an opportunity to speak, to offer themselves as listeners whose presence would enable her to testify to the sexual trauma of slavery. Beginning her account of sexual harassment with the phrase "I cannot tell," Jacobs reminds her reader that, just as Linda is silenced by Dr. Flint, she herself is censored by the hypocritical morality of a culture that implicitly sanctioned the sexual exploitation of slave women by law, even as it proscribed explicit reference to this practice in public discourse. The lack of such a listener, both in the narrative and at the moment of its production, means that much of this story of sexual exploitation is, in Felman and Laub's word, "annihilated."[2] But Jacobs compensates for these culturally imposed silences precisely by calling her reader's attention to slavery's conspiracy of silence.

If silence is not an appropriate response to the kind of vicarious witnessing that testimony engenders, neither is the excessive, unproductive emotionalism that the antebellum culture of sentiment tended to foster. Jacobs makes this quite clear in her portrayal of Linda's second testimonial encounter, in which the slave girl is interrogated by her mistress concerning Dr. Flint's sexual harassment:

"Will you answer truly all the questions that I ask?"

"Yes, ma'am."

"Tell me, then, as you hope to be forgiven, are you innocent of what I have accused you?"

"I am."

She handed me a Bible, and said, "Lay your hand on your heart, kiss this holy book, and swear before God that you will tell me the truth."

I took the oath she required, and I did it with a clear conscience.

"You have taken God's holy word to testify your innocence," said she. "If you have deceived me, beware! Now take this stool, sit

down, look me directly in the face, and tell me all that has passed
between your master and you."

I did as she ordered. As I went on with my account her color
changed frequently, she wept, and sometimes groaned. . . . She
pitied herself a martyr, but she was incapable of feeling for the
condition of shame and misery in which her unfortunate, helpless
slave was placed. (Jacobs 33)

In a chapter titled "The Jealous Mistress," which is immediately
preceded by "The Trials of Girlhood," Jacobs portrays the slave girl's
verbal interaction with her mistress as a trial in a courtroom as constricted as the "justice" it dispenses. This scene exposes the radical in-
stability of plantation justice as Linda shifts from defendant to victim
and back again, and Mrs. Flint by turns plays Linda's accuser, the clerk
who administers the oath, the cross-examining lawyer for the prosecu-
tion, and both judge and jury. Implicitly, the scene demonstrates the
necessity of the alternative court of public opinion in which the female
slave witness can give her testimony and receive a fair hearing. Furthermore, as Deborah Garfield points out, by "[p]reempting Linda's account of her own vulnerability, Mrs. Flint rescripts herself as the martyr of the drama and Linda as co-conspirator in the debauchery," and
"thus becomes an unsavory type within the text of [editor Lydia Maria]
Child's 'delicate' reader, who might eclipse a concern for the slave's sufferings with that of her own embattled image" (Garfield 113). Mrs.
Flint thus provides yet another negative example against which *Incidents*'s projected readers can pattern their own responses to the female
slave's testimony. (And testimony it most emphatically is; Jacobs is careful to cast the "innocent" slave girl's speech in testimonial, as opposed
to confessional, terms: "I took the oath she required, and I did it with
a clear conscience.") Mrs. Flint is a model of inappropriate behavior
because, although herself a witness to Dr. Flint's lasciviousness and
brutality ("she watched her husband with unceasing vigilance"), she
has "no sympathy" for the slave girl and, rather than using her own
power to protect "the young and innocent among her slaves," appropriates Linda's testimony for her own cathartic purposes and thus fails to
take action on behalf of the "unfortunate, helpless slave" (Jacobs 31).

Incidents's third testimonial encounter, which occurs between Linda
Brent and her grandmother, anticipates two other possible responses of
Jacobs's projected readership to her narrative: contempt and pity. Linda
recalls the day she finally shares her experiences with the older woman:

I went to my grandmother. My lips moved to make confession, but
the words stuck in my throat. . . . I think she saw something un-

usual was the matter with me. The mother of slaves is very watchful. She knows there is no security for her children. After they have entered into their teens, she lives in daily expectation of trouble. This leads to many questions. If the girl is of a sensitive nature, timidity keeps her from answering truthfully, and this well-meant course has a tendency to drive her from maternal counsels. Presently, in came my mistress . . . and accused me concerning her husband. My grandmother, whose suspicions had been previously awakened, believed what she said. She exclaimed, "O Linda! has it come to this? I had rather see you dead than to see you as you now are. You are a disgrace to your dead mother." She tore from my fingers my mother's wedding ring and her silver thimble. "Go away!" she exclaimed, "and never come to my house, again." Her reproaches fell so hot and heavy, that they left me no chance to answer. . . . How I longed to throw myself at her feet and tell her all the truth! (Jacobs 56–57)

The imagined scenario in which the slave girl's testimony is solicited by the sympathetic maternal listener contrasts sharply with Linda's experiences. Unlike the "sensitive" slave girl whom "timidity keeps from answering truthfully" the maternal figure's concerned, probing inquiries, Linda, who "wanted to confess" (56) to her grandmother, actively seeks out the older woman as an audience. But, rather than offering "maternal counsels," Linda's grandmother behaves in a remarkably unmaternal, unsympathetic fashion, believing Mrs. Flint's false testimony against her, refusing to give Linda a hearing, and figuratively sentencing her to death. Nevertheless, Linda continues to hope that, if her grandmother will only consent to hear her testimony, sympathy will win out over condemnation: "I thought if she could know the real state of the case . . . she would perhaps judge me less harshly" (57). When Linda finally shares her story with her grandmother, the older woman "listen[s] in silence" and, while refusing to "forgive" Linda, does express "pity" for her (57).

Once again, we might read this scene as an allegory of the production and reception of *Incidents* itself: the slave girl "confesses" her traumatic experiences to what she believes to be a sympathetic female audience, only to be silenced by the competing, false testimony of a slaveholder, she and her story figuratively "annihilated," in Felman and Laub's terminology, by an unsympathetic audience. Alternatively, when the slave girl finally *does* tell her story, she is haughtily condescended to as an object of pity. Linda's grandmother displays the responses Jacobs fears

Incidents's projected readership may have: judgment manifested as either contempt or pity. Sandra Gunning argues that the grandmother's "acceptance of Brent's narrative (which has a cathartic effect for Brent) signals the potential for a transformed relationship between speaker and reader" (Gunning 147). I am suggesting, however, that Jacobs portrays the grandmother's response as but one step on the road to this transformation, and an unsatisfactory one at that. Moreover, as I will demonstrate in my discussion of subsequent testimonial encounters in *Incidents*, Jacobs ultimately rejects catharsis, whether on the part of the speaker or the reader, as an impediment to her larger abolitionist, feminist political project of testifying against slavery.

Interestingly, Jacobs engages in confessional rhetoric more in this chapter, "A Perilous Passage in the Slave Girl's Life," than in any other to this point: Linda speaks of "confessing" to the reader her affair with Sands (Jacobs 56); she longs "to confess" to her grandmother that she is "no longer worthy of her love" (56); and, in the passage cited above, she struggles "to make confession" to her grandmother. But just as Linda's confessional posture makes her vulnerable to the contempt and pity of her censorious grandmother, Jacobs makes it quite clear that this chapter's confessional rhetoric exposes its author to censure from her projected audience. In the two celebrated apostrophes to her projected reader that frame Linda's confession of her affair with the white congressman, Mr. Sands, Jacobs's contrast of the legal powerlessness of the female slave with the comparatively privileged legal status of her white, Northern readership calls attention to how confessional discourse only serves to reinforce the unequal power relations between the two:

> O, ye happy women, whose purity has been sheltered from childhood, who have been free to choose the objects of your affection, whose homes are protected by law, do not judge the poor, desolate slave girl too severely! If slavery had been abolished, I, also, could have married the man of my choice; I could have had a home shielded by the laws; and I should have been spared the painful task of confessing what I am now about to relate. (54)

> Pity and pardon me, O virtuous reader! You never knew what it is to be a slave; to be entirely unprotected by law or custom; to have the laws reduce you to the condition of chattel, entirely subject to the will of another. . . . I know I did wrong. No one can feel it more sensibly than I do. . . . Still, in looking back, calmly, on the events of my life, I feel that the slave woman ought not to be judged by the same standards as others. (55–56)

Coupling "pity" with "pardon" and suggesting that her readers' comparatively privileged status in American society blocks their ability to sympathize with the female slave, Jacobs highlights how confessional discourse only serves to consolidate her readers' superior power and authority by placing them in a position to judge both *Incidents* and its author. But by contrasting the position of the slave woman, who is "unprotected by law," with that of her white reader, who is "protected by law," Jacobs challenges her audience's right to pass judgment on those for whom there is no justice. More than simply questioning the "standards" by which slave women are "judged," Jacobs effectively rejects judgment as an appropriate mode of response to the female slave's testimony, much as she rejects confession as the appropriate mode in which to articulate that testimony.[3]

So far, I have suggested an allegorical relationship between Jacobs's account of Linda Brent's testimonial encounters in slavery and the production and reception of *Incidents* itself. Through this relationship Jacobs alerts her readers to the pitfalls of narrative transmission, especially when narrative must be transmitted in confessional language. I want to turn now to Jacobs's rendering of three important testimonial encounters in the North. In these scenes, Jacobs presents her Northern readership with model responses that are much closer to home, both geographically and culturally, for all three involve the genteel responses of sympathetic Northerners.

Upon arriving in Philadelphia, Linda is taken in by the Reverend Jeremiah Durham, an African Methodist Episcopal preacher she meets on the wharf, to whom she "frankly" tells the history of her children's parentage. Durham responds politely but somewhat disapprovingly, "Your straight-forward answers do you credit; but don't answer every body so openly. It might give some heartless people a pretext for treating you with contempt" (160). Noting that the "word *contempt* burned me like coals of fire," Linda responds to Durham, "God alone knows how I have suffered; and He, I trust, will forgive me" (161). Linda makes it quite clear that if "God alone knows" her suffering, then God alone is qualified to judge her. And, although it is evident that Linda's Philadelphia benefactor does not himself judge her, the thrice repeated word "contempt" highlights the correspondence between his response and that of Linda's grandmother, as well as the responses Jacobs anticipates from *Incidents*'s projected readers. The North, it appears, is not so different from the South after all; indeed, Linda's behavior after the exchange with Durham suggests the parallels between the minister's attempts to silence her in the North and the silence, invisibility, confinement, and isolation that characterized her existence in the South: "glad to shut out the world for a while," Linda retires to her room, the Northern counterpart of her attic "retreat," and reflects on Rev. Durham's words, which "brought up great shadows from the mournful past" (161).

As affected as she is by his words, Linda is less concerned with Reverend Durham's response to her narrative than with that of his wife, who, by embodying key attributes of both Linda Brent and the narrative's projected readers, has the potential to symbolically bridge the gulf between them: an African-American woman like Linda, she, like the reader, is "surrounded by her husband and children, in a home made sacred by protecting laws" (160). Linda recalls that, parting with Mrs. Durham after her five-day stay, "I longed to know whether her husband had repeated to her what I had told him. I supposed he had, but she had never made any allusion to it. I presume it was the delicate silence of womanly sympathy" (162). Carla Kaplan has perceptively observed that in *Incidents* "silence is radically coded. Whereas white silence is presented as shameful and cowardly, black silence is valued, privileged, and protected. Whereas whites are called upon to speak out against the outrages of the Fugitive Slave Act . . . the ability to keep silent is an index, among blacks, of trustworthiness and reliability" (Kaplan 112). As I have demonstrated, however, there are several moments in *Incidents* when such racial coding does not apply and Jacobs implicitly indicts her fellow slaves for their reluctant complicity in slavery's conspiracy of silence. Here, however, Mrs. Durham's silence is coded, in gendered as opposed to racial terms, as "the delicate silence of womanly sympathy."

Linda Brent's second testimonial encounter in the North provides a clue as to why in this section of her narrative Jacobs presents silence not as guilty complicity but as exemplary feminine sympathy. In this scene, Linda has found work and lodging as a nurse in the household of the Bruce family, but she is soon forced to leave her new home for a second time when her whereabouts are revealed to Dr. Flint. Although she likes Mrs. Bruce and "longed for some one to confide in," Linda does not inform her employer of her fugitive status or her children's history. The renewed threat to her safety, however, makes her regret never having shared her story with her female employer:

> I had not concealed it merely on account of being a fugitive; that would have made her anxious, but it would have excited sympathy in her kind heart. I valued her good opinion, and I was afraid of losing it, if I told her all the particulars of my sad story. . . . But the sadness of my face attracted her attention and, in answer to her kind inquiries, I poured out my full heart to her, before bed

time. She listened with true womanly sympathy, and told me she would do all she could to protect me. (Jacobs 180)

In her "Preface," Jacobs insists that she tells her story not "to excite sympathy for [her] own sufferings" but, rather, "to arouse the women of the North to a realizing sense of the condition of two millions of women at the South." In this scene Linda Brent, still a slave, has faith that her story would "excite sympathy" in her auditor, but is almost silenced by her fear of losing the "good opinion" of her designated audience. Unlike Linda's fellow slaves, her grandmother, and Reverend Durham, Mrs. Bruce actively solicits the female slave's testimony; like Mrs. Durham, she receives the slave woman's troubled history "with true womanly sympathy." Despite the differences in their racial status, Mrs. Durham and Mrs. Bruce share not only feminine sympathy but also a willingness to protect the fugitive slave: upon meeting Mrs. Durham, Linda is "sure that she had comforted other weary hearts, before I received her sympathy" (160), and Mrs. Bruce, upon hearing Linda's story, promptly arranges for her safe escape from New York. Jacobs sanctions "the delicate silence of womanly sympathy" as long as it is accompanied by direct action "on behalf of [her] persecuted people."

In keeping with her project of providing *Incidents*'s target white Northern female readership with exemplars upon which to pattern their own behavior, Jacobs offers, through the first Mrs. Bruce and her successor, the widowed Mr. Bruce's second wife, two white female characters who engage in sympathetic acts of civil disobedience to protect the female slave. The second Mrs. Bruce offers her own child to Linda when she again attempts to escape the Fugitive Slave Law, so that the authorities will be forced to reveal Linda's whereabouts to her if she is captured. We can read these exemplary white characters as both models of and correctives to white abolitionist behavior: both Mrs. Bruces listen to Linda's story and respond not by silencing, appropriating, censuring, or pitying the bondswoman, but by joining her in resisting the laws of slavery, much as Jacobs would have her own audience do.

Linda Brent's final and most crucial testimonial encounter—"The Confession" of her affair with Mr. Sands to her daughter Ellen in the chapter of the same name—foregrounds the tensions between confessional and testimonial discourse that dwell beneath the surface of the narrative's previous encounters. In this chapter Linda finally discloses to Ellen, who is about to leave for boarding school, her adulterous relationship with Mr. Sands, only to have the girl protest, "O don't mother! Please don't tell me any more" (188). But Linda persists, determined that Ellen should know about her father, falling silent when Ellen admits that she has already learned his identity. Jacobs registers her narrator's mixed emotions:

> [Ellen] hugged me closer as she spoke, and I thanked God that the knowledge I had so much dreaded to impart had not diminished the affection of my child. I had not the slightest idea that she knew that portion of my history. If I had, I should have spoken to her long before; for my pent-up feelings had often longed to pour themselves out to some one I could trust. But I loved the dear girl the better for the delicacy she manifested toward her unfortunate mother. (189)

Garfield is quite right in characterizing this scene as "a revised template for the exchange between speech and ear that Jacobs wishes her white audience to imitate and for which her narrative, with its array of faulty listeners, has steadily prepared that audience" (Garfield 119). Ellen's response is both unobtrusive and sympathetic, which leads Linda Brent to identify her daughter as the ideal audience to whom to "trust" her story. But what are we to make of the fact that Ellen's reaction nevertheless has the effect of silencing her mother, much as the less sympathetic responses of Linda's fellow slaves, her grandmother, and Reverend Durham do? Garfield argues that because Ellen "curtails Brent's disclosures not out of . . . [a] porcelain politesse, but out of an insight into her mother's excruciating history," this chapter "restores to 'Confession' its sentimental cachet—as the sign of communion and regeneration" (120, 119). I would like to suggest, however, an alternative reading which argues that, by revising the purpose of Linda Brent's insurgent speech, this chapter, rather than restoring confession, represents Jacobs's ultimate rejection of confessional discourse as the appropriate vehicle for the slave woman's story.

Early in *Incidents*, describing the sexual exploitation endured by the female slave, Jacobs asserts that "[t]he felon's home in a penitentiary is preferable" to that of "a favorite slave" domiciled with "an unprincipled master and a jealous mistress," explaining that unlike the silenced slave woman, the felon "may repent, and turn from the error of his ways, and so find peace" (Jacobs 31). Throughout most of *Incidents*, confession seems to represent for Linda Brent, as for the felon, "peace" in the form of catharsis: this is why she "longed . . . to confide in" her fellow slaves, her grandmother, even Mrs. Flint. Unable to achieve catharsis in the South, Linda continues to seek out a sympathetic listener in the North, in the person of Reverend Durham. Durham's response suggests, however, that such "peace" is unattainable due to the dominant culture's emphasis on respectability and delicacy: this is why Linda resists sharing her story with Mrs. Durham and Mrs. Bruce, preferring to remain silent rather than risk censure. In "The Confession," however, Linda seems finally to have found "peace" in her daughter's exemplary, sympathetic, unobtrusive response. Suggesting that the time for catharsis has passed ("I should have spoken to her long before; for my pent-up feelings had often longed to pour themselves out to some one I could trust"), Linda tells her daughter about her affair with Sands not to achieve psychological "peace" but to provide the girl with important information concerning her parentage. If confession, on the one hand, provides catharsis for its speaker and, on the other, endows its auditor with the authority "to judge, punish, forgive, console, and reconcile," in Foucault's words, testimony is characterized by a very different set of effects, as this chapter suggests. Testimony allows the speaker to document the crimes she or he has witnessed but, perhaps more importantly, it also edifies and therefore potentially transforms its audience. Here, although Ellen already possesses the information Linda imparts, the latter's testimony has the effect of bringing the two closer together, much as it does with the first Mrs. Bruce. And once again, although Ellen urges her mother to remain silent, testimony is followed by further speech which in turn becomes a form of abolitionist activism.

Jacobs concludes the six-paragraph chapter titled "The Confession" with an apparently incongruous summary of Linda's activities after her daughter's departure for boarding school. Linda responds to her brother's request to join him in "opening an anti-slavery reading room in Rochester"; although this venture "was not successful," due to the fact that abolitionist "feeling was not general enough to support such an establishment," Linda nevertheless describes finding "warm antislavery friends there," especially "Isaac and Amy Post," with whom she lived "nearly a year" (189). The reference to the Posts marks the first time Jacobs identifies white characters by their actual names rather than by pseudonyms; this chapter marks the point at which the "eye-witness to the cruelty" of slavery becomes the author of the testimonial slave narrative, for it is the events described at the close of this chapter — the fugitive's public anti-slavery activities and her introduction to the Posts — which, historically, culminated in Jacobs's authorship and publication of *Incidents in the Life of a Slave Girl*. Although the reading room "was not successful" and Linda eventually returns to employment in the Bruce household, *Incidents* itself testifies to the narrator's ability to transform herself from a confessing victim of slavery into an outspoken abolitionist activist. "The Confession" indicates the necessity of a corresponding shift in rhetorical goals and strategies on the part of both abolitionists and African Americans: in order to be effective, speech can no longer be private, domestic, confessional, and cathartic, effecting change only in its individual speaker; instead, it must be public and testimonial, changing the status quo by effecting a transformation in its audience.

Early in *Incidents*, after recounting Dr. Flint's harassment of young Linda, Harriet Jacobs demands of her audience, "In view of these things, why are ye silent, ye free men and women of the north? Why do your tongues falter in maintenance of the right?" (29–30). By documenting the female slave's sexual harassment and concubinage—by giving her Northern, white audience a firsthand "view" of slavery's exploitation of women—Jacobs forces her reader to witness the gendered brutality of slavery. Placing her reader in the role of vicarious witness to slavery, she also reminds her audience of the responsibility that reading as a form of witnessing engenders. Once they have read, in *Incidents*, of the female slave's sexual victimization, once they have witnessed this largely unspeakable and unspoken aspect of slavery, Jacobs suggests, her readers have a duty to respond to her text with words: by taking the witness stand and testifying against the crime of slavery in the American court of public opinion. The very act of reading the testimonial text implicates the reader in "a network of complicity" (Felman and Laub 193): like the auditors portrayed in *Incidents*, Linda Brent, and by extension Harriet Jacobs herself, the reader must decide whether to comply with the unspeakable state of affairs *Incidents* portrays by remaining silent, or to speak out "in maintenance of the right." Jacobs thus transforms her account of the "trials" of the slave's "girlhood" into a trial that not only arraigns slavery and its perpetrators in the court of public opinion but also calls upon its passive witnesses— *Incidents*'s Northern, white, female audience—to join her in testifying against the crime of slavery. Jacobs, aware that the female slave's necessarily sexually explicit testimony is always in danger of being received as confession and its speaker subject to either censure or pity, carefully traces Linda Brent's move away from a confessional stance in the South to a more liberated testimonial stance in the North. Equally important, however, is the transformation Jacobs seeks to effect in her audience by providing them with a series of models upon which to pattern their response to her own narrative of sexual exploitation. Jacobs insists upon her readers' "response-ability" for slavery, their obligation to join her in both speaking out and acting against slavery. By doing so, Harriet Jacobs helped to forge a testimonial literary tradition that continues today.

Notes

1. Garfield observes that through scenes of what she calls "speech" and "hearing," Jacobs "gradually builds towards an implicit and tenuous pact with her reader in which the captive, not the white apologist of Southern patriarchy or the white reader, secures a pedagogical austerity" (Garfield 116). Discussing the "epistemic challenge" posed by Jacobs's "white readers' inevitably dual response of approbation and judgment," Ernest, citing Stepto, finds that Jacobs must "teach her readers to *hear* and understand the whole truth" (Ernest 180–181). Kaplan also employs Stepto's "discourse of distrust" theory to read *Incidents*, concluding, however, that Jacobs does *not* attempt to train her reader in the appropriate response to her text: "Jacobs' presumption seems to be that narration lacks this power, that the reader will not change, and that the mechanics of the narrative encounter are insufficient to the task of moral transformation" (Kaplan 111).

2. Focusing on Jacobs's reluctance to speak more plainly of her sexual exploitation while a slave, critics, reading her narrative as one of "quiet desperation" (Morrison 104), have emphasized the role of silence in *Incidents*. Pointing out that Jacobs provides very little information about the specifics of Dr. Flint's harassment of Linda or the nature of her affair with Mr. Sands, scholars have persuasively argued that these silences expose the inadequacy of both the traditional male-authored slave narrative and the sentimental novel as literary vehicles for Jacobs's story (see Smith 224–225; Jacobs xxi). It is my contention, however, that reading *Incidents* as a testimonial text allows us to reevaluate the role of silence in the narrative and to appreciate Jacobs's outspoken critique of the silence surrounding slavery.

3. My reading is consistent with that of Hazel Carby, who notes, "In contrast to the expected pattern of a confessional passage, which called for the unconditional acceptance of the judgment of readers," in these apostrophes "Jacobs attempted to deflect any judgmental response of moral condemnation through consistent narrative reminders to the reader that the material conditions of a slave woman's life were different from theirs" (Carby 58).

Works Cited

Andrews, William L. *To Tell a Free Story: The First Century of Afro-American Autobiography, 1760–1865*. Urbana: University of Illinois Press, 1986.

Barnes, Gilbert H., and Dwight L. Dumond, eds. *Letters of Theodore Dwight Weld, Angelina Grimké Weld, and Sarah Grimké, 1822–1844*. 2 vols. New York: Da Capo, 1970.

Beverley, John. "The Margin at the Center: On *Testimonio* (Testimonial Narrative)." In *De / Colonizing the Subject: The Politics of Gender in Women's Auto-biography,* edited by Sidonie Smith and Julia Watson, 91–114. Minneapolis: University of Minnesota Press, 1992.

——. "'Through All Things Modern': Second Thoughts on Testimonio." *Boundary 2* 18, no. 2 (1991): 1–21.

Carby, Hazel V. *Reconstructing Womanhood: The Emergence of the Afro-American Woman Novelist.* New York: Oxford University Press, 1987.

Douglass, Frederick. *My Bondage and My Freedom.* 1855. In *Autobiographies,* edited by Henry Louis Gates, Jr., 103–452. New York: Penguin, 1994.

——. *Narrative of the Life of Frederick Douglass, An American Slave, Written by Himself.* 1845. Edited by Houston A. Baker, Jr. New York: Viking-Penguin, 1982.

Ernest, John. "Motherhood beyond the Gate: Jacobs's Epistemic Challenge in *Incidents in the Life of a Slave Girl.*" In *Harriet Jacobs and* Incidents in the Life of a Slave Girl: *New Critical Essays,* edited by Deborah M. Garfield and Rafia Zafar, 179–198. Cambridge: Cambridge University Press, 1996.

Felman, Shoshana, and Dori Laub. *Testimony: Crises of Witnessing in Literature, Psychoanalysis, and History.* New York: Routledge, 1992.

Fisher, Philip. *Hard Facts: Setting and Form in the American Novel.* New York: Oxford University Press, 1985.

Foucault, Michel. *The History of Sexuality, Volume 1: An Introduction.* Translated by Robert Hurley. 1976. Reprint, New York: Vintage-Random House, 1990.

Garfield, Deborah M. "Earwitness: Female Abolitionism, Sexuality, and *Incidents in the Life of a Slave Girl.*" In *Harriet Jacobs and* Incidents in the Life of a Slave Girl: *New Critical Essays,* edited by Deborah M. Garfield and Rafia Zafar, 100–130. Cambridge: Cambridge University Press, 1996.

Garvey, T. Gregory. "Frederick Douglass's Change of Opinion on the U.S. Constitution: Abolitionism and the 'Elements of Moral Power.'" *American Transcendental Quarterly,* n.s., 9, no. 3 (1995), special issue on Frederick Douglass: 229–243.

Gunning, Sandra. "Reading and Redemption in *Incidents in the Life of a Slave Girl.*" In *Harriet Jacobs and* Incidents in the Life of a Slave Girl: *New Critical Essays,* edited by Deborah M. Garfield and Rafia Zafar, 131–155. Cambridge: Cambridge University Press, 1996.

Jacobs, Harriet A. *Incidents in the Life of a Slave Girl, Written by Herself.* 1861. Edited and with an introduction by Jean Fagan Yellin. Cambridge: Harvard University Press, 1987.

Kaplan, Carla. "Narrative Contracts and Emancipatory Readers: *Incidents in the Life of a Slave Girl.*" *Yale Journal of Criticism* 6, no. 1 (1993): 93–120.

Morrison, Toni. "The Site of Memory." In *Inventing the Truth: The Art and Craft of Memoir,* edited by William Zinsser, 101–124. Boston: Houghton Mifflin, 1987.

Nelson, Dana D. *The Word in Black and White: Reading "Race" in American Literature, 1638–1867.* New York: Oxford University Press, 1993.

Samuels, Shirley, ed. *The Culture of Sentiment: Race, Gender, and Sentimentality in Nineteenth-Century America.* New York: Oxford University Press, 1992.

Sekora, John. "Black Message/White Envelope: Genre, Authenticity, and Authority in the Antebellum Slave Narrative." *Callaloo* 10, no. 3 (1987): 482–515.

Smith, Valerie. "'Loopholes of Retreat': Architecture and Ideology in Harriet Jacobs' *Incidents in the Life of a Slave Girl.*" In *Reading Black, Reading Feminist: A Critical Anthology,* edited by Henry Louis Gates, Jr., 212–226. New York: Penguin-Meridian, 1990.

Sommer, Doris. "'Not Just a Personal Story': Women's *Testimonios* and the Plural Self." In *Life/Lines: Theorizing Women's Autobiography,* edited by Bella Brodzki and Celeste Schenck, 107–130. Ithaca: Cornell University Press, 1988.

Starling, Marion Wilson. *The Slave Narrative: Its Place in American History.* 2nd ed. Washington, D.C.: Howard University Press, 1988.

Stepto, Robert B. "Distrust of the Reader in Afro-American Narratives." In *Reconstructing American Literary History,* edited by Sacvan Bercovitch, 300–322. Cambridge: Harvard University Press, 1986.

———. "I Rose and Found My Voice: Narration, Authentication, and Authorial Control in Four Slave Narratives." In *The Slave's Narrative,* edited by Charles T. Davis and Henry Louis Gates, Jr., 225–241. New York: Oxford University Press, 1985.

Tompkins, Jane. *Sensational Designs: The Cultural Work of American Fiction, 1790–1860.* New York: Oxford University Press, 1985.

Weld, Theodore Dwight. *American Slavery As It Is: Testimony of a Thousand Witnesses.* 1837. Reprint, New York: Arno/New York Times, 1969.

Young, James E. *Writing and Rewriting the Holocaust: Narrative and the Consequences of Interpretation.* Bloomington: Indiana University Press, 1988.

Yúdice, George. "*Testimonio* and Postmodernism." *Latin American Perspectives* 18, no. 3 (1991): 15–31.

Four

Water Rites
Navigating Passage and Social Transformation in American Slave and Travel Narratives

Richard Hardack

The American slave narrative emerges as an ideological inversion of the white American travel narrative, which is a tale of travel and social passage masking a tale of confinement and immobility. Where the white travel narrative, contrary to expectations, typically inters its protagonists, the slave narrative stages a never wholly successful attempt to liberate its protagonist through rituals of travel. Though itself ostensibly a chronicle of confinement and immobility, the slave narrative stakes but also masks its own claims to the allegedly liberating motifs of the white travel narrative. The crucial differences between the genres stem from the social circumstances of their writers. Male and female slaves, or their forbears, are brought to America by ship as involuntary seafarers, and lose their status as social beings in the process. By contrast, white men sometimes escape lower- and middle-class white society (or themselves) by going to sea, and so elevate their social status. Yet at the end of many white travel narratives, the protagonists are barely better off than when they started, if they are even still alive to tell the tale; at the end of many slave narratives, the protagonists have gained a hard-won transformation of social status. In sociological terms, such outcomes predominate because white travel narratives invoke a ceremonial affirmation of status rather than the ritualistic transformation of identity that slave narratives do.

An earlier version of this article, "Water Pollution and Motion Sickness: Rites of Passage in Nineteenth-Century Slave and Travel Narratives," appeared in *ESQ: A Journal of the American Renaissance* 41, no. 1 (1995): 1–40. I thank the editors for permission to reprint parts of that essay.

Given the anthropologist Mary Douglas's definition of taboo as a proscription of that which violates categories and is hence contradictory,[1] to be a black runaway, particularly a female black runaway who then writes about her experience, is to achieve marginality in motion, to transgress a series of borders and restrictions. On many levels, however, the slave narrative tells of the rite of passage thwarted, of a ritual partly generated and controlled by the master and of a genre confronting other master narratives. Still, in what the anthropologist Victor Turner calls the betwixt and between period,[2] where categorical positions are suspended and master and slave may confront one another on equal footing or even change positions—as Frederick Douglass does in his several confrontations with his ex-master Covey—the rite of passage also promises to destabilize the relationship between travel and slave narrative. How far that passage reasserts or transforms the power of masters, how far it can transform the slave, and how much it must affirm the existing order become the central questions of the slave narrative. As a ritual act of personal transformation and transportation, the slave narrative declares its author free and must make a polemical call for the liberation of all other slaves, yet it cannot achieve this social transformation through the same methods of *individual* passage and ritual transformation it has just advocated. (The slave narrative must always be part palimpsest, erasing certain elements deemed insufficiently representative of slavery, hiding details regarding escape, and incorporating motifs from other genres; but it does not erase its own memory.) The freedom of Frederick Douglass and Harriet Jacobs then stands against the bondage of all other slaves, for such is their bind: they must declare themselves free yet simultaneously still enslaved with their race. The failure, or rather incompleteness, of the slave narrative is necessitated by the juxtaposition of a particular self which would pass through and a race which has as yet been passed over. In the meantime, the runaway slave is authorized to write only by an act of physical passage, a return across sea, while remaining in a state of liminality or transition, still part-slave, never completely transformed. As a result of the importance of travel and transition, the implicit focus of many slave narratives is on water itself, the medium of passage; where white sailors often become slaves, slaves often figuratively or literally free themselves as sailors. The often inverted representations of liberating or contaminated water and liminal travel in slave and travel narratives are closely linked indices of how the two genres become mutually defining and intertextual.

Where white travel narratives frequently become tales of incarceration in whaling ships or other vessels, slave narratives often construct trajectories not just of liberation, but of "authentic" travel, which is imagined as a form of transgression. Slave narratives inscribe a variety of passages which cross dangerous social and physical barriers, producing the pollution which arises from a confusion of social categories. Several "fake" white travel narratives, like Poe's *Narrative of Arthur Gordon Pym*, and hybrid narratives which combine aspects of the slave and travel genres, such as Melville's *Benito Cereno*, also focus on the interface between race and travel. At the end of *Pym*, only the putative secondary author is left to tell the tale of mutiny and passage; in *Benito Cereno*, the slave mutiny, the liminal event, can't even be witnessed directly. In these tales, the journey's true liminality is either entirely called into question through the motifs of repetition and circularity, or staged completely outside the narrative; as a result, the social transformation the genre is supposed to provide cannot transpire. The lack of a real journey even precludes the possibility of social affirmation for the white characters. While the slave narrative can't depict many aspects of the slave's flight to freedom for reasons of security, it can fully document the rituals of passage and hence afford social transformation to the slave.

The mid-nineteenth-century white travel narrative often incorporates elements of the slave narrative, recounting how white men are effectively imprisoned and denied all constitutional rights aboard brigs. (As Ishmael laments in the first chapter of *Moby Dick*, echoing Redburn in complaining of the sea-captain's right to order him about, "who ain't a slave?") The slave narrative then inverts the polarities of the travel narrative, evident particularly in its representations of water, pollution, and the forms of passage. The slave narrative, as well as the distinct but related genre of the captivity narrative, might then be seen as a mirror inversion of the travel narrative, and vice versa.

Like many slave narratives, Melville's *Typee*, for example, raises questions of autobiographical authenticity, revealing that most putatively factual white travel narratives are as "contaminated" by fiction as the slave narrative. It is no accident that Poe's *Narrative of Arthur Gordon Pym* is also a *Narrative* like Douglass's or other slave writers'. (*Pym* should be situated in a purely ironic framework as a fake captivity narrative which masquerades as a travel narrative by appropriating the motifs of the slave narrative.) Where white travel narratives dismantle themselves as fictions, slave narratives try to reconstruct themselves as facts. The subject of this essay is not white travel narratives, but transformation in slave narratives; but the questions of liminality, transformation, slavery, and water-pollution are inextricable from the issue of genre. Poe's *Pym* and Melville's *Benito Cereno*, which play with issues of credibility involved in the liminal transformations of travel, thus set up the context for the discussion of Douglass and Jacobs which follows. As William Lloyd Garrison notes in his preface to Douglass's 1845 autobiography, "tell [white readers] of . . . scenes of pollution and blood . . . and they affect to be greatly indignant at such enormous exaggerations."[3] In other words, the issue of pollution in both slave and travel narratives can't be separated from the credibility of the slave narrative; liminality finally becomes a function of genre. Slave narratives cross not just the polluting borders of slavery, but those between themselves and white travel narratives; water, the substance which joins them and which is often transmuted to blood, thus becomes the contested site for both genres.

According to Mary Douglas, "place in the hierarchy of purity is biologically transmitted," and "boundary pollution" is often reflected in the variety of our bodily fluids; seemingly neutral or pure (unpolluted) water then serves as the basic medium, itself a linguistic discourse for culture.[4] Even if, as the code preceding the message, water in a semiotic context is not exactly equivalent to the message, it affords both the specific and abstract space for transition, and in fact may determine the form and content of the message. Even in his "Appendix," where he clarifies his position regarding conventional religion, Douglass consistently uses the terminology of contamination: "He who is the religious advocate of marriage robs millions of its sacred influence, and leaves them to the ravages of wholesale pollution" (*NFD*, 121). In violation of the categories of white society, and uncertain how far those categories could or should be rehabilitated, Douglass must somehow use what is situated as a tainted discourse or genre to reclaim a pure one, and discover the sources of corruption. By tracing the paths of this pollution, one can also trace the relationship between nineteenth-century slave and travel narratives.

In all the primary texts addressed in this article, captivity is juxtaposed with travel, and the passage from slave to sailor, or the reverse, is marked by the degree of each character's liminality. Douglass's *Narrative*, Jacobs's *Incidents in the Life of a Slave Girl*, Poe's *Pym*, and Melville's *Benito Cereno* are all accounts concerned with race, slavery, authorial veracity, liminality, and, except for Jacobs's, with the ways being at sea perpetuates or inverts captivity on land. *Pym* and *Benito Cereno* might be thought of as slave narratives rather than travel narratives, much as Douglass's slave narrative could be considered a travel narrative. If anything, we should regard *Pym* as an inversion of the slave narrative, a failed, parodic attempt at self-definition through travel. Emblematically, Pym moves perpetually—if through staccato repetition— toward, rather than away from, "the *white* curtain of the South."[5] To the extent that it lays bare the otherwise hidden assumptions behind most white travel narratives and exaggerates their ideological imperatives, *Pym* actually becomes emblematic of the genre.

Pym addresses himself, "principally, if not altogether," to readers who have never been to sea, and such a disingenuous disclaimer marks his tale as a parodic travel narrative; only naive readers who have never been on a voyage—analogous to naive readers who only know either Northern or Southern misrepresentations of slavery—could believe that Poe has (*NAGP,* 105). "As [his] readers may not all have seen these" new climates and their inhabitants, Pym leaves the dubious reader at a pole opposed yet equivalent to the blacks—for whose "ignorance . . . we were not prepared," and which seems affected to Pym. In other words, on the one hand, only blacks and dubious readers would doubt the veracity of Poe's inverted slave narrative, but, on the other hand, no reader of Poe could be dull enough to take his tale seriously (*NAGP,* 152, 169). Ignorance, credibility, gullibility—and the affectation of these traits—along with the inexpressible nature of the liminal are then the first issues at stake in all these narratives. Melville, whose work here occupies a position between Poe's and Douglass's, addresses himself to the Delanos of the world, people who have perhaps been to sea, or should have been, and yet remain blind to what they have witnessed. While Melville's tale at least echoes its author's actual travels, *Pym* cannot engage the liminal because even its narrator never sets out to sea, never genuinely encounters any other, and is never marginalized like Cereno. Pym claims that no event in the course of human experience is as destabilizing as this "living inhumation" he specializes in, casting him "beyond the remotest confines" of hope, "never to be conceived"; but Pym remains always only on the verge of this inconceivable passage (*NAGP,* 182). He never passes through the stages of liminal transformation. The narrative drifts toward the other, the black, who in both works is unmasked only after a prolonged period of deceit. In *Pym* the unmasking is a hoax; in *Benito Cereno,* unmasking is itself the hoax.

In many ways, *Pym* can be considered to embody everything of which the slave narrative is falsely accused. Pym's perpetual admissions of inaccuracy are feints whose final effect is quite similar to Swift's in *Gulliver's Travels* (a notoriously unreliable and multiprefaced sea narrative); we construct a wholly untrustworthy, self-aggrandizing narrator whose every protestation of sanity, innocence, and credibility further transforms him into a bullying fraud or a dangerous con man. Pym, the son of "a respectable trader in sea-stores," has become a disreputable trader in sea-stories, whose only transition is from mild to intense sickness. No liminal transformations can occur in a narrative that holds both accuracy and travel itself in a "miserable existence [of] captivity" (*NAGP,* 185). Any possible ritual passage involved in the shift to the *Grampus,* where Pym leaves the grandfather who would disown him, would occur during his time of captivity: a period normally devoted to the liminal struggle, when identity and position are most threatened. But Pym exists in a vacuous isolation, whether alone or with his upper-deck doubles; his own liminality, trickery, and isolation never impinge on Pym, which is what enables him to forget each captivity as soon as it ends. Unlike that of the slave narrator, Pym's whole purpose is to erase history, and especially captivity, as soon as it has occurred. Beyond anything else, beyond John Irwin's sense of its obsession with psychological doubling, inhumation, and death and rebirth, *Pym* is a text about the alleged "impermeability" of horror and, by direct implication, of slavery.[6] Untouched by the liminal events he describes, Pym effectively imagines he can live in the midst of slavery or defilement without ultimately being contaminated by it.

Pym then inverts, or one could say inadvertently restores, the framework of credibility applied to slave narratives; as most white travel narrators would attest, sailors, not slaves, are the most untrustworthy story-tellers. Not only is his memory suspect and his narrative identity always recursive, but Pym's models for narration are all liars, from Swift to Poe. Even within *Pym,* sailors are never trustworthy story-tellers, as evinced in their spurious, nonchalantly Gulliveresque story of having drowned thirty or forty persons—Pym and his companions—at sea. Pym now suspects more than half of Augustus's oceanic stories to have been fabrications, "wonders in the ways of deception"; Peters, for some reason unavailable to give his deposition (like Poe), and Augustus, dead, cannot, as Melville's Toby could, come forward to testify (*NAGP,* 64, 207). Pym's fictitious life, bound so closely to the editor who prefaces his work and testifies for him, depends "upon lying close" (*NAGP,* 80). (And the nautical notion of "lying-to" is laboriously invoked thereafter.) Presumably, if Poe inverts a paradoxical Southern assumption that slaves, while incapable of telling the truth, are simultaneously too simpleminded to substitute fiction for reality, his narrator is situated as too sublimely complex to let reality intrude on fiction.

In its repetition of inhumation, its gothic warping of captive space, *Pym* foreshadows Jacobs; but where Jacobs is unable to leave her liminal space, Pym is only unwilling. *Pym* proposes a captivity endlessly if discontinuously repeated, giving the illusion of progress, based on the future position of the writer, who has precisely arrived without traveling; the narrative's greatest hoax lies in this promise of motion. In contrast, Babo is trying to gain a haven, a new home, unlike Pym, who is trying to regain his old one; inexplicably but persistently bound southward, "earnestly bent" on falling in various stages, Pym can only reaffirm the old South. The (fictional) white travel narrative tends ceremonially to affirm an old identity rather than transform it. In his "species of second childhood," Pym's every "fear is fully confirmed," his first childhood and old self reified, while his passage, which would reflect his presumed surroundings, is denied *(NAGP,* 130, 192). The actual slave narrative then must navigate the labyrinth of self-erasing fictions Poe locates at the heart of white travel narratives which effectively usurp the structural positions of slaves.

Credibility is the first crucial issue the slave confronts in expressing his liminality. Because blacks could not bear witness, could not be protected by or inscribed within the law, the reader of the slave narrative becomes a criminal, an abettor of the black writer; the reader is liminalized by the very strength of the work. Since blacks were not supposed to be writing, the slave narrative begins its existence as an anomalous and liminal text. (Blacks in slave narratives primarily address, and in effect argue with, white men, and attempt to supplicate white women readers; white men in travel narratives, in degrees of solitude, argue among themselves and attempt to ignore white women. Where the white travel narrative putatively seeks the reader's sympathy and trust, the slave narrative seeks to transform the reader's political stance.) Even within a sympathetic community, the slave narrative must remain narrowly mimetic, and this limitation also fetters the slave as writer. Where the travel writer could portray the fabulous as the real, the slave writer could only seem to portray the real as the fabulous. Paradoxically, to the extent that the narrative would serve as a testimony of fact and a legal document, any mimetic representation dilutes the liminal force of the narrative if the embrace of a fractured realism is all blacks should be able to manage; the mere truth itself becomes insufficient to the narrative's political purpose.

Like the travel narrative, the slave narrative must claim that its seeming exaggerations represent facts—but it inverts this prescription. The question of the slave narrative's genre is a vexed one: as John Sekora asks in "Is The Slave Narrative a Species of Autobiography?" "Does it matter that the slave narrative as a form begins fully encased in the trappings of another—some would say white and hostile—literary mode?"[7] The white travel narrative, white autobiography, and white sponsorship form a secondary border around the slave narrative, another border the slave must pass. The slave narrative then has to present a mixture of romance and naturalism, captivity and travel along with the two identities of the slave, of slave/free, black/white, illiterate (oral)/

writing; these oppositions are mirrored in "the double relation of master and father," and perhaps also of master and mast, sale and sail. In *The Narrative of the Life of Frederick Douglass* and Harriet Jacobs's *Incidents in the Life of a Slave Girl*, the slave narrator attempts to appropriate the authority of the travel narrator while also subverting his assumptions.

The slave narrative is a genre of crossed borders, particularly borders marked by water—a fluid threshold, indistinct and indefinable, which also transforms what it conducts. In Douglass, the black who accidentally crosses the border to another plantation and the black who "flees" to a stream to "escape" a scourging cross a double boundary. If a slave can be punished or killed arbitrarily, if plantation discourse is precisely arbitrary, unpredictable and unaccountable, then crossing the water boundary turns an already liminal figure into a site of conflicting genres, identities, and attributes. Unlike the white who "fled" with impunity to his father's residence upon having killed a servant, the fleeing black man, whether marked by water or tar, has nowhere to claim asylum (*NFD*, xiii). The attempt to authorize the slave narrative's discourse by a simple appropriation of the literary functions of the travel narrative could not succeed; in the end such a narrative also has no place to seek asylum. Each slave-writer is already a criminal, a transgressor, before he has even begun to write; contrary to initial expectations, mere writing, itself a "crime," will not serve to free or transform the slave. A ritual transformation of the self must be invoked to transform a slave into a free man.

Many aspects of the slave narrative emulate the travel narrative, and such imitations of the master at first provide the only way to be freed of him. Still, the slave narrative remains as much a construct of the white society which set up the white travel narrative as is slavery itself. The very whiteness of Garrison's preface reveals the frame of Douglass's narrative; not only are the *Narrative*'s internal events a response to white society, but its skeletal structures, its own passages, are partly determined, skewed, by a superimposed genre. Before Douglass begins, someone must ease the reader's safe passage into this dangerous work. The imagined audience of the slave narrative is indignant at "exaggerations, wholesale misstatements, such abominable libels," and this reader sets the boundaries of discourse and transformation (*NFD*, xi–xii).[8] Garrison must vouch at length to this audience for Douglass's integrity by crediting him with no imagination (repeatedly in these "wholesale" or pecuniary terms). Though its names have been changed, the slave narrative must purportedly be maintained as a truthful account, and its representation of blood and pollution can't be "discredited," in the monetary terms of truth, by Northern whites who have no knowledge of slavery.

Throughout this essay, I adapt the distinction between ceremony which affirms and ritual which transforms that Victor Turner develops in "Betwixt and Between: The Liminal Period in *Rites de Passage*."[9] The slave narrative typically offers a set of conventionalized rites of passage, involving for example suffering, cooking, reading, and physical passage. Douglass's history invokes some presumably straightforward transformations: "the dark night of slavery closed in upon me," he writes, "and behold a man transformed into a brute" (*NFD*, 75). Slavery transforms man into liminal brute; the slave narrative, liminal itself, must transform him back: "You have seen how a man was made a slave; you shall see how a slave was a made a man." The two positions are incommensurate, and interbreeding between the two species—the two beings Douglass has been, slave and man—produces the mule of social discourse, the mulatto, the writer of the slave narrative (*NFD*, 77). (Jacobs's chapter "The Slave Who Dared to Feel Like A Man" evinces a similar awareness of the social transgression of the slave who crosses this line between "species.") Douglass tries to use transformation—which is figured as absolute—rather than mere conversion—which is figured as gradual—to transcend the dichotomies and binary oppositions Henry Louis Gates observes in his narrative.[10] In addition to his use of irony, Douglass circumvents dualities—of genre, race, and social status, and even the duality between natural signifier and constructed signified that Gates identifies—by allowing himself, in his state of liminal transformation, at least temporarily, to encompass both sides of any binary. Douglass thus achieves an all-inclusive "largeness" sought by white transcendental writers like Emerson and Whitman. The rite of passage is thus itself effectively liminalized for Douglass, complicated by a second taboo overlaid on the original restrictions or conventions of passage. It is as he is "fast approaching manhood" that Douglass runs into his brick wall, for as a slave he is unable to pass or move, and is consistently "mangled" instead (*NFD*, 100).

Much is of course made of Douglass's ritual of personal passage in the narrative, but the most interesting aspects of such transformation-become-transgression are expressed in terms of liquid. This association of water, and polluting and cleansing liquid, with the slave's passage to manhood can serve as the focus of comparison of two broad types of "travel" literature. The slave narrative, like the white travel narrative, is a chronicle of social transformation, one which typically occurs in some site—the ocean, the river, a removed space—defined against the geography of "normative" society. The waters mark the borders of slavery in all areas, from the farthest shore to the nearest body:

> We could see no spot, this side of the ocean, where we could be free. . . . At every gate through which we were to pass, we saw a watchman—at every ferry a guard—on every bridge a sentinel. . . . [slavery]—its robes already crimsoned with the blood of millions, and even now feeding itself greedily upon our own flesh. (*NFD*, 92)

On this side of the ocean, all liminal markers—every gate, every ferry passage, every bridge—represent not just the slave's potential freedom, but his potential recapture and death in water; the signs of water are themselves fluid. The threat of cannibalism central to the period's social discourse about slavery first manifests itself in the slave narrative in slavery's bestiality, and finally in its frenzied consumption of slaves. The starved slave is literally bled dry by a parasitic slavery. Slaves in passage find themselves "as if in the midst of wild beasts, whose greediness to swallow up the trembling and half-famished fugitive is only equaled by that with which the monsters of the deep swallow up the helpless fish upon which they subsist" (*NFD*, 112). The drama played out on the human body is thus analogous to the larger drama of passage played out in the journey. During the forced expatriation from Africa, slaves are in a sense consumed in the hold of the ship, surrounded by water, interred and transformed by white society. This passage must be reversed by the slave's own revision of the white travel narrative.

Douglass consistently depicts starvation and slavery's cannibalism in liquid terms: to escape bloodhounds, one must cross the right rivers, purify one's blood. At several points in the narrative, the black man is figuratively devoured, shedding his martyr's blood, but the transubstantiation fails, and at first all passage is denied: "Now it was starvation, causing us to eat our own flesh;—now we were contending with the waves, and were drowned . . . [torn] by the fangs of the terrible bloodhound," and the fugitives are virtually drowned in their own blood after "swimming rivers" to reach an opposite wilderness (*NFD*, 93). The slave's very blood is tainted, infused with slavery and the blood of slaveholders. Still, only persistence in the water route can offer the slaves an untraceable, invisible passage: Douglass would navigate directly "up the Chesapeake Bay . . . it was our purpose to turn our canoe adrift, and follow the guidance of the north star. . . . Our reason for taking the water route was, that we were less liable to be suspected as runaways; we hoped to be regarded as fishermen" (*NFD*, 94). Though cast adrift, while he is a fisherman—and perhaps finally a fisher of men—on these waters, while pursuing that north star, Douglass would be safe. The water, with his liminal guise of fisherman, would act as catalyst for his transformation into a free man, or at least give him the temporary appearance of one. But the slaves' "passes" can protect them only "while on the bay," and water's limited access at first thwarts Douglass's escape (*NFD*, 94).

Throughout the *Narrative*, social and geographic markers are established with images of water. Douglass's first master was "called Captain Anthony—a title which, I presume, he acquired by sailing a craft on the Chesapeake Bay"; his overseer's name was Plummer, and his master Captain Auld can also be included in this roll (*NFD*, 24). The line between captains and masters, and even between captains and fathers, is blurred from the start of Douglass's text. Naming, and renaming, necessitates a form of watery baptism: Douglass of course receives his last name from the "Lady of the Lake" (*NFD*, 114). One's freedom is marked by a social sanction to control and navigate waters. The blurring between people and ships is apparent in the generic naming of vessels, and this blurring of mastery, if not pronouns, is emphasized throughout the text: Colonel Lloyd

> was able to keep in almost constant employment a large sloop, in carrying [products] to market at Baltimore. This sloop was named Sally Lloyd, in honor of one of the colonel's daughters. My master's son-in-law, Captain Auld, was master of the vessel; she was otherwise manned by the colonel's own slaves. (*NFD*, 27)

(A slave at sea is at least "manning" a boat.) "If a slave is convicted of any high misdemeanor," he is "put on board the sloop and carried to Baltimore" to be sold. Baltimore thus enters the story as another liminal site, a port offering either freedom or reinscription under new masters. Living on a plantation "on the border of Miles River," Douglass begins to suspect that the bordered river is always up for grabs; twin-shored, its waters are double-sided, the space of passage itself (*NFD*, 27–28). Though his initial experiences are inconclusive, Douglass eventually proceeds to free-shipping in his mind: when he "reached New Bedford, I visited the wharves, to take a view of the shipping. Here I found myself surrounded with the strongest proofs of wealth. Lying at the wharves, and riding in the stream, I saw many ships of the finest model" (*NFD*, 115). And so ships, wealth, and freedom come to be conflated in Douglass's imagination. As he is "walled in" by the edge of his transformed surroundings, Douglass begins the process of recommercializing vessels whose use had been purely "escapist" and whose prior economic task pertained to enslavement. The slave ship is turned upside down to provide a freedom ride; in the liminal state of slavery, all oppositions can be inverted. It is then "from the wharves" (*NFD*, 116) that Douglass approaches the town itself.

Douglass associates fluency and affluence through images of passage, and the complex relationship between slavery, education, and freedom is saturated by water. The results of learning to read eventually "would flow" to Douglass, and his path to literacy would thus be crucially untraceable (*NFD*, 50). The ability to read and then to travel provides the ability to reconfigure oneself, to attain wealth/currency and every imaginable social fluency. But waters are mostly contaminated for Douglass, and in the South the waters are frequently and explicitly poisoned; under slavery, Douglass had "imbibed" misconceptions of the North (*NFD*, 115). Douglass's dissolution is typically expressed in liquid terms: "I was made to drink the bitterest dregs of slavery. . . . I sank down again," etc. (*NFD*, 75). Repeatedly, when Douglass is beaten, it is only "the blood [which] ran freely" (*NFD*, 78). In danger of bleeding to death, Douglass wanders through the "bogs and briers," the wilderness bordering the waters of separation (*NFD*, 79). Liminal blood—conceived as representing a state between white and black, internal and external— becomes a mark of the slave; Douglass causes "the blood to run" on Covey, but has "no blood" drawn from him, and so moves away from "the bloody arm of slavery" (*NFD*, 82–83). Douglass's passage to manhood is here expressed in the control of bloodshed, even as the master regulates slavery as if it were a system of waterworks. To maintain the "safety valves" which relieve the mounting pressures of slavery, the master compels the slave to "dissipation . . . [to] drink of his own accord," and by so doing swallow his position, "drink it down" (*NFD*, 85). When he recalls the Christians breaking up his Sabbath school, Douglass's "blood boils as [he] thinks of [their] bloody manner," of the "bloody-minded" and "blood-thirsty kidnappers" who literally feed off slaves (*NFD*, 89, 103, 117).

Douglass's passage from slavery is therefore achieved through blood and liquid, through "the blood stained gate," a kind of floodgate (*NFD*, 25). The transformation of Douglass's mistress, restored to her old image, also transpires in water, or a water catalyzed by blood:

> The heart of my once overkind mistress was again melted into pity. My puffed out eye and blood-covered face moved her to tears. . . . [She] washed the blood from my face, and, with a mother's tenderness. . . . [Master Hugh] gave expression to his feelings by pouring out curses. (*NFD*, 102)

Douglass here characterizes his position in the fluid language of melting, bleeding, tearing, washing, and pouring; what is mangled becomes mingled. His mistress's cruelty dissolves in the face of his own liminality, but his master still curses him in the same liquid terms. By the bay, Douglass in turn, "with no audience but the Almighty, would pour out my soul's complaint, in my rude way, with an apostrophe to the moving multitude of ships," not men (*NFD*, 76). Water is reclaimed from the depths as Douglass works through his passage; slaves who spend their Sundays by the water fishing, incurring the displeasure of masters, become Douglass's ideals. His depiction of pollution appropriates the symbolic pieties of Christian typology for his own purposes: Douglass would turn tainted blood back to pure water.

To escape a scourging, a slave "ran and plunged himself into a creek, and stood there in the depth of his shoulders, refusing to come out," as if safe in a marginal or sacred position where he cannot be scathed (*NFD*, 40). But such demarcations offer no sanctuary: "His mangled body sank out of sight, and blood and brains marked the water where he had stood." Again, blood and the mangled body are used as markers of slavery, ones that are only partially washed away. The marks of defilement and guilt on those "stained with [their] brother's blood" leave traces in water where none should be (*NFD*, 40–41). Many slaves attempt to reach freedom at creeks and shores only to be so "stained." Water should but often cannot erase the signs of trespass, leaving the slave far more visible than he would want to be; a slave "get[s] beyond the limits" and "at this trespass, Mr. Bondly took offense, and with his musket came down to the shore, and blew its deadly contents into the poor old man" (*NFD*, 42). Trespass and pollution are then indissociable for the slave, whose normal position is liminal at best, and whose position in transit is doubly marginalized. As Melville would argue, slavery is itself a thing writ in water, leaving no normally accessible trace of itself; when slavery does leave traces, it is through the body and blood of the slave.

A variety of pollutions appear throughout the slave narrative; reminders of "mutilations and brandings, of scenes of pollution and blood," or of the "impossibility of touching *tar* without being defiled," occur almost at set intervals in the *Narrative* (*NFD*, 33: emphasis in original). The defilements of blood pollution, the contaminations of slavery, cannot be cleansed even in water, unless one travels through that water to a new destination; travel finally purges pollution, undoes the effects of the forced journey from Africa to America. During three joyful days prior to a voyage, Douglass "spent the most part of all these days in the creek, washing off the plantation scurf and preparing myself for my departure." Yet even as he would desire to purge himself for this passage, Douglass is also told he "must get all the dead skin off my feet and hands before I could go to Baltimore." Douglass must wash off his past without washing off his identity. He scrubs until not just "the mange, but the skin" is washed off before he sails out on the Miles River. After he has bathed himself, washing off not blackness but the tar of pollution, Douglass takes what he hopes will be his last look at the plantation (*NFD*, 44).

The ship provides the horizon to a man who is trapped in social desolation, kept to the present, without knowledge of time or space. On board ship, Douglass begins the process of looking forward to freedom and back to slavery; he "there spent the remainder of the day," like the bulk of transformative time in the river itself, "in looking ahead, interesting myself in what was in the distance rather than in things near by or behind" (*NFD*, 46). Yet of course Douglass can tell us so only precisely in looking back, in writing his narrative of the past. Though he has no time to go on shore at Annapolis, Douglass's voyage to Baltimore has "opened the gateway to all my subsequent prosperity" (*NFD*, 46–47). Having opened this gate, Douglass here speaks of his role as chosen baby; Douglass becomes, at least for a time, the baby Moses, separated from his family, drawn in by Pharaoh's daughter in his basket, finally to be elevated to the ruling caste and freedom, if not to lead his own exodus. But as Douglass himself begins to suggest, some of his identity rubs off in the water, and transformation can remove as much as it adds; travel no longer represents a "pure" experience, but belongs as much to slavery as to freedom. In biblical terms, none of the slave generation can survive passage to the holy land; to be transformed from slave to freeman is to die and lose the old self. "Travel to" necessitates a kind of death: the sickness, transformative cleansing, and rebirth of the self.

From this point, Douglass is keen to keep travel and water uppermost in mind: on leaving for Baltimore, he "paid particular attention to the direction which the steamboats took to go to Philadelphia," and "deemed this knowledge of the utmost importance" (*NFD*, 64). But at no point can Douglass divulge his disguise, reveal that he escaped by dressing as a seaman and only then rode the railroad to freedom in the garb of the professional traveler. (The diluted evidence, however, is at least aesthetically perceptible throughout the text, for Douglass could never eradicate the "deep structure" or representational logic of his narrative.) Douglass, as always invoking appropriate names, "took passage with Captain Row in the schooner Wild Cat, and after a sail of about twenty-four hours, found myself near the place of my birth" (*NFD*, 59). Douglass also returns, this time free, to the Lloyd plantation later in his life; all such ventures are figured in slightly mythic terms in this narrative, and the journey out remains potentially the journey back. He does not return home, but travels to, and so creates, a new past.

Douglass spends a considerable portion of the narrative at the water's edge, on the brink of both baptism and drowning. Covey's house itself

> stood within a few rods of the Chesapeake Bay, whose broad bosom was ever white with sails from every quarter of the habitable globe. Those beautiful vessels, robed in purest white, so delightful to the eye of the freeman, were to me so many shrouded ghosts, to terrify and torment me with thoughts of my wretched condition. (*NFD*, 76)

Douglass's subsequent paean to these sexual yet still spectral ships— pure white, as Garrison emphasizes in his preface, yet to Douglass terrifying—again typically associates seraphic salvation with passage through water. Douglass identifies himself with the ships, with north-swimming bodies:

> You are loosed from your moorings, and are free; I am fast in my chains, and am a slave! . . . You are freedom's swift-winged angels, that fly round the world; I am confined in bands of iron! . . . O that I were on one of your gallant decks, and under your protecting wing! . . . O that I could also go! Could I but swim! . . . The glad ship is gone; she hides in the dim distance. . . . I will take to the water. This very bay shall yet bear me into freedom. The steamboats steered in a north-east course from North Point. I will do the same. (*NFD*, 76)

As Douglass models himself upon the ship, his first thought of freedom is that he will be able to travel without a pass; freedom means passage without marginality (*NFD*, 77). But the liminality of passage is reflected in the unreliability of the boat, the man of war, the man of letters; Douglass emblematically cannot swim, and nothing is yet delivered. Though they are neutral, Douglass needs to reconfigure ships and methods of passage as exigently favoring his side.

A ship's master or captain is often little better than a rank pirate, barely more than the slave master buoyed; Douglass makes the homology transparent: "Captain Auld was not born a slaveholder. He had been born a poor man, master only of a Bay craft. He came into possession of all his slaves by marriage." The master of ships becomes master of men. In the genealogy of passages, slavers and pirates are equally demonic, and to the fleeing slave "a band of pirates never looked more like their father, the devil" (*NFD*, 98). Even at the shipyards of Baltimore,

Douglass cannot work freely as a calker on the two aptly named "large man-of-war brigs," and must regard all the men at the shipyard as prison-masters as well as captains. "The right of the grim-visaged pirate upon the high seas is exactly the same" as the right of the master to take Douglass's freely earned wages, and pirating and slavery—often called "man-stealing" in anti-slavery literature—are seen as economically, and geophysically, interchangeable. Douglass can see no reason why he should each week "pour the reward of my toil into the purse of my master," why his *currency,* his fluidity, should be drained into another's pocket (*NFD,* 104, 107). Douglass thus must bypass the wrong kind of ships: "I suppose I felt perhaps as one may imagine the unarmed mariner," the literally crippled and divided laborer, "to feel when he is rescued by a friendly man-of-war from the pursuit of a pirate" (*NFD,* 111). In Douglass's scenario, the slave/pirate ship must be transformed along with its passenger. The man-of-war is thus potentially salvaged, and when Douglass does keep his pay and finds a job, it is in essence one of waterworks, "at the ship yard near the draw-bridge" (*NFD,* 109).

Still, what starts out as a captivity narrative and attempts to end as a travel narrative can get lost or tainted in the translation. The terms of captivity continue to "contaminate" those of the travel narrative. Douglass is so terrified by the sight of the whipping of his aunt "that I hid myself in a closet, and dared not venture out till long after the bloody transaction was over" (*NFD,* 26). By the book's end, the "bloody transaction," a transgression of blood, of liquid, is inscribed as the rite of passage itself, but it still cannot be witnessed (*NFD,* 27). The passage is then tainted, for the same blood shed to fight for freedom is defiled by slavery; but the blood which serves as a locus of pollution comes to measure and determine both transgression and passage itself. In Douglass's *Narrative,* the liminality which is not witnessed until it is over ultimately produces a real transformation rather than Poe's static affirmation of social position.

Even more than Douglass, Harriet Jacobs inverts the structures of white travel narratives. Hidden on the very grounds of slavery for seven years, she encounters a liminality not just of passage, but of extreme immobility. For the even more closeted and hidden Jacobs, no flight north can alter her interior fluidity: "I was the only nurse tinged with the blood of Africa."[11] Jacobs's narrative is also structured around the transformations of blood and water. Jacobs too must conceal herself until the bloody transactions are over, for emergence from the liminal state can serve only to interiorize and make portable the external conflict's violent transgressions. For Jacobs, passage occupies a taboo space; it can't be witnessed for reasons of security, for the sake of still suffering slaves, but also because, like the unwitnessed mutiny of *Benito Cereno*, it is a violation and a mystery. Some portion must be reserved for the eyes of the gods, and only the too familiar aftermath, viewed after a period of liminal hiding, is recountable to the white reader:

> It is not necessary to state how [Benjamin] made his escape. Suffice it to say, he was on his way to New York when a violent storm overtook the vessel. . . . To port they went. There the advertisement met the captain's eye. . . . the Captain laid hold on him and bound him in chains. . . . Before reaching [New York] Benjamin managed to get off his chains and throw them overboard.

He escaped from the vessel, but was pursued, captured, and carried back to his master (*I,* 34–35). Once more, the connection between captain and capturer is made evident, and the travel narrative collapses back into a captivity narrative. The ship captain always remains a potential slaver. Recalling her description of Benjamin's escape, Jacobs later continues (like Douglass, still needing to conceal specific details of her journey),

> I was to escape in a vessel; but I forbear to mention any further particulars. I was in readiness, but the vessel was unexpectedly detained several days. Meantime, news came to town of a most horrible murder committed on a fugitive slave, named James. . . . [Grandmother's] excessive fear was somewhat contagious.

Again, no overt connection is made between the two events (just as there would be none in the case of Douglass and Mr. Ruggles), yet the displaced murder is somehow associated with the movement to the ship, and the contagious fear arises from a taboo encroachment, from a boundary crossed. Resembling Douglass in moving from a position of relative security to one of suffering, Jacobs is unlike Douglass in remaining for so long in her liminal gestation before achieving passage. In her own narrative framework, Jacobs is bent into liminal shape for so long that she can never fully assume any other "normative" position.

The *de rigueur* imitation of a sailor, whether in Douglass or Jacobs—and at least in the modified form of train/river passage for William and Ellen Craft, who traveled to freedom along both land and water routes—signals a final break with the South. After an almost biblically exaggerated seven-year confinement comes a necessarily abrupt transition from captivity to ship travel which is as bizarre as any such shift in *Pym*. Jacobs's disinterment comes through her impersonation of the male sailor:

> I had not the slightest idea where I was going. Betty brought me a suit of sailor's clothes. . . . It was a long time since I had taken a walk out of doors. . . . He took me into his boat, rowed out to a vessel not far distant, and hoisted me on board. We three were the only occupants of the vessel. . . . They said I was to remain on board till near dawn, and then they would hide me in Snaky Swamp till she could be returned to confinement. (*I*, 169–170)

Unable to escape the search any boat proceeding north would endure, Jacobs must pass through Snaky Swamp, the polluted waters of slavery itself, only to be temporarily returned to solitary confinement, to a kind of living death in the midst of human communities. Yet as a sailor, in attaining a liberation only promised by most white travel narratives, Jacobs achieves the transformation Benjamin at first cannot.

Upon Jacobs's escape, her identity is further rendered liminal, as the boundaries of self are crossed, as the 'second Linda' is added to the first, doubling the passengers. As for William and Ellen Craft, for Jacobs a blending of identities is the ferryman's price in such transactions.[12] Fanny too must hide in a "very small cabin" after being carried on board "half-dead with a fright." Harriet continues to spy from her "loophole," as the discussion of detention, weather, and boarding follows. After the ship begins moving, the blurring continues in both directions: with his light complexion, Peter is misidentified by the Captain as a white pursuer. The whole episode transforms in the midst of passage, as the slave half of the waters gives way to the free. Even if she is "showed to a little box of a cabin," forced briefly to reenact her confinement, Jacobs is treated well by the captain and sailors. Though she had "heard that sailors were rough and sometimes cruel," and while she worries about their fate after their passage is paid for, and is, like Douglass, made "suspicious of everybody" (*NFD*, 239–240), Jacobs is harbored aboard ship. For all its confusion, the scene initiates her transition; as she is "fairly sailing on Chesapeake Bay," it is spring, her exhilaration is indescribable, and she believes she sees her first sunrise on free soil, from the other side of the water. The transitional quality, from still cramped shipboard space to a space of gradually unfolding freedom, the emblematic Chesapeake Bay, is emphasized: "Constant exercise on board the vessel, and frequent rubbing with salt water, had nearly restored the use of my limbs" (*I*, 242). Sea water is the slave's salve. But virtually every slave's ship passage must begin in doubt and only gradually turn upon better fortune: "I knew that colored passengers were not admitted to the cabin. I was very desirous for the seclusion of the cabin . . . to avoid observation" (*I*, 273).

For Jacobs is still not entirely free, and each transition requires a repeat performance; while in transition, Jacobs must return to confined space, and again the captain must come to her aid, intervening and providing a room below decks. With regard to questions of genre and liminality, Jacobs's reinterments then make sense of Poe's endless mock captivities. Poe tries to exploit the liminal authority of a genre which he cannot inhabit, and to which he has access only through an appropriation by inversion; Jacobs is freed, however, as a result of a liminality which threatens to keep her from any fixed position. Despite the continuation of Jacobs's liminality, the waters primarily transform danger to familiar security, and finally Jacobs's brother is successfully transformed from slave/person to seaman and back to person: "my attention was attracted by a young man in a sailor's dress. . . . [I] beckoned to the sailor, and in less than a minute I was clasped in my brother's arms" (*I*, 257). His position as whaler/sailor has given him freedom, but also, according to the myths of the sea, allowed him to pass through categories. In this staged recognition scene, the brother emerges from his liminal state. Jacobs too is partially reborn: "shut up in a living grave for years," Jacobs "sat at [her] loophole, waiting for the family to return from the grave," awaiting her own rebirth. Jacobs emerges from what is literally a "trap-door," and her lingering marginality becomes a threat to her self, but also to her potential enemies.

For Jacobs, "[t]here are no bonds so strong as those which are formed by suffering together," and Jacobs must remain an outsider in the North, still bound even when she proclaims herself "Free at Last." The most dangerous part is indeed over; Jacobs has passed through, and will not be captured in transit, but she can never be completely "deliminalized": the passage remains partial. The next generation is still doomed, the old generation cannot enter the promised land; we stay in the dry desert: "So then, after all I had endured for their sakes, my poor children were between two fires; between my old master and their new master! And I was powerless" (*I*, 209). This particular state of "betweenness" precisely marks the gendered liminality Jacobs endures. Though her children are also finally freed, Jacobs's own body "still suffers" from her imprisonment, "to say nothing of [her] soul" (*I*, 224). Between comes betwixt itself as a set of terms, and passage remains the most dangerous state for Jacobs, while captivity is actually the safest. As Jacobs crouches in her immobile home, "[t]he opinion was often expressed that I was in the Free States. . . . Yet there was no place, where slavery existed, that could have afforded me so good a place of concealment." Jacobs is safer being a spy in the house of slavery than a free person in New York; the transformation doesn't work, for she cannot move except without moving altogether. As Jacobs reminds us, "I do not sit with my children in a home of my own. I still long for a hearthstone of my own, however humble" (*I*, 302). Though the narrative demands that Jacobs claim that passage has, in a positive sense, left her high and dry, she is in fact still in the midst, caught between two fires, when she needs to be all washed up.

Once Jacobs has achieved passage, one of her primary goals in the North is to desegregate public transportation. But she never witnesses the same absence of prejudice which she encountered during the entirety of her trip to England. Even in the North, the fugitive slave law continues to destabilize her position. Social mobility for the slave remains tied to physical mobility, to the manner of travel; unless the slave in some form manages to pass for white, once passage ends, social position backslides. Passage for the slave is never fully achieved; she is left stranded or shipwrecked, stuck in the liminal position of the perpetual traveler.

Coda

On an island, a Friday become Robinson Crusoe, Douglass can never get rid of the slave songs, which he could not understand while "within the circle," and which "still follow" him as incessantly as the threat of recapture. What he too cannot leave behind is the position of the cast-out, the castaway: "The singing of a man cast away upon a desolate island" might sooner be construed as joyous than that of a slave, and the comparison carries broad implications for issues of genre and passage (*NFD*, 31–32). Douglass and Jacobs have completed their journeys, but find themselves on islands of safety rather than safely harbored. The social deaths of the sailor and the castaway are compared with that of the slave, and their situations merge; as Douglass or Jacobs might attest, there are as many unknown spies on board ship, in the unknown officers, as on the plantation in the familiar overseer and the slaveholder's minions (*NFD*, 36). The narrative cannot entirely succeed, for in order to remain effective, its message must be completely disguised, left liminal. But in a relatively acceptable seaman's disguise, the black slave narrative can then infiltrate the white world in terms too subversive to be immediately apprehended.

The transformation from bondage to freedom alters, but does not erase, the peculiar position of the slave; white men remain either untrustworthy or Douglass's victims in his debt to them, for example in his inability to reveal their names. It is as if the act of helping Douglass transforms Mr. Ruggles, who is "now afflicted with blindness, and is himself in need of the same kind of offices" which Douglass once received from him. The slave narrative's final claim is that slavery, not blackness, is contagious, liminal, poisonous—its effects can't be stopped, and once transformation begins, it runs rampant over all; it is slavery whose travel cannot be contained. As long as slavery exists even in vestigial forms, the former slave remains, with all the term's resonances, a carrier; and he can only be cured by a variety of parasitic or— given slavery's blood lore—vampiric acts (*NFD*, 112). The variously titled Douglass has swallowed the fisherman, but "Marshal Douglass," returning to the death-bed of a palsied Captain Auld who now sheds tears, insists on being called not Marshal, but Frederick, and is left speechless.[13]

At the tail end, like some journeys, the slave's travel narrative would take us where for the present we don't want to go—in this case downstream to *Huckleberry Finn*. For the moment, it is worthwhile instead to look back to *Pym* and *Benito Cereno* and wonder who is alive to tell the tale in the slave narrative. The Douglass who once had to remind the reader he was still liminal, still in danger of being returned as a fugitive, must now assert his non-liminality. But until Douglass manages to escape the Garrison in its present incarnation, his craft will never be his own, and his ship will never come in. Though her unconventional "non-marriage" narrative ends with Jacobs insisting she is free, Jacobs, inadvertently or through editorial interpolation, writes that "it is a privilege to serve her who pities my oppressed people" (*I*, 303). Pity and its crocodile, or snake, tears may tragically mark Jacobs's end in her beginning. From water we come, and at the close of Jacobs's narrative, as the author gathers the years "passed in bondage," to water we return: "for with those gloomy recollections come like light, fleecy clouds tender memories of my good old grandmother, floating over a dark and troubled sea" (ibid.). Unless they would erase their pasts entirely, time between times, former slaves can only endure the tides.

Notes

1. Mary Douglas, *Purity and Danger: An Analysis of the Concepts of Pollution and Taboo* (London: Routledge and Kegan Paul, 1966).

2. Victor Turner, "Betwixt and Between: The Liminal Period in *Rites de Passage*," in *The Forest of Symbols: Aspects of Ndembu Ritual* (Ithaca: Cornell University Press, 1967).

3. *Narrative of the Life of Frederick Douglass, an American Slave, Written by Himself* (New York: Signet, 1968), xi; hereafter cited parenthetically as *NFD.*

4. Douglas, *Purity and Danger,* 125.

5. Edgar Allen Poe, *The Narrative of Arthur Gordon Pym,* in *Collected Writings of Edgar Allen Poe,* vol. 1, *The Imaginary Voyages* (Boston: Twayne Publishers, 1981), 208; hereafter cited parenthetically as *NAGP.*

6. John Irwin, *American Hieroglyphics: The Symbol of the Egyptian Hieroglyphics in the American Renaissance* (Baltimore: Johns Hopkins University Press, 1980), 185.

   Poe's amnesiac narrator might be compared to Nietzsche's perpetually forgetful animals, an image suggested in a different context in "'When Man Falls': Gravity in Stephen Crane's Urban Sketches," a paper delivered by Mary Esteve (University of Washington) at the Western Humanities Conference, University of Oregon, October 1994.

7. John Sekora, "Is the Slave Narrative a Species of Autobiography?" in *Studies in Autobiography,* edited by James Olney (New York, Oxford University Press, 1988), 102–106. Sekora also asks in another piece, "Does it matter that the earliest of slave narratives [Briton Hammon's 1760 *Narrative*] is not at all about the legal institution of Anglo-American slavery? . . . that the immediate model for this significant black story may be an insignificant white youth? . . . Does it matter for autobiography if personal, individual experiences and language are suppressed in favor of the orthodox and the conventional?" ("Black Message/White Envelope: Genre, Authenticity, and Authority in the Antebellum Slave Narrative," *Callaloo* 10, no. 3 [summer 1987], 488).

   In other words, the slave narrative becomes a hybrid but representative genre, transmuting individual men into representative ones. Sekora also notes that John Marrant's doctored conversion story becomes largely impersonal and emblematic, though his "tale of 'crossing the fence, which marked the boundary between the wilderness and the cultivated country,'" could still be read as a highly bowdlerized or filtered account of the ritual transformation of a black man in a culture alien to him. As Kim Benston demonstrates in "I Yam What I Am: The Topos of Un(naming) in Afro-American Literature" (in *Black Literature and Literary Theory,* edited by Henry Louis Gates, Jr. [New York: Methuen, 1984], 151–172), Douglass, whatever his true name, becomes his representative self in African-American literature by assuming this name (162).

   I argue elsewhere that white male transcendental writers attempt to transcend the confines of a Jacksonian self-reliant male individuality; they define themselves by deifying a possessive nature—one which takes control of their voices and bodies, separates them from families, and effectively sacralizes the alienating effects of slavery. (This nature represents everything outside the white male self, and is finally coded as black and female.)

It is Douglass, for example, and not white transcendentalists, who seeks to construct a Jacksonian self he never possessed, even if he never entirely invests himself in that project without discomfort. White sponsorship and intervention cannot be entirely separated from the slave narrative, and in Douglass's case should emphatically be considered in light of the narrative's own hybridized attempt to cast off that interference while still using some of the ideological narratives of that mediation. Such interference produces what we might call an unusually high level of genre contamination; the slave narrative incorporates elements of white travel narratives, sentimental or domestic fictions, institutional sanctions and introductions, even as these forms incorporate elements of the slave narrative.

Though cautious of the generalization, I would argue that it is primarily African-American writers who focus on the liminality of middle-passage. Several examples indicate that, in addition to other factors, nationality inflects the context of transformation in slave narratives. In *The History of Mary Prince, a West Indian Slave*, Prince is not liminally transformed by or through her experiences. Partly as a result of the conventions imposed by white publishers, Prince's narrative bears some of the familiar motifs of passage; but in her narrative, water is portrayed in almost consistently negative terms. Prince's cruel slave-master, Captain I——, is not redeemed by any counterpoint of cleansing waters. Prince begins her narrative, "I was born at Brackish-Pond, in Bermuda. . . . Captain Williams, Mr. Darrel's son-in-law, was master of a vessel which traded to several places in America and the West Indies." In effect, Prince is only transferred from one slave-island to another, from the West Indies to England. While traveling to England with her mistress, Prince finds the ship's steward is kind to her on board. But once in England she remains locked into the role of slave: a doctor tells Prince that she "was a sickly body and the washing did not agree with me. But Mrs. Wood would not release me from the tub, so I was forced to do as I could. I grew worse, and could not stand to wash." As a woman and a West Indian, Prince does not seem interested in any version of Douglass's male, American self-transformations in water (*The History of Mary Prince, a West Indian Slave*, in *Six Women's Slave Narratives*, with a foreword by Henry Louis Gates, Schomberg Library [New York: Oxford University Press, 1988], 1, 18–19).

In *The Life of Olaudah Equiano*, Equiano, like Douglass, strenuously objects to being given a name, Gustavus Vasa, by his master, but ultimately accepts it. More British than American, Equiano is also an actual sailor, a status which informs his approach to water, liminality, and transformation. Equiano provides no definite pattern in his attitude toward the ocean or travel, adapting his opinion as circumstance dictates. While noting, for example, that "every heart on board gladdened on our reaching the shore, and none more than mine," Equiano can also observe that "every day now brought me nearer my freedom, and I was impatient till we preceded again to sea" (*The Life of Olaudah Equiano*, edited by Paul Edwards [Hong

Kong: Longman, 1988], 1, 33, 9, 106, 134). Where even Dana posits that death at sea is always sadder than on land, for no marker can locate our graves, or where Melville asserts in the opening paragraph of *Moby Dick* that going to sea is like committing suicide, or that the divine Pacific can rob the sailor of his bordered identity, Equiano attributes no special liminality or narrative emphasis to the medium of his passage (Richard Henry Dana, *Two Years before the Mast: A Personal Narrative* [New York: Signet, 1964], 39).

Still, parallels exist between Douglass's *Narrative* and Dana's *Personal Narrative*. Particularly with regard to water's dual or liminal state, Douglass would probably concur with Dana, e.g., that "a sailor's life is at best but a mixture of a little good with much evil. . . . the beautiful is linked with the revolting, the sublime with the commonplace, and the solemn with the ludicrous" (Dana, *Two Years*, 40).

8. According to Garrison, Douglass will narrate "facts": "I am confident that [this narrative] is essentially true in all its statements. . . . nothing exaggerated; nothing drawn from the imagination, that it comes short of the reality, rather than overstates a single fact" (*NFD*, vi, x).

9. Turner, "Betwixt and Between," 95. In Turner's terms, the slave is the quintessential liminal, invisible man seeking to transform his social status —one denied him in middle passage—through the transitions of the rite of passage.

10. Henry Louis Gates, Jr., "Binary Oppositions in Chapter One of *Narrative of the Life of Frederick Douglass, an American Slave, Written by Himself*," in *Figures in Black: Words, Signs, and the "Racial" Self* (New York: Oxford University Press, 1987), 80–97.

11. Harriet Jacobs, *Incidents in The Life of a Slave Girl*, Schomberg Library Edition, edited by Lydia Maria Child (New York: Oxford University Press, 1988), 266; hereafter cited parenthetically as *I*. Though Douglass and Jacobs both finally achieve freedom, Jacobs's *Incidents* ends with her identity essentially unchanged; her incidents do not affect her inner identity, and her status is relatively unaffected by passage. (Turner's model of male transformation, as Carolyn Walker Bynum and others argue, might not apply to the less "disrupted" narratives used to frame women's lives. See Bynum, *Fragmentation and Redemption: Essays on Gender and the Human Body in Medieval Religion* [New York: Zone, 1991].)

12. The slave narrative should in certain respects be considered a form of travel narrative, but almost never is, as evidenced by Janis Stout's book *The Journey Narrative in American Literature: Patterns and Departures* (Westport, Conn.: Greenwood, 1983), which includes an analysis of escape, class mobility, quests, and the motivations of the white traveler, and sections on Cooper, Melville, Twain, and others. Stout's book is typical of its critical genre in containing no mention of any slave narrative; the slave passage typically could not be strictly considered a land journey in any case, but

one that traverses several geographies. As Homi Bhabha would argue, such omissions reflect a general suppression of the intertextuality of western and "non-western" genres. But it is, I would argue, also a "feint" of the white travel narrative, an attempt to safeguard its own truth claims, which excludes the slave narrative from being considered a form of travel literature.

It is also important to explore the historical role of shipboard mutiny and the status of such off-shore events: e.g., as John Blassingame notes, a slave revolt occurred in 1826 on board a Mississippi River steamer. See John W. Blassingame, *The Slave Community* (New York: Oxford University Press, 1979), 206. For an important discussion of the role of shipping and travel in black culture, see Paul Gilroy's *The Black Atlantic* (London: Verso, 1993) and Carl Pedersen's "Sea Change: Middle Passage and the Transatlantic Imagination" (in *The Black Columbiad: Defining Moments in African American Literature and Culture*, ed. Werner Sollers and Maria Diedrich [Cambridge: Harvard University Press, 1994], 42–51). Gilroy "settle[s] on the images of ships in motion across the spaces between Europe, America, Africa, and the Caribbean as a central organizing symbol for the enterprise [of cultural transmission]. . . . It is particularly important that . . . both Wedderburn and sometime associate Davidson [nineteenth-century black political writers] had been sailors, moving to and fro between nations. . . . Their relationship to the sea may turn out to be especially important for both the early politics and poetics of the black Atlantic world. . . . [As Linebaugh says,] 'the ship remained perhaps the most important conduit of Pan-African communication before the appearance of the long-playing record'" (Gilroy, 4, 12–13).

In response to the queries of recent critics, particularly Deborah Mc-Dowell and Winifred Morgan, concerning the representative nature of Douglass's text, its paradigmatic status as an authoritative male narrative of slavery, I would note that Douglass's manipulation of the tropes of white travel narratives makes him relatively assimilable to white audiences, despite the fact that Douglass is also using another genre to subvert the assumptions of that audience. For McDowell, see her "In The First Place: Making Frederick Douglass and the Afro-American Narrative Tradition," in *Critical Essays on Frederick Douglass*, edited by William Andrews (Boston: G. K. Hall, 1991); for Morgan, see her "Gender-Related Difference in the Slave Narratives of Harriet Jacobs and Frederick Douglass," in *American Studies* 35, no. 2 (fall 1994): 73–94.

13. See Houston Baker, *The Journey Back* (Chicago: University of Chicago Press, 1980), 45, and Douglass's *The Life and Times of Frederick Douglass* (Toronto: Collier, 1962), 442.

PART II

RACE AND SLAVERY

Five

James Forten and
"The Gentlemen of the Pave"
Race, Wealth, and Power in
Antebellum Philadelphia

Julie Winch

James Forten—whose name I never mention but my heart
swells within me . . . James Forten, a coloured man . . .
stood side by side with American freemen and . . . bared
his bosom in defence of this country.
—Frederick Douglass, April 24, 1849, New York City

When wealthy African-American sailmaker James Forten died in March
of 1842, he was eulogized in the anti-slavery press as a staunch sup-
porter of abolition and a champion of causes ranging from women's
rights to temperance. However, although he was actively committed to a
reform agenda he hoped would bring about the moral rebirth of America,
it is clear from his personal correspondence that Forten saw himself
primarily as "a man of business," "a gentleman of the pave," someone
intimately connected with the commercial life of one of the nation's
premier ports.[1] And that was how many of Philadelphia's white "gentle-
men of the pave" saw him. They had bought sails from him over the
years, borrowed money from him, made loans to him, traded real estate
with him, mulled over the state of the market with him, and gossiped
about him. In short, to a certain extent they had admitted him to their
fraternity. Now they came to St. Thomas's African Episcopal Church to
pay their final respects to him. At his funeral sea-captains and merchants rubbed shoulders with abolitionists and social reformers in a display of respect for a remarkable individual who had had a foot in both
camps.

James Forten was born on September 2, 1766, in a modest home in
Philadelphia's Dock Ward, a few blocks from the wharves and ware-
houses that lined the banks of the Delaware. In a city where the vast
majority of black people were slaves, James Forten was freeborn.[2] His

father, Thomas Forten or Fortune, had himself been born free in Philadelphia, but he was the grandson of an African slave brought to the
fledgling colony of Pennsylvania in the 1680s.[3] James's mother, Margaret,
had probably spent many years in bondage. The evidence suggests that
she and Thomas had delayed marrying and producing children until
they could secure her freedom. Most of her contemporaries bore their
first child when they were in their early to mid-twenties, but Margaret
Forten was forty-one when James's sister, Abigail, was born, and forty-
four when she gave birth to her son.[4] Under Pennsylvania law, if Margaret had been a slave when she and Thomas began their family, their
children would have inherited her legal status and not his. As it was, one
of the most valuable legacies Margaret and Thomas bestowed on their
children was their freedom.

Thomas Forten gave his son another early advantage; he taught him
the rudiments of a skilled trade. Thomas was a craftsman, a journeyman
sailmaker in the sail loft of white sailmaker Robert Bridges and a small-
scale contractor in his own right.[5] He knew not only how to cut and sew
sails but how to fashion canvas into everything from tents and wagon
cloths to "Speaking Trumpets."[6] Thomas Forten was not a wealthy
man, but his skill and ingenuity kept his family in modest comfort.
Lawmakers might dismiss the two or three hundred free people of color
in Philadelphia at the time of James Forten's birth as "idle, slothful and
. . . burdensome,"[7] but the Fortens hardly deserved such epithets.

The Bridges sail loft became school, playroom, and workplace to the
young James Forten. He earned his first few pennies sweeping the floor
of the loft, gathering up scraps of twine and canvas, and melting bees-
wax and shaping it into convenient pieces for the journeymen to wax
their sewing thread with. And as soon as he could handle a palm and a
needle, Thomas began teaching him how to sew neatly and quickly. In
time he might be able to secure an apprenticeship, or at least be able to
work as a craftsman rather than as an unskilled laborer.

In 1773 tragedy struck the Forten household. Thomas Forten died
suddenly, leaving his family on the edge of financial disaster. Margaret
Forten struggled to keep a home together for herself and her two children, but her ambition extended beyond paying the rent and putting
food on the table. She was determined to give her son a formal education. At considerable sacrifice to herself, for James was seven years old
and eligible to be sent out to work full-time, she enrolled him in the
Friends' African School. The school, founded by Quakers at the urging
of white abolitionist Anthony Benezet, a friend of the Fortens, was virtually the only institution in the city where African-American children
could receive an education.[8] For two years, at least on a part-time basis,

James Forten studied reading, writing, and "ciphering" at the African School. His education would stand him in good stead as a businessman and as a reformer. In years to come, his neat copperplate writing graced receipts and ledgers as well as petitions to Congress and the Pennsylvania legislature.

In 1775 several factors combined to put an end to James Forten's formal schooling. To begin with, the African School was often closed for weeks at a time. The deepening conflict with Britain caused serious disruptions in trade, and that meant Quakers, many of whom were merchants, could no longer be so charitable. After all, maintaining the school and paying the kind of salary that would attract and retain a good teacher was an expensive proposition. Closer to home, the Forten family was sinking inexorably into poverty. Margaret Forten could not continue to keep her son out of the workforce, even on a part-time basis. He had to go out to work. Anthony Benezet found him his first job, clerking for a white grocer and cleaning the store.[9] It was not what he had been trained for, and not what his parents had hoped for, but at nine years of age James Forten was too young to do much else. He was certainly too young to begin a formal apprenticeship in Robert Bridges's sail loft. He had to take what he could get and count himself fortunate to be able to help support his family.

The Revolution became a crucial reference point in James Forten's life, as it did in the lives of so many of his contemporaries. It marked him physically and emotionally. Not quite ten years old, he stood in the statehouse yard on July 8, 1776, and heard Sheriff John Nixon read the Declaration of Independence to the people for the first time.[10] It spoke of all men being created equal, and being entitled to liberty, and yet he knew that it was the British who seemed to be the friends of liberty for black people. Barely had the war begun when the British promised freedom to the slaves of rebel masters if they rallied to King George's standard. Forten saw black and white men marching together through the streets of his native city to meet the British in battle,[11] and yet he knew that most leading revolutionaries, George Washington included, shrank from advocating the abolition of slavery, or the granting of equality to black men. But if the new nation's leaders deftly avoided the issue of slavery, Pennsylvania legislators did not. In 1780 they passed the Gradual Abolition Act. True, it stopped far short of freeing the thousands of slaves in the state. Children born to slave women after the passage of the Act would be held as indentured servants until they were in their mid-twenties. Nothing was said about the rights of free people of color. But the preamble to the Act did link abolition to the Revolutionary cause. The lawmakers rejoiced "that it is in our power to extend a portion of that freedom to others, which hath been extended to us." They went on to declare:

> It is not for us to inquire, why, in the creation of mankind, the inhabitants of the several parts of the earth were distinguished by a difference in . . . complexion. It is sufficient to know, that all are the work of an Almighty hand.[12]

The messages were mixed, and James Forten had a choice of loyalties before him as he grew from a child to a young man with the war still raging. Should he put his faith in the Patriot cause, with all its contradictions, or should he remain a loyal subject of King George?

The Fortens remained in Philadelphia through the nine-month British occupation, with James and his mother and sister seeking whatever work was to be had. After the British abandoned the city in the spring of 1778, Philadelphia emerged as a major center for privateering. Sailmaker Robert Bridges was one of many businessmen who combined patriotism with profit. He owned or partly owned six "cruisers," and James Forten may well have worked in his sail loft, helping to make or repair their sails.[13] Eventually, in the summer of 1781, a few weeks short of his fifteenth birthday, Forten decided to try his luck on a privateer. He signed on for a cruise with Stephen Decatur, Sr., on his new vessel, the 450-ton *Royal Louis*. Needing a complement of two hundred men and boys, Decatur could pay scant attention to such issues as race. Indeed, as slaveowners learned to their cost, privateering captains were only too willing to sign on runaway slaves as well as free men.

It is easy to see why Decatur would have welcomed Forten. He had never been to sea before, but he was young, strong, eager to serve, and with his knowledge of sailmaking he might be useful when the *Royal Louis*'s sails needed running repairs. Forten was the sort of recruit Decatur could use, but why would Forten risk his life for the Patriot cause? In later years he would argue that patriotism alone had motivated him. For instance, when he was a successful man of business, "an honorable gentleman," a member of Congress, visited his sail loft and urged him to apply for a pension for his wartime service. Forten answered, "I was a volunteer, sir."[14] It was not a pension he wanted. It was equality. Patriotism may have been uppermost in Forten's mind in after years. However, other considerations probably weighed equally heavily with him as a young man. There was the prospect of making money. Decatur had an impressive list of prizes to his credit. His crew could look forward to good pickings. James Forten may also have welcomed the chance to see more of life than the streets and wharves of his native Philadelphia. Money-making and a longing for adventure went hand in hand with at least a glimmer of hope that a Patriot victory would mean full citizenship at some time in the future. James Forten talked his reluctant mother into letting him go and he sailed with the *Royal Louis* on her maiden voyage in search of prizes.[15]

The first voyage of the *Royal Louis* was a great success. Decatur cruised the waters between the Loyalist strongholds of New York City and Charleston, South Carolina, intercepting merchantmen. Most captains surrendered without firing a shot when they realized the strength of their adversary. The *Royal Louis* had twenty carriage guns and was more than a match for a lightly armed trading vessel. However, Forten did see action on that first voyage. The *Royal Louis* encountered the armed brig *Active*, which put up surprisingly fierce resistance, given her size and the number of her guns, for she was smaller and more lightly armed than her opponent. When the *Active* finally struck her colors, the privateers discovered that she was carrying vital dispatches from Admiral Rodney in the Caribbean to Admiral Graves in New York City. Decatur seized the dispatches and forwarded them to General Washington, who then knew exactly what the enemy's strength was, and when and how the Royal Navy planned to rescue the luckless Cornwallis and his army from the Yorktown peninsula.[16] In this small way Decatur and his crew had helped bring about the British surrender.

In the fall of 1781, though, it was far from certain that James Forten would live to see an American victory. On the *Royal Louis*'s second cruise she was captured in an encounter with a British man-of-war. Forten and the rest of the crew found themselves prisoners aboard HMS *Amphion*, bound for the prison-hulk *Jersey* in New York's Wallabout Bay.[17] That was bad enough, but Forten's fear was that he would be sent not to the *Jersey* but to Barbados or Jamaica. He had heard rumors that the British enslaved their black prisoners. However, the domestic needs of the British captain saved him. The *Amphion*'s captain, John Bazely, had his two sons on board. Fourteen-year-old John Jr. was a midshipman with duties to perform, but his younger brother, Henry, was on the *Amphion* as his father's servant, an ill-defined assignment that left him with a great deal of time on his hands.[18] Bored and often idle, he was a danger to himself and others on a man-of-war. Among the prisoners from the *Royal Louis* Captain Bazely spotted a young African-American sailor and was "struck with his honest and open countenance." James Forten found himself under orders to play nursemaid to Henry Bazely and keep him out of mischief. What began as a less than welcome task soon grew into a friendship between the two youths.

> During one of those dull and monotonous periods which frequently occur on ship-board, [they] were engaged in a game of marbles, when with signal dexterity and skill, the marbles were

upon every trial successively displaced by the unerring hand of Forten. This excited the surprise and admiration of his young companion, who, hastening to his father, called his attention to it.

Bazely asked Forten if he could repeat the feat, "and assuring the Captain that nothing was easier for him to accomplish, the marbles were again placed in the ring, and in rapid succession he redeemed his word."[19] After that, Bazely took a friendly interest in the young Philadelphian, giving him greater freedom than his fellow captives.

As the *Amphion* approached New York and Bazely made ready to discharge his prisoners, Henry begged his father to spare his new friend. Bazely considered the matter, sent for Forten, and made him an extraordinary offer. Would he come to England as Henry's companion, to be educated with him and sponsored by the Bazely family? To the utter astonishment of father and son, Forten rejected the offer, insisting, in the words of his son-in-law and biographer, Robert Purvis: "I have been taken prisoner for the liberties of my country, and never will prove a traitor to her interest." Captain Bazely was left with no option but to send him to the prison-hulk, although he did give him a letter for the *Jersey*'s commander asking that he be treated no differently from the other prisoners and exchanged as soon as possible.[20]

Forten endured seven months of captivity on the *Jersey*, battling smallpox and malnutrition, seeing men die around him, and undoubtedly regretting at times the offer he had rejected. With youth and strength on his side, he survived. He was exchanged in the spring of 1782. Rowed ashore, he was left to make his own way back to Philadelphia. To the mother and sister who had long since given him up for dead, he appeared almost a stranger. He was gaunt and haggard. His feet were cracked and swollen. He had walked from New York to Trenton barefoot until someone took pity on him and gave him an old pair of shoes. Scurvy had caused his hair to fall out in great clumps. But he was alive and he was home.[21]

His wartime experiences did not deter James Forten from venturing off to sea again. In the spring of 1784, with the war over, he signed on for a voyage to England in company with his sister Abigail's new husband, William Dunbar.[22] They sailed with Thomas Truxtun, a privateersman turned merchant and, like Decatur, a future commander in the United States Navy. The crossing was uneventful, and William Dunbar was soon on his way back to his young wife. However, James Forten was discharged at his own request in London. It is tempting to imagine him heading to Dover, where the Bazelys lived, presenting himself on their doorstep, and reclaiming the friendship of father and son.[23] Alas, there is not a scrap of evidence to suggest that Forten ever saw the Bazelys again after he left the *Amphion*. He was on his own in England. He stayed a year, most likely working in one of the sail lofts along the Thames. The war had left many dockyards desperately short of skilled workers, and if Forten had to toil for his first few shillings as a common laborer, he soon did better for himself.[24] Nor would the fact that he was black have hindered him. Hundreds of men and women from Africa and the Caribbean had made their homes in the dockside communities along the Thames, and they had been joined in the previous couple of years by African-American Loyalists—some freeborn, and others slaves who had escaped to British lines in the American war, served in the British army, and been evacuated with the white Loyalists at war's end.[25]

James Forten could have stayed in England, but he chose not to. In 1785 he was back in Philadelphia. His travels over, he entered into an apprenticeship with his father's old employer, Robert Bridges. This was no ordinary apprenticeship. To begin with, at nineteen Forten was several years older and more experienced than the majority of apprentices. Advancement came quickly for him. Within a year he was the foreman at the loft, with Bridges quelling a minor rebellion in the workforce to keep him in that position.[26]

In the normal course of events James Forten might have expected to continue as foreman for the rest of his working life, employed by Bridges, and then by whichever of his sons or sons-in-law succeeded to the business. However, as Forten may have known from the moment he signed his indentures, or as he soon learned in conversation, that was not Bridges's intention.

Robert Bridges had become a sailmaker through force of circumstances. His father, Edward, had been carving out a career for himself as a merchant when he died, at age thirty-two, in 1741. His widow, Cornelia, found herself in much reduced circumstances. Robert was not quite two when Edward Bridges died.[27] As soon as he was judged able to work, he was bound out to learn a trade. He had become a sailmaker not out of choice but out of necessity. For twenty years, through the commercial upheavals of the 1760s and 1770s, as well as the Revolution itself, Bridges had struggled, but he had prospered. He was determined that his children would do better still. His sons were not destined to become craftsmen; they would become merchants and professional men. As for his daughters, he intended that they should marry merchants and professional men, not craftsmen. His designated successor in the sail loft was not a son or a son-in-law but his foreman.

James Forten had a complex relationship with the Bridges family. He lived for a time in the Bridges home on Front Street. Robert Bridges might not have cared for slavery, but he was no abolitionist. In the 1780s his home contained a free man of color, Abraham, and two slaves, Pitt and Sophia. Freedom came for Pitt and Sophia only with Bridges's death.[28] Robert Bridges's encouragement of his foreman was based not so much on principles as on mutual respect. As for Forten, he developed close ties with various members of the Bridges family, eventually naming a son for Robert Bridges and a daughter for Bridges's daughter Harriet. As a wealthy entrepreneur, he would assist Bridges's widow and an unmarried daughter, and he would enter into what proved to be an unprofitable business relationship with the husband of yet another daughter.

In 1792 James Forten became a homeowner. Robert Bridges bought him a small frame house on Shippen Street in Southwark. Lying along the Delaware and south of the city, Southwark was home to many who earned their living from seafaring and the maritime trades. Forten was to pay Bridges back in installments.[29] Bridges's generosity was probably combined with a wish to bind a trusted junior partner closer to him. It may also have been a token of appreciation for the sail-handling device Forten reportedly designed and which the Bridges loft adopted.[30]

James Forten's years as Bridges's foreman were crucial to his business success in many ways. He mastered the technological aspects of his craft, and he also learned how to deal with suppliers, ships' captains, and shipowners—white men who no doubt looked askance at Bridges's choice of a successor. Then there was the vexed issue of interacting with white workingmen, at first as an equal and then as a superior. There had been problems when Bridges promoted Forten. What would happen when Forten took over the sail loft? In fact, when Bridges retired in 1798, the workers split into two camps. The apprentices had indentured themselves to Bridges to be instructed in the "mystery" of sailmaking. Latterly they had worked under Forten's direction. They knew him to be highly skilled, and now they "all, with one consent, agreed to take him as their new master."[31] But the journeymen were worried. In 1798 no other major business enterprise in the city was owned by an African American. The journeymen did not have the years invested in the business that the apprentices did. They were more mobile, and there were other sailmakers along the Delaware they could work for. Their main concern was whether Forten could pay them on a regular basis. Could he keep Bridges's customers? Eventually Bridges came to Forten's rescue with moral and financial support, and there was no exodus of journeymen.[32]

Forten never forgot Bridges's decision to stand by him, train him, and promote him. Nor did he forget his early labor troubles as a master. Once secure in his position as owner of the loft at 95 South Wharves, he set about integrating the workforce. As a first step, he brought his relatives into the business. Brother-in-law William Dunbar died in the Seamen's Hospital in New York in February 1805, and Abigail found herself a widow with four children to raise. James Forten provided for them. Abigail's daughter, Margaret, married shortly after her father's death. Forten offered an apprenticeship to her husband, George Lewis, a freeborn black migrant from Delaware. He also found room in the sail loft for two of Margaret's brothers, Nicholas and William.[33] That left the baby of the family, Forten's namesake, James Forten Dunbar. He was only six when his father died, and his uncle took a special interest in him. In 1810 Forten secured seamen's protection papers for young James and sent him to sea. What seemed heartless—separating a young boy from his family and exposing him to the dangers of life at sea—was no more than what many other parents and guardians, black and white, were doing, and Forten took pains to get his nephew signed on with captains he knew and trusted. As for young Dunbar, seafaring agreed with him. Over the next two decades he made eight overseas voyages to Cuba, England, China, and the East Indies, as well as innumerable coasting trips. When he was ashore in Philadelphia for any length of time, he joined his elder brothers and his brother-in-law in the sail loft.[34]

In time, Forten took his father-in-law and his sons into the business. In 1805, when he was thirty-nine, James Forten married nineteen-year-old Charlotte Vandine. It was his second marriage. His first, in 1803, had ended after only seven months with the death of his young wife.[35] Charlotte Vandine's father, George, was a longtime resident of the city. He was of mixed European, African, and Native American ancestry, and the census-takers and compilers of the city directories were mystified as to his precise racial identity, sometimes describing him as black and sometimes as white. Forten knew George Vandine and his wife, Alice, from St. Thomas's African Episcopal Church, where they worshiped and where he was a vestryman.[36] George had been a sugar refiner and a "dealer." Now, thanks to his daughter's marriage, he had the chance to become a sailmaker. Eventually he left the Forten sail loft and went into business on his own.[37]

In the 1820s James Forten, Jr., and Robert Bridges Forten began learning their father's trade and preparing to succeed him. A decade later they were joined by their younger brothers, Thomas and William. But James Forten wanted to do much more than ensure the financial well-being of his family. Again and again he lamented the fact that there were so few employers of Robert Bridges's stamp prepared to train young African-American men in a skilled trade. Writing to abolitionist William Lloyd Garrison in 1831, he observed, "If a man of color has children, it is almost impossible for him to get a trade for them, as the journeymen and apprentices generally refuse to work with them, even if the master is willing, which is seldom the case."[38] In another letter he declared, "[I]f the whites will give us our rights, establish good schools for our children as well as theirs, give them trades, and encourage them after they have become masters of their trade, they will have nothing to fear: they will find us as true to this our country and home, as any class of persons."[39] If few white masters would train young black men in skilled trades, then African-American masters must make a commitment to do so. James Forten's sail loft at 95 South Wharves produced two generations of black sailmakers.

James Forten began in a small way. In July 1805 he consulted the Indentures Committee of the Pennsylvania Abolition Society and took on a young black boy, Samuel Elbert, as an indentured servant. Elbert was bound out to Forten to work in the sail loft for five years and five months.[40] Then Forten sought out other young African-American men: Pennsylvania natives Joseph Waterford and Charles Anthony; a migrant from Delaware, James Cornish; and New Englanders Shadrack Howard and Ezra P. Johnson, who were relatives of his old friend the merchant and sea-captain Paul Cuffe. Waterford was with Forten for twenty-five years, as apprentice and then as foreman. In time, his son, Joseph Jr., came into the business. Eventually, lured by prospects in California in the 1850s, the Waterfords moved to San Francisco.[41] In the mid-1840s Charles Anthony joined forces with George Bolivar, a wealthy free black settler from North Carolina who was another of Forten's apprentices, to purchase the business from Forten's heirs.[42]

Like Joseph Waterford and his son, other apprentices took the skills learned at Forten's loft to succeed elsewhere. Two apprentices left him in the 1820s to go to Haiti and establish their own sail lofts there. Forten probably approved of their desire to emigrate, for he was greatly interested in the progress of the black republic. One man settled in Port-au-Prince and the other in Cap Haitien, and both prospered.[43]

Occasionally, though, an apprentice disappointed Forten. That was the case with Francis Devany, a young ex-slave from South Carolina. Forten trained him and then watched him leave for Liberia. As far as James Forten was concerned, the West African colony was rooted in the desire of hostile white Americans to rid the United States of free people of color. He had briefly been interested in the notion of a place of refuge on the West African coast—a haven for ex-slaves from America, a mission station for evangelizing the African continent, and a base from which to begin the suppression of the slave trade. He had even talked and corresponded with some of the white men who organized the American Colonization Society. However, Forten's initial enthusiasm had soon waned when he heard more talk of deporting free people of color and less of ending slavery. Although he publicly announced his change of heart, the officers and agents of the ACS made repeated efforts to win him over. They understood that, as a highly successful and very articulate free man of color, he could do much to advance their cause, especially if he could be persuaded to endorse their African colony and lead an exodus of free people of color to Liberia. Forten rebuffed every approach, fearing the real goal of the ACS was to remove from the United States thousands of free black men and women who could help the slaves in the South win their liberty. The project also smacked of forced deportation. He was not at all sure that free people would have any say in whether or not they emigrated. He would have nothing to do with the Society or the Liberian colony. Francis Devany, however, saw economic opportunities in Liberia. He went, did well, and joined with other settlers and with the American Colonization Society's leadership in attacking Forten. Forten deplored Devany's actions, but he was not a vengeful man, and no doubt regretted the younger man's death in 1833 from consumption at age thirty-six.[44]

Although he was a strong advocate for African-American employment opportunities, at no point did James Forten consider dismissing his white workers. He kept those who had worked for Bridges and hired more. Deeply committed to the idea of integration, he was determined to have a workforce in which black men and white worked harmoniously together. They were required to obey the rules he set down, labor faithfully, and subscribe to his values, attending church and abstaining from the use of alcohol, but race made no difference in his sail loft.

Paying a man's wages, whether that man was black or white, gave an employer power, and Forten was not reluctant to use that power. One day toward the end of October 1822, Congressman Samuel Breck was out for a stroll in Philadelphia when he was "accosted" by "a Negro man named Fortune or Forton . . . offering his hand to me." Breck was surprised, but, "knowing [Forten's] respectability," he stopped to shake hands. Forten then informed Breck, no doubt with the utmost politeness, that the congressman was in his debt.

> [H]e told me that at my late election to Congress, he had taken 15 white men to vote for me. In my sail-loft . . . I have 30 persons at work . . . and among them are 22 journeymen—15 of whom are

white . . . All the white men went to the poles [*sic*] and voted for you.

That chance meeting led Breck to ponder the peculiar status of men of color. In Pennsylvania they could legally vote if they were tax-payers; but, at least in the eastern part of the state, "owing to custom, prejudice or design, they never presume to approach the hustings, neither are they . . . summoned upon juries."[45] Yet Forten, although effectively disfranchised, had at his command fifteen votes to give to the candidate of his choice in an era where the secret ballot was still decades away.

So much for the workers and Forten's control over them. But without orders all the workers at the sail loft would go unpaid. As events showed, James Forten was very successful in retaining Robert Bridges's customers and gaining new ones. The sail loft was on the premises of the powerful mercantile firm of Willings & Francis. The three partners gave Forten many commissions.[46] In gratitude he named one of his sons Thomas Willing Francis Forten. A near neighbor of the firm of Willings & Francis was merchant Louis Clappier, and Forten apparently received orders from him. He also did work for "many other [merchants] of like character."[47]

One major advantage for Forten was that he was beginning in business as Philadelphia's merchants were entering the lucrative China trade. They needed to fit out their vessels with the finest quality sails for the long voyage around the Cape of Good Hope and the equally grueling encounter with the shoals and typhoons of the South China Seas. Skimping and hiring a less than proficient sailmaker could mean the loss of a vessel. If Forten's loft produced the best sails then that fact outweighed all other considerations.

Many new clients came to Forten with orders. A valued customer in the 1820s, for instance, was Irishman Patrick Hayes, nephew of Commodore John Barry. Hayes had substantial interests in the China trade and in commercial ventures with Cuba. He was a Warden of the Port of Philadelphia, and his son Thomas, who commanded several of his vessels, was married to Commodore William Bainbridge's daughter. In an association that lasted well over a decade, Forten supplied sails and sailmaker's gear, did repairs, and consulted with Hayes about redesigning sail plans for his vessels. Forten's loft even turned out a canvas cover for the captain's piano.[48]

James Forten learned early in his career the importance of diversifying his investments. When he took over the sail loft he was still living in the house on Shippen Street. In 1803, with orders coming in steadily, he made his first foray into the real estate market. He bought a lot in

Southwark, built a house, and rented it out. In 1806 he moved with his young wife from Southwark to the city proper, purchasing a three-story brick house on Lombard Street. Then he began looking for suitable investments. In 1809 he acquired a second house on Lombard. As the nation headed into its second war with Britain, Forten used a substantial part of his savings to buy a lot in Blockley Township, just outside Philadelphia, and another house in the city. The outbreak of war brought a sharp upturn in property values, and Forten acquired more real estate, most of it in the Lombard Street neighborhood. The end of the War of 1812 led to economic upheavals, but for those like Forten who survived it with their fortunes intact, there were real estate bargains as fellow merchants went to the wall. In the space of four years, from 1816 to 1820, Forten added considerably to his properties. He sold real estate as well—and almost always at a profit.[49] He rented out various properties to tenants from many segments of Philadelphia society, and he used his profits to acquire bonds, mortgages, bank stock, and shares in various companies.[50] He prided himself on the fact that "he never . . . took an advantage of his neighbor in the time of emergency or pecuniary embarrassment," and that he studiously avoided "the genteel kind of swindling that some professedly 'good' people practice under the . . . name of *note shaving*."[51] But he was no fool. When debts went unpaid, he would ask for payment in person and then in writing. Sometimes he would approach a friend or relative of the delinquent, as he did when one of Samuel Breck's in-laws got into difficulties.[52] But if he had to he would go to court—to the Philadelphia District Court, to the Court of Common Pleas, and in one instance to the Pennsylvania Supreme Court. And his lawyers (he hired the best) invariably won.

For more than four decades James Forten was an active participant in a complex network of credit arrangements. He loaned money to many other businessmen and he in turn secured loans. His credit transactions almost always involved men Forten knew as neighbors, either at South Wharves or on Lombard Street, or as customers. These men borrowed from him; they also loaned money to him. Whether at any given time one was a debtor or a creditor depended on many variables.

But buying and selling, borrowing and lending—the business transactions only constitute a part of the equation. What did the predominantly white business community think of James Forten? He had his friends: iron merchant Thomas Ash; sea captain Daniel Brewton, a comrade-in-arms from the Revolution; William Deas, for whom he named a son; and a handful of other merchants. Then there were hundreds of acquaintances, like Captain Charles Perry, who carried word of Forten's success as a businessman to Havana, Cuba, and saddled him with a most unlikely commission.[53] The likes of Perry never quite knew what to make of James Forten. They certainly gossiped about him. In 1831, when Harriet Forten married Robert Purvis, the son of an Anglo-Scottish cotton merchant and his mulatto mistress, the story went around that James Forten had made "some sacrifice of his fortune" to buy "a whiter species" of husband for his daughter.[54] It made a good story except for a few crucial facts. Robert Purvis, who could have "passed," chose to identify himself as a man of color, he was a committed abolitionist, and he was wealthier than his father-in-law.

For James Forten the inescapable fact was that, try as he might to be a "gentleman of the pave" who happened to be of African descent, he was, to all but a handful of men in Philadelphia's business community, a man of color first. They saved his letters because, as one observed, it was a novelty to have a letter from "a Negro gentleman."[55] Samuel Breck, who admired him for his respectability and his Revolutionary War service, paid him a back-handed compliment. He was "a black *gentleman* . . . [who] by his urbane manners, manly and correct deportment, deserves the epithet I have used, maugre [in spite of] his black face."[56] As the editor of the *Herald of Freedom* observed, to "[t]he white men in Philadelphia . . . [i]t would have seemed a sort of sacrilege to despise [Forten], and they made him an exception to his race."[57]

It was this contradiction that puzzled an English visitor, Sir Charles Lyell, who happened to be in Philadelphia at the time of James Forten's death. He witnessed his funeral and was struck by the sight of thousands of people, rich and poor, following his coffin to St. Thomas's Church or standing in the street to watch the cortege pass by. Lyell asked about Forten and was impressed to learn of his success in business.

> I was rejoicing that his colour had proved no impediment to his rising in the world, and that he had been allowed so much fair play as to succeed in over-topping the majority of his white competitors, when I learnt, on further inquiry . . . that, not long before his death, he had been especially mortified, because two of his sons had been refused a hearing at a public meeting where they wished to speak on some subject connected with trade which concerned them.[58]

It was that painful realization that he and his children could advance so far and no further in an America that sanctioned slavery and racial proscription that motivated James Forten to devote so much of his wealth and his time to the twin causes of anti-slavery and social reform. But that is the other half of James Forten's story . . .

Notes

1. This emerges again and again from his letters to fellow reformers and to business contacts. See, for example, James Forten to William Lloyd Garrison, July 28, 1831, Anti-slavery Manuscripts, Boston Public Library (hereafter BPL).

2. At the time of James Forten's birth, about 20 percent of male laborers in Philadelphia were slaves. Philadelphia had about 1,400 slaves out of a total population of 18,000. Gary B. Nash, *Forging Freedom: The Formation of Philadelphia's Black Community, 1720–1840* (Cambridge: Harvard University Press, 1988), 9–10.

3. Stephen H. Gloucester, *A Discourse Delivered on the Occasion of the Death of Mr. James Forten, Sr., in the Second Presbyterian Church of Colour in the City of Philadelphia, April 17, 1842, before the Young Men of the Bible Association of Said Church* (Philadelphia: I. Ashmead, 1843), 18.

4. For evidence of Margaret Forten's age see *Poulson's American Daily Advertiser*, May 31, 1806.

5. See, for example, Thomas Fortune to Lambert Cadwalader, August 25, 1770, Cadwalader Collection, Historical Society of Pennsylvania (hereafter HSP).

6. In 1767 Forten was working for Bridges when he received an order to outfit the surveying party determining the Mason-Dixon line with marquees, tents, wagon covers, speaking trumpets, and a special canvas covering for the valuable telescope. Mason & Dixon, Pennsylvania Misc. Papers, Penn and Baltimore, Penn Family, 1756–1768, HSP.

7. Edward R. Turner, *The Negro in Pennsylvania: Slavery—Servitude—Freedom, 1639–1861* (Washington, D.C.: American Historical Association, 1912), 56.

8. At various times one of the city's Anglican churches hired a catechist to teach African-American adults and children the elements of literacy.

9. Robert Purvis, *Remarks on the Life and Character of James Forten, Delivered at Bethel Church, March 30, 1842* (Philadelphia: Merrihew and Thompson, 1842), 3.

10. "Great Men." Unidentified newspaper clipping in Anna Julia Cooper, *Personal Recollections of the Grimké Family* (Washington, D.C.: For the Author, 1951), 10.

11. James Forten to William Lloyd Garrison, February 23, 1831, BPL.

12. Roger Bruns, ed., *Am I Not a Man and a Brother: The Antislavery Crusade of Revolutionary America, 1688–1788* (New York: Oxford University Press, 1977), 446–447.

13. Library of Congress, *Naval Records of the American Revolution, 1775–1788* (Washington, D.C.: Government Printing Office, 1906), 217, 254, 325, 390, 409, 438.

14. Purvis, *Remarks*, 11.

15. Ibid., 4.

16. *The Freeman's Journal*, August 22, 1781; *Pennsylvania Gazette*, August 22, 1781. On the importance of the dispatches see French Ensor Chadwick, *The Graves Papers and Other Documents Relating to the Naval Operations of the Yorktown Campaign, July to October, 1781* (New York: For the Naval History Society, 1916), xiv–xvi, lxvi–lxvii.

17. *Amphion*, Master's Log, ADM 52/2133, Public Record Office (hereafter PRO), London.

18. *Amphion*, Muster, ADM 36/9561, PRO.

19. Purvis, *Remarks*, 5–6.

20. Gloucester, *Discourse*, 21–22; Purvis, *Remarks*, 6. Forten, his name spelled "Fortune," was taken aboard the *Jersey* as prisoner #4102. *Jersey* Muster, ADM 36/9579, PRO.

21. Purvis, *Remarks*, 7–8.

22. Ibid., 8.

23. Frederick Arthur Crisp, *Visitation of England and Wales* (n.p.: Privately printed, 1909–11), vol. 16, 100.

24. Ralph Davis, *The Rise of the English Shipping Industry in the Seventeenth and Eighteenth Centuries* (London: Macmillan, 1962), 62–64, 66–68, 70–71, 78.

25. On the black community in London in the 1780s see James Walvin, *Black and White: The Negro and English Society, 1555–1954* (London: Allen Lane, 1973), 47–57, 61, 72, and Gretchen Gerzina, *Black London: Life before Emancipation* (New Brunswick: Rutgers University Press, 1995).

26. Purvis, *Remarks*, 9.

27. Edward L. Clark, ed., *A Record of the Inscriptions on the Tablets and Grave-Stones in the Burial-Grounds of Christ Church, Philadelphia* (Philadelphia: Collins, 1864), 525. Records of Christ Church, Baptisms, Marriages, Burials, HSP.

28. Will of Robert Bridges, Will Book Y, p. 281, #24 (1800), Philadelphia City Archives (hereafter PCA).

29. Philadelphia County Deeds, T.H., Book 179, 244, 248, PCA.

30. Purvis, *Remarks*, 8.

31. Gloucester, *Discourse*, 23.

32. *National Anti-Slavery Standard*, March 10, 1842.

33. Records of St. George's Church, Philadelphia, 1785–1856, HSP. Philadelphia City Directories, 1811, 1813, 1814, 1816, 1817.

34. Seamen's Protection Papers, Box 18 (1810, A–F), Record Group 41, National Archives. *Maritime Records—Alphabetical—Masters and Crews, 1798–1800*, series V, vol. 13 (1819), 123; vol. 15 (1821), 27; vol. 17 (1823), 163, 226; vol. 19 (1825A), 122; vol. 21 (1826A), 59; vol. 24 (1828), 118; vol. 33 (1838), 298. Philadelphia City Directories, 1825, 1829, 1830.

35. *Poulson's American Daily Advertiser*, November 14, 1803; June 2, 1804; December 13, 1805.

36. William Douglass, *Annals of the First African Church in the United States of America, Now Styled the African Episcopal Church of St. Thomas* (Philadelphia: King and Baird, 1862), 107–110.

37. Philadelphia City Directories, 1810, 1811, 1813, 1817, 1819, 1820, 1822.

38. James Forten to William Lloyd Garrison, February 3, 1831, BPL.

39. Forten to Garrison, in *Liberator*, March 19, 1831.

40. Indenture of Samuel Elbert (1805), Pennsylvania Abolition Society Papers, HSP.

41. James de T. Abajian, comp., *Blacks in Selected Newspapers, Censuses, and Other Sources: An Index to Names and Subjects* (Boston: G. K. Hall, 1977), vol. 2.

42. Henry M. Minton, *Early History of Negroes in Business in Philadelphia* (Nashville: AME Sunday School Union, 1913), 16.

43. Benjamin Hunt, *Remarks on Hayti as a Place of Settlement for Afric-Americans; and on the Mulatto as a Race for the Tropics* (Philadelphia: T. B. Pugh, 1860), 6.

44. *African Repository and Colonial Journal*, vol. 10 (May 1834), 90.

45. Nicholas B. Wainwright, ed., "The Diary of Samuel Breck, 1814–1822," *Pennsylvania Magazine of History and Biography* 102 (October 1978), 505.

46. *North American*, March 5, 1842.

47. Gloucester, *Discourse*, 23.

48. Barry-Hayes Papers, Independence Seaport Museum, Philadelphia.

49. Philadelphia County Deeds; Philadelphia County Mortgages, PCA.

50. Will of James Forten, Will Book 15, p. 445, #87 (1842), PCA.

51. Gloucester, *Discourse*, 22.

52. See, for instance, James Forten to Samuel Breck, July 22, 1828, Breck Papers, HSP.

53. Alonso Munoz to James Forten, June 24, 1817, in Pennsylvania Abolition Society Minutes, 1800–1824, 260, HSP. *Poulson's American Daily Advertiser*, July 14, 1817. Forten was asked to arrange for the education of a young West African prince, the grandson of a slave trader.

54. Abraham Ritter, *Philadelphia and Her Merchants, as Constituted Fifty and Seventy Years Ago* (Philadelphia: The Author, 1860), 46–47.

55. Endorsement on James Forten to Samuel Breck, July 22, 1828, Breck Papers, HSP.

56. Diary of Samuel Breck, 1832–33, HSP.

57. *The Herald of Freedom* in *Liberator*, April 8, 1842.

58. Sir Charles Lyell, *Travels in North America* (London: Longman, Brown, Green and Orme, 1843), 207.

Six

David Walker, African Rights, and Liberty

Verner D. Mitchell

The first difference which strikes us is that of colour . . .
that immoveable veil of black which covers all the emotions of the other race. . . . This unfortunate difference of
colour, and perhaps of faculty, is a powerful obstacle to
the emancipation of these people.
—Thomas Jefferson, *Notes on the State of Virginia*, 1787

Millions of [whites], are this day, so ignorant and avari-
cious, that they cannot conceive how God can have an attribute of justice, and show mercy to us because it pleased
Him to make us black—which colour, Mr. Jefferson calls
unfortunate! ! ! ! As though we are not as thankful to our
God, for having made us as it pleased himself, as they,
(the whites,) are for having made them white.
—David Walker, *Appeal to the Coloured Citizens of the
World*, 1830

Answering Jefferson from exile, after having traveled from his native
North Carolina to Boston, was the author, orator, entrepreneur, and
freedom fighter David Walker. Walker responded foremost by speaking
to the importance of blacks themselves refuting Thomas Jefferson's assertions of black inferiority. His *Appeal, in Four Articles; Together with a
Preamble, to the Coloured Citizens of the World, but in Particular, and Very
Expressly, to Those of the United States of America* (1830) thundered
throughout the antebellum period and beyond. Why, Walker asks, would
one who enacted laws making it a punishable crime for the African
people he held in captivity to learn to read and write find it noteworthy
that the captives remained illiterate?[1]

Has Mr. Jefferson declared to the world, that we are inferior to the
whites, both in the endowments of our bodies and our minds? It is
indeed surprising, that a man of such great learning, combined
with such excellent natural parts, should speak so of a set of men
in chains. I do not know what to compare it to, unless, like putting

one wild deer in an iron cage, where it will be secured, and hold another by the side of the same, then let it go, and expect the one in the cage to run as fast as the one at liberty. (Walker 10)

Merely an unassuming autodidact, Walker nonetheless unsettles the core of Jefferson's musings on difference. Would even a child, much less a learned scholar, expect a shackled deer to outpace one at liberty? Why then, asks Walker, would a man of great learning think "differently" of a set of men in chains? Sixty-five pages later, Walker ends his *Appeal* with an assessment of a sizable quotation from the *Declaration of Independence*. This choice enables him structurally and thematically to conclude his argument as he began: with the reader's eyes fixed on the contradictions between the cornerstone of America's inaugural narrative and the realities of American slavery and racism.

Walker's demand that the nation finally deliver on its promise of unalienable rights for all is one which has been echoed down through the years, perhaps most poignantly during the 1960s by Martin Luther King, Jr., and Malcolm X. Today King is best remembered for having successfully trumpeted the moral efficacy of non-violent resistance and Malcolm for his strident call, "By any means necessary." Their means, then, clearly differed, yet it is equally clear that they sought a common end, one which Walker had articulated over a century before. As Malcolm explains in his *Autobiography*, "[I]f white Americans could accept the Oneness of God, then perhaps, too, they could accept in *reality* the Oneness of Man—and cease to measure, and hinder, and harm others in terms of their 'differences' in color" (Malcolm and Haley 341). King similarly looked beyond superficial differences and accentuated the oneness of man, perhaps most famously during his August 28, 1963, "I Have a Dream" speech. He dreamed of a day "when all of God's children, black men and white men, Jews and Gentiles, Catholics and Protestants, will be able to join hands" (King 650).

The above discussion, along with offering some sense of *Appeal*'s import as an enabling text, provides a framework through which to view what the historian Vincent Harding terms "David Walker and . . . the Great Tradition of Black Protest" (Harding 83). This essay locates Walker at the fore of that Great Tradition.

Although not much is known of Walker's early years, we do know that he was born on September 28, 1785, in Wilmington, North Carolina, to a free mother and an enslaved father, who had died a few months before his son's birth. Born of a free mother, under North Carolina's laws Walker was thereby free. We know from his own statements that he was largely self-educated and that he traveled through many of America's twenty-four states, in both the South and the North. We also have a helpful sketch of his physical appearance, thanks to his widow, Eliza. During an interview with the Reverend Henry Highland Garnet, Mrs. Walker described her husband as having been "prepossessing, being six feet in height, slender and well-proportioned. His hair was loose, and his complexion was dark"[2] (Garnet 44).

During his travels Walker saw firsthand and up close the horrors of American slavery. His *Appeal* is, as a consequence, replete with vivid descriptions of these indignities. The cumulative drain that came from repeatedly witnessing "barbarous cruelties" from within the belly of the beast, as it were, accounts in large part for Walker's decision in or around 1825 to uproot and move to Boston. "This is not the place for me—no, no," he declared. "Certainly I cannot remain where I must hear their chains continually, and where I must encounter the insults of their hypocritical enslavers. Go, I must" (Garnet 41). Exacerbating the harsh sounds of enslaved people's clanking chains were the enslavers' verbal "insults," a gauntlet of dehumanizing affronts which, quite naturally, weighed very heavily on Walker. At the core of slaveholding society, in Walker's view, was a continual and incessant stream of insulting laws, edicts, sermons, and other learned teachings, promulgated to secure the allegedly God-ordained positions of white masters and black slaves. Representative of the insults which Walker found so painful is the following North Carolina Supreme Court ruling, a juridical edict which masterfully delineates white people's "place" in Walker's native state.

> What acts in a slave towards a white person will amount to insolence it is manifestly impossible to define—it may consist in a look, the pointing of a finger, a refusal or neglect to step out of the way when a white person is seen to approach. But each of such acts violates the rules of propriety, and if tolerated, would destroy the subordination, upon which our social system rests. (Aptheker, *Revolts*, 55)

Unwilling, in turn, to maintain his place, Walker realized that remaining free necessitated that he promptly steal away from the South.

Of major importance to Walker was the opportunity Boston afforded him to work to free his shackled brothers and sisters. He seemed indeed determined to ensure that those still enslaved would not suffer his father's ultimate fate under slavery. Within months of his entrance into Massachusetts, Walker was actively engaged in organized resistance: 1) serving as Boston agent for the New York–based *Freedom's Journal* (which in March of 1827 had become the first black-owned and

-operated newspaper in the United States), 2) holding meetings on behalf of the paper at his home in Boston,[3] 3) writing and publishing his
Appeal, 4) dispatching three successive editions of *Appeal* deep into the
South, 5) serving as secretary of the city's African Masonic Lodge, and
6) delivering anti-slavery speeches to Boston audiences large and small.
"Whatever his podium," observes Charles M. Wiltse, Walker's "theme
was the same: slavery degrades the man, corrupts the body, destroys the
soul. If the master will not free the slave, the slave must seize his own
freedom, at whatever cost in blood, because death is better than life
under such conditions" (Wiltse viii).

Along with fostering acts of resistance throughout the slaveholding
South, from Virginia down the coast to Georgia and west to Louisiana,
Walker's unabashed calls for freedom and dignity triggered a similarly wide-ranging number of demands for his capture, dead or alive. In
June 1830, Walker was found near the doorway of his 42 Brattle Street
clothing shop, having been felled by an assassin. "Few doubted," notes
Wiltse, "that the most eloquent voice in the battle for Negro freedom
had been violently stilled" (xi). Rather than flee to Canada as friends
advised, Walker had chosen to remain in Boston and fight. "I will
stand my ground," he vowed. "Somebody must die in this cause" (Garnet 43).

He had not made this decision lightly. Instead, like King and Malcolm and a host of others, Walker knew full well that remaining in
America, even in the North, ensured that he would in all likelihood be
killed: "Why do the Slave-holders or Tyrants of America and their advocates fight so hard to keep my brethren from receiving and reading
my Book of Appeal to them?" he asked. "Why do they search vessels,
&c. when entering the harbours of tyrannical States, to see if any of
my Books can be found, for fear that my brethren will get them to read?
. . . I expect some will try to put me to death, to strike terror into others, and to obliterate from their minds the notion of freedom, so as to
keep my brethren the more secure in wretchedness" (Walker 22, 72).
Resolved, as Malcolm and King would in like manner be during the
next century, Walker continued tossing lifelines to his enslaved brothers
and sisters, defiantly proclaiming, "I would suffer my life to be taken
before I would submit" (22).

Before examining the substance of these lifelines, let us consider
briefly the response in Georgia and North Carolina, and most especially
in Virginia, states where, as Herbert Aptheker explains, "Walker's revolutionary *Appeal* had penetrated . . . and had provoked unrest" (Aptheker, *Revolts,* 281). We actually need travel no further than the third
edition of *Appeal* itself to find a candid snapshot. For as Walker details,

coming fast on the heels of the first and second editions of his "Appeal to my brethren" was a Georgia law "prohibiting all free or slave persons of colour, from learning to read or write." "Another law," Walker continues, "has passed the *republican* House of Delegates, (but not the Senate) in Virginia, to prohibit all persons of colour, (free and slave) from leaning to read or write, and even to hinder them from meeting together in order to worship our Maker ! ! ! ! ! !" (Walker 53)

As for North Carolina, a similar train of events was set in motion by the September 1830 discovery of *Appeal* in Walker's hometown. After confiscating several copies, the Wilmington chief of police promptly penned a letter to the governor, warning him that the book "throughout express[ed] sentiments totally subversive of all subordination in our slaves" (Eaton 323). (Governmental officials in South Carolina, Louisiana, and Georgia had reached the same conclusion the prior year.) The subsequent discovery of *Appeal* circulating amongst the black citizenry in Fayetteville and New Bern further alarmed many of the state's white citizens. The last straw evidently came on November 15, 1830, when a captured runaway confessed that "Walker's pamphlets had been brought from Wilmington [to New Bern], weapons had been stored away, and captains appointed for the projected uprising on Christmas day" (Eaton 331). Posthaste, the state legislature scurried into secret session. And by the ninth of December 1830, less than four months after the Wilmington police chief's initial letter, North Carolina law held that persons convicted of writing or circulating publications "the evident tendency whereof would be to excite . . . resistance in the slaves or free Negroes" should, for the first offense, be imprisoned and whipped, and for the second offense "suffer death without benefit of clergy" (Eaton 331–332).

The mayor of Savannah, Georgia, did his colleagues to the North one better. During the summer of 1829, a number of "suspicious" fires swept across various parts of Augusta and Savannah; soon afterward, local police seized sixty copies of *Appeal*. The incensed Savannah mayor then wrote to his counterpart, Mayor Harrison Gray Otis of Boston, demanding that Walker be arrested and punished (Wiltse x; Aptheker, *Revolts*, 281). Mayor Otis, to his great credit, observes Henry Highland Garnet, "replied to the Southern Censor, that he had no power nor disposition to hinder Mr. Walker from pursuing a lawful course in the utterance of his thoughts." Garnet adds that subsequent to this reply,

A company of Georgia men then bound themselves by an oath, that they would eat as little as possible until they had killed the youthful author. They also offered a reward of a thousand dollars for his head, and ten times as much for the live Walker. (Garnet 43)

Without belaboring this succession of outraged and panicked reactions, it would not be overstating the case simply to conclude, as does Dolan Hubbard, that Walker's narrative "shook the psyche of the nation, found its ideals wanting, and intensified the growing national debate on slavery" (Hubbard 331). In short, Walker had dared insist, at the risk of his life, that the nation bridge the vast gap between its rhetoric and its actions.

Further shaking the country's psyche, particularly in and around Southampton County, Virginia, was a thunderous explosion in August of 1831 (fourteen months after Walker's death). Led by the Reverend Nat Turner, a cadre of six men captured and swiftly executed fifty-five slavers, including men, women, and children. Perhaps best capturing the ensuing panic is the following account by Mrs. Lawrence Lewis, niece of President Washington:

[I]t is like a smothered volcano—we know not when, or where the flame will burst forth but we know that death in the most horrid forms threatens us. Some have died, others have become deranged from apprehension since the South Hampton affair. (Aptheker, *Revolts*, 306–307)

Rumors have long persisted that Walker's appeal to his "enslaved brethren" provided the chief inspiration for "enslaved" Turner's intrepid attack. Was Turner in fact listening as Walker cried out,

Oh! my coloured brethren, all over the world, when shall we arise from this death-like apathy?—And be men! ! . . . They know well that the Aborigines of this country, (or Indians) . . . would not rest day or night, they would be up all times of night, cutting their cruel throats. But my colour, (some, not all,) are willing to stand still and be murdered by the cruel whites. (Walker 62–63)

Many scholars do not believe that there was a direct link between Walker's *Appeal* and Turner's revolt. Others disagree, pointing to the timing of key events. Between September 1829 and June 1830, Walker published three editions of *Appeal;* eight months afterward (coincident with a February 1831 solar eclipse), Turner decided to attack. He set July 4, 1831, as D-day, but ill health forced him to delay until the twenty-second of August (Harding 94–95).

But did *Appeal* actually reach Southampton County? Or more to the point, did it reach Turner prior to his uprising? Virginia's Governor

John Floyd, for one, certainly thought so. "I am fully persuaded, the spirit of insubordination which has, and still manifests itself in Virginia," writes Floyd in a November 19, 1831, letter to his South Carolina counterpart, "had its origin among, and eminated from the Yankee population, upon their first arrival amongst us, but most especially the Yankee pedlers and traders."[4] He identifies two specific pedlars—William Lloyd Garrison and David Walker. Their "incendiary publications"—together with the urgings of black preachers, by whom "often from the pulpits these pamphlets and papers were read," asserts Floyd —produced "the Southampton affair." Floyd was by no means alone. Nonetheless, it is the visionary power of *Appeal* that attracts us; whether or not it was a catalyst for slave revolts is not critical.

The Bostonian novelist, editor, and essayist Pauline Elizabeth Hopkins supports my reading. In her essay on Walker's son, "the eminent Negro barrister" Edward Garrison Walker, Hopkins observes that Walker's famous *Appeal* "was strong in sentiment, cogent in its reasonings, and breathed the thoughts of a man of powerful mind." She adds, "Right here we have the most interesting fact in the history of the abolition movement: this appeal was *the very first step taken in the attempt to arouse the people of the United States to the enormity of the crime of slavery* and the deep disgrace it was bringing upon the country. . . . These men could not withstand the evidence, and soon the very lives of the brightest ornaments of American thought and culture were absorbed in the warfare against slavery" (359; Hopkins's emphasis).

Among the brightest of these was a twenty-nine-year-old woman who in February of 1833 (less than three years after Walker's demise) approached the stage in Boston's African Masonic Hall. Standing at what I prefer to envision as the very podium from which Walker had launched similar salvos, Maria W. Stewart boldly called her audience to action:

> The unfriendly whites first drove the native American from his much loved home. Then they stole our fathers . . . and brought them hither and made bond men and bond women of them and their little ones . . . and now that we have enriched their soil, and filled their coffers . . . [t]hey would drive us to a strange land. But before I go, the bayonet shall pierce me through. African rights and liberty is a subject that ought to fire the breast of every free man of color in these United States. . . . Where is the man that has distinguished himself in these modern days by acting wholly in the defence of African rights and liberty? There was one— although he sleeps, his memory lives. (Stewart 26, 33–34)

Stewart was obviously speaking from beneath (what W. E. B. Du Bois later termed) the veil, for to have done otherwise might well have resulted in her suffering Walker's fate. Given their own positions within the veil, however, we can be certain that her Bostonian listeners knew of which distinguished defender of African rights and liberty, now asleep, she spoke.

In her 1831 essay "Religion and the Pure Principles of Morality," Stewart bids her readers, "Prove to the world that you are neither ourang-outangs, or a species of mere animals, but that you possess the same powers of intellect as the proud-boasting American" (40). Walker also deemed it imperative that such ungenerous characterizations not go unanswered, that they be thoroughly and decisively rebutted. He underscores this point on *Appeal*'s very first page: "It is expected that all coloured men, women and children, of every nation, language and tongue under heaven, will try to procure a copy of this *Appeal* and read it, or get some one to read it to them, for it is designed more particularly for them." Fully cognizant, moreover, of the measure of Thomas Jefferson's influence, in particular, Walker thinks it important that blacks themselves come forward and answer the former president's charges. "This very verse, brethren, having emanated from Mr. Jefferson, a much greater philosopher the world never afforded, has in truth injured us more, and has been as great a barrier to our emancipation as any thing that has ever been advanced against us" (Walker 27).[5] He implores all black men "to buy a copy of Mr. Jefferson's 'Notes on Virginia,' and put it in the hand of [your] son. For let no one of us suppose that the refutations which have been written by our white friends are enough— they are *whites*—we are *blacks*" (14–15; Walker's emphasis).

Clearly Walker realizes that refutations solely from whites would of necessity reinforce Jefferson's argument. For if, as Jefferson posits, blacks are mentally deficient beings lacking full facility with language, it follows that they require the assistance of more capable agents. Walker, however, has no patience with such inanity. Thus he sidesteps the friendly whites and addresses his black brethren directly, so as to accentuate more vigorously their own human agency. And with the friendly white intermediaries removed, Walker's brethren (enslaved and free) can stand with Jefferson shoulder to shoulder, man to man.

For his part, Walker launches a four-pronged rebuttal grounded in the annals of ancient Africa (dating from before the Arab invasions of the seventh century AD). Initially, he delivers a series of riveting, first-hand accounts of black people's lives under American slavery. He paints pictures of families being torn asunder on auction blocks, of children being chained and branded, of overseers disrupting worship services by beating worshippers "as they would rattle-snakes" (37). In a particularly gruesome passage, he shows a son being forced to take his mother, "who bore almost the pains of death to give him birth, and by the command of a tyrant, strip her as naked as she came into the world, and apply the cow-hide to her, until she falls a victim to death in the road" (21). With these scenes, Walker shamelessly plays upon his readers' emotions. By so doing he aims to blast open the door, and in his words, allow all the world "to enter more fully into the interior of this system of cruelty and oppression" (6).

While scrutinizing slaveholding society, an overwhelmed Walker at one point pauses and sighs, "Oh my Lord! too horrible to present to the world" (21). Although he does manage to proceed, by the end of the presentation he is so drained that he stops, mid-sentence, and cries out, "Oh Heaven! I am full! ! ! I can hardly move my pen! ! ! !" (22) A number of important things are happening here. First, in cataloguing myriad "cruelties," Walker the artful traveler gently grasps his readers' hands and maneuvers them deep into the interior of enslaved people's lives. Appropriately, unlike W. E. B. Du Bois's "car-window sociologist," Walker's prose snatches genteel readers from "the suburbs" and forces them to face the very bowels of American slavery (Du Bois 113; Walker 6). The multiple exclamation points, for instance, work in conjunction with other tactically placed devices—italics, bold print, words of varying height, words written entirely with upper-case letters—to recreate an oral dynamic. Collectively, these devices modulate the narrative's tone and rhythm, ensuring that the reader pauses and lingers, smells and tastes, sees and feels. Walker's vividly expressive written language thus functions in much the same manner as the animated oral performances of black preachers like Dr. Martin Luther King, Jr., in "I Have a Dream" and the Reverend John Jasper in "The Sun Do Move." Finally, the above passage astutely calls attention to Walker the author, with his pen in hand, a strategic positioning which may have been the model for Frederick Douglass's famous syncretic passage, "My feet have been so cracked with the frost, that the pen with which I am writing might be laid in the gashes" (Douglass 72).

During the second part of his rebuttal Walker moves away from emotive appeals and relies more heavily on logos or appeals to logic. At this point he could well have written, "Let us sit, put aside our surface differences, and reason together as intelligent, thinking humans." As one who is himself rational, Walker assumes that given sufficient evidence other thinking people will see that notwithstanding our "woolly heads" and our "immoveable veil of black" we are neither subhuman nor naturally designed to labor as beasts of burden. Here again, he deems it important first to appeal specifically to his "coloured brethren," although he knows full well that people are listening throughout the color spectrum, on both sides of the Mason-Dixon line, and on both sides of the Atlantic:

> [R]emember that we are men as well as they. They have no more right to hold us in slavery than we have to hold them, we have just as much right, in the sight of God, to hold them and their children in slavery and wretchedness, as they have to hold us, and no more. (Walker 11)

Attuned to the crippling effects of mental bondage, a condition Frederick Douglass would explore fifteen years later in great detail, Walker here acts to impede widespread assaults on enslaved people's sense of their own humanity. "You must remember," he implores, that "God has been pleased to [make us] men as well as they" (11).

That said, he directs his gaze more openly upon a wider audience. In a move designed to locate slavery as the root cause of enslaved Africans' current wretchedness, he presents a rather lengthy dissertation, detailing lucidly and with passion ancient African accomplishments. Taking center stage are wise legislators, talented architects, and "that mighty son of Africa, HANNIBAL" (20). In sum, Walker's descriptions, much like those in the *Aeneid* of flourishing Carthage under Queen Dido's reign, bespeak a wise and learned people. And if the enslaved Africans in America spring from a wise and learned people, reasons Walker, what judgment must follow? That is, what conclusion logically follows for adjudicators who are rational thinkers and, equally important, persons of goodwill?

> When we take a retrospective view of the arts and sciences—the wise legislators—the Pyramids, and other magnificent buildings—the turning of the channel of the river Nile, by the sons of Africa or of Ham, among whom learning originated, and was carried thence into Greece, where it was improved upon and refined. Thence among the Romans, and all over the then enlightened parts of the world, and it has been enlightening the dark and benighted minds of men from then, down to this day. I say, when I view retrospectively, the renown of that once mighty people, the children of our great progenitor I am indeed cheered. (20)

Overstepping by far the bounds of nineteenth-century American propriety, Walker daringly creates a counternarrative, one openly celebratory of African intellect, beauty, character, and worth. Most important, as his forebears had done for the Romans and the Greeks, he aims to enlighten benighted minds.

During the third part of his rebuttal, Walker offers an olive branch. Once again, he presumes that reasonable movements should result when reasonable, thinking persons gather and reason together.

> I speak Americans for your good. We must and shall be free I say, in spite of you. You may do your best to keep us in wretchedness and misery, to enrich you and your children; but God will deliver us from under you. . . . Throw away your fears and prejudices then . . . and treat us like men, and we will like you more than we do now hate you. (70)

To make clear the precise terms of his appeal, Walker, much like his friend and neighbor Maria W. Stewart, conveys forcefully the unacceptability of all designs advancing removal or colonization. Rather than act to preclude mixture and thereby reserve the land for the few, he envisions a tolerant, abundant mosaic. In short, he struggles valiantly, as Toni Morrison might say, to transform a racist house into an enlightened, non-racist home:[6] "tell us no more about colonization, for America is as much our country, as it is yours.—Treat us like men, and there is no danger but we will all live in peace and happiness together" (70).

Finally, cautiously not ruling out the possibility of his interlocutors' proving rigid and unyielding, Walker ends with a stern appeal. Here I imagine him trusting that should appeals to emotion, logic, and ethics all fail to impede racism and greed, surely the assurance of certain death will succeed and thereby stay the Armageddon he feels is otherwise sure to come: "wo, wo, will be to you if we have to obtain our freedom by fighting" (70). "Perhaps they will laugh at or make light of this," he adds for those who are especially hard of hearing, "but I tell you Americans! that unless you speedily alter your course, *you* and your *Country are gone*! ! ! ! ! ! For God Almighty will tear up the very face of the earth! ! !" (39) It merits stressing, once more, that Walker issues the above warning not out of hatred for whites, as has occasionally been charged, but out of an intense concern for the world's people, most particularly its oppressed colored citizens. Throughout his *Appeal* he repeatedly weighs not the phenotype but the deed. Hence at various junctures he decries a colored woman's "ignorant and deceitful actions," he excoriates "coloured men . . . in league with tyrants, selling their own brethren into *hell upon earth*,"[7] and he lovingly praises whites who show themselves human:

Those among them [white Americans], who have volunteered their services for our redemption, though we are unable to compensate them for their labours, we nevertheless thank them from the bottom of our hearts, and have our eyes steadfastly fixed upon them, and their labours of love for God and man.[8] (22)

Walker's great concern, then, as a lover of God and man, is to call all Americans away from ignorance, intolerance, and greed, to an acknowledgment of our common humanity. Only then, he exhorts, can the American people stay the civil war or Armageddon he so accurately foretells. Even "[i]f you cannot or will not profit," he concludes, "I shall have done my duty to you, my country and my God" (3).

Appeal to the Coloured Citizens of the World is significant not only for its eloquence, candor, and artistry, but by virtue of its very existence. It aggressively belies myths of black illiteracy, incompetency, and intellectual inferiority. Moreover, beginning with the strategically placed titular phrase "Coloured Citizens of the World," Walker signals that his is through and through a boldly transgressive discourse. At a historical time and place when blacks were deemed mentally arrested creatures incompetent to speak even about themselves, Walker's double-edged prose raises them to the status of fully human agents not only in America but on the world stage. Turning one revolution, it simultaneously braves the bowels of American slavery, graphically exposing at the cost of his life the intellectual and moral bankruptcy of reified difference as a despotic tool. Maria W. Stewart's "distinguished defender of African rights and liberty" sleeps. Resounding down through the ages nonetheless are his fervid rejoinders to the ideological pillars undergirding America's perverse system of human servitude.

Notes

1. "During the years of Thomas Jefferson's presidency [1801–1809]," notes Robert McColley, "Virginia discouraged the education of Negroes, required that newly freed Negroes should leave the state, and decided that contraband Negroes should be sold into slavery" (McColley 183).

2. For a photograph of Walker's son, see *The Colored American Magazine* 2, no. 5 (March 1901): 372. Edward Garrison Walker, Esq. (1830–1901), became the first African American to serve in the Massachusetts Legislature, taking his seat in 1866. For more on Walker, see Clarence G. Contee's entry, "Edward [Edwin] Garrison Walker," in the *Dictionary of American Negro Biography* (New York: Norton, 1982): 63.

3. Walker lived in Ward 5, on the northern border of the city's mostly black Beacon Hill community. The U.S. Census for 1830 lists him as head of household of a family of nine. The members of his family, listed under his name by age and sex only, include five children, a man between ages twenty-four and thirty-five, and two women between twenty-four and thirty-five. One of these, we know, was his wife, Eliza Walker; the others must, for now, remain unknown.

4. The letter is dated eight days after Turner's execution (Library of Congress, Manuscript Division).

5. In his germinal study *White over Black: American Attitudes toward the Negro, 1550–1812*, Winthrop D. Jordan concludes that Jefferson's remarks on black inferiority "constituted, for all its qualifications, the most intense, extensive, and extreme formulation of anti-Negro 'thought' offered by an American in the thirty years after the Revolution" (481).

6. Toni Morrison, "Home," keynote address at "Race Matters: Black Americans, U.S. Terrain," a conference at Princeton University, April 28, 1994. An excerpt of this speech that includes Morrison's full sentence—"How can we convert a racist house into a race-specific, non-racist home?"—appears in the May 11, 1994, issue of *The Chronicle of Higher Education*, p. A-10.

7. Here Walker builds on a topic he had earlier broached during his December 1828 address to the Massachusetts General Colored Association: "[W]e see, to our sorrow, in the very midst of us, a gang of villains, who, for the paltry sum of fifty or a hundred dollars, will kidnap and sell into perpetual slavery, their fellow creatures! . . . Brethren and fellow sufferers, I ask you, in the name of God, and of Jesus Christ, shall we suffer such notorious villains to rest peaceably among us?" (*Freedom's Journal*, December 19, 1828, 295).

8. Prominent among the many "volunteers" was Elijah H. Burritt, a white printer in Milledgeville, Georgia. Accused in February 1830 of circulating copies of Walker's *Appeal*, as Herbert Aptheker explains, Burritt "was finally forced to flee for his life in the middle of the night when a hostile mob attacked his dwelling" (Aptheker, *One Continual Cry*, 47).

Works Cited

Aptheker, Herbert. *American Negro Slave Revolts*. New York: International, 1974.
———. *One Continual Cry: David Walker's* Appeal to the Colored Citizens of the World, *1829–1830*. New York: Humanities Press, 1965.
Douglass, Frederick. *Narrative of the Life of Frederick Douglass, an American Slave, Written by Himself.* 1845. Edited by Houston A. Baker, Jr. New York: Penguin, 1982.

Du Bois, W. E. B. *The Souls of Black Folk*. 1903. New York: Vintage, 1990.

Eaton, Clement. "A Dangerous Pamphlet in the Old South." *The Journal of Southern History* 2, no. 3 (August 1936): 323–334.

Floyd, John. "Letter to James Hamilton, R., Governor of South Carolina." Richmond, November 19, 1831. Library of Congress, Manuscript Division.

Garnet, Henry Highland. "A Brief Sketch of the Life and Character of David Walker." 1848. In *One Continual Cry: David Walker's Appeal to the Colored Citizens of the World, 1829–1830*, edited by Herbert Aptheker, 40–44. New York: Humanities Press, 1965.

Harding, Vincent. *There Is a River: The Black Struggle for Freedom in America*. New York: Vintage, 1983.

Hopkins, Pauline E. "Famous Men of the Negro Race: Edwin Garrison Walker." *The Colored American Magazine* 2, no. 5 (March 1901): 358–366.

Hubbard, Dolan. "David Walker's *Appeal* and the American Puritan Jeremiadic Tradition." *The Centennial Review* 30, no. 3 (summer 1986): 331–346.

Jefferson, Thomas. *Notes on the State of Virginia*. 1787. Edited by William Peden. Chapel Hill: University of North Carolina Press, 1955.

Jordan, Winthrop D. *White over Black: American Attitudes toward the Negro, 1550–1812*. Chapel Hill: University of North Carolina Press, 1968.

King, Martin Luther, Jr. "I Have a Dream." 1963. In *Crossing the Danger Water*, edited by Deirdre Mullane, 647–650. New York: Anchor, 1993.

Malcolm X and Alex Haley. *The Autobiography of Malcolm X*. 1964. New York: Ballantine, 1987.

McColley, Robert. *Slavery and Jeffersonian Virginia*. Urbana: University of Illinois Press, 1978.

Morrison, Toni. "Home." Keynote address. "Race Matters: Black Americans, U.S. Terrain," a conference at Princeton University, April 28, 1994.

Stewart, Maria W. "Religion and the Pure Principles of Morality, the Sure Foundation on Which We Must Build." 1831. In *Maria W. Stewart: America's First Black Woman Political Writer*, edited by Marilyn Richardson, 28–42. Bloomington: Indiana University Press, 1987.

Walker, David. *Appeal, in Four Articles; Together with a Preamble, to the Coloured Citizens of the World, but in Particular, and Very Expressly, to Those of the United States of America*. 1830. Edited and with an introduction by Charles M. Wiltse. New York: Hill and Wang, 1965.

Wiltse, Charles M. Introduction to *Appeal, in Four Articles . . .*, by David Walker. New York: Hill and Wang, 1965.

Seven

African-American Protest and the Role of the Haitian Pavilion at the 1893 Chicago World's Fair

Barbara J. Ballard

> America could find no representative place for a colored man, in all its work, and . . . it remained for the Republic of Hayti to give the only acceptable representation enjoyed by us at the Fair.
> —Ida B. Wells, *The Reason Why the Colored American Is Not in the World's Columbian Exposition*, 1893

In 1893, at the age of seventy-five, Frederick Douglass came to the World's Columbian Exposition. Douglass—runaway slave, abolitionist, orator and author, newspaper editor and preeminent African-American leader—had been a Civil War recruiter, an adviser to Lincoln, and a diplomat. From 1889 to 1891 he had served as consul general to Haiti and chargé d'affaires for the Dominican Republic. He resigned his post because of the controversy around the U.S. bid for a coaling station and naval base in Haiti's Môle Saint Nicolas. Now, as the World Columbian Exposition opened, Douglass had served his people and nation for half a century. Because of his former relationship to Haiti, the Haitian government appointed Douglass to co-manage its pavilion.

He came with several prominent black activists who organized to denounce the absence of "acceptable" black American representation. With him were the journalist and anti-lynching leader Ida B. Wells; her soon-to-be spouse, Chicago lawyer and newspaper editor Ferdinand Barnett; and the Virginian educator, author, and newspaper editor I. Garland Penn.

Douglass, Wells, Barnett, and Penn's protest took two forms. First

Parts of this chapter have appeared previously in "A People without a Nation," *Chicago History: The Magazine of the Chicago Historical Society* 28, no. 4 (Summer 1999).

was the publication of an expository pamphlet titled *The Reason Why the Colored American Is Not in the World's Columbian Exposition,* and second was an adoption of the Haitian pavilion as the site for black American protest and representation at the Fair.

An act of Congress established the 1893 World's Columbian Exposition in Chicago to celebrate the four hundredth anniversary of Columbus's discovery of the New World. The Exposition promised to be all things to all people. It would be a display of the extraordinary commercial, technological, industrial, and cultural attainment of western civilization in general and of the United States in particular. The Chicago World's Fair, as it was popularly called, was also an economic venture calculated to open new domestic and international markets. In the end it netted millions of dollars for the city of Chicago and exposition financiers.[1] For the general public, it was a great amusement park designed to enhance national pride and capture the fair-goer's imagination with the achievements of his or her particular nation and the exotica of the unfamiliar.

The Exposition was to be international in scope; the United States invited many national and ethnic groups from around the world to participate. American women, at least those who were white, won the battle to erect a building dedicated to their achievements.[2] Only three decades from slavery, many African Americans in the United States hoped to illustrate at the Fair how far the race had progressed since emancipation. However, the Fair managers declined to include an exhibition representing black America. Similarly, they excluded African Americans from the planning, administration, and national ceremonies of the event and, according to David Burg, even though millions of blacks resided in America and generations of black slaves had contributed uncompensated labor to building the nation, the Exposition managers did not invite any African-American dignitaries to appear on the dais for the opening of the Fair.[3]

In a survey of black newspapers from 1890 to 1893, Rudwick and Meier have shown that African-American leaders did not agree on the role blacks should play at the Chicago World's Fair, or how they should respond to their exclusion from equal participation.[4] Yet Douglass, Wells, Barnett, and Penn were emphatic about the need for African-American representation. For them the World's Columbian Exposition was a contested space—an ideological and cultural playing field in which black people could display their contributions, progress, and potential.

In a contemporary journal, Douglass charged that the Fair managers were either deliberately attempting to insult black people or bowing to

Southern racial attitudes. He maintained that black people had a right to representation at the Fair because their labor helped create America's wealth and black men had defended the nation in all its wars. Furthermore, "The presence of one of this race in a prominent position," Douglass declared, "would speak more for the civilization of the American republic than all the domes, towers, and turrets of the magnificent buildings, that adorn the Exposition grounds."[5]

At the Fair visible and hidden symbols reflected national and international politics and race relations. The very arrangement of the fairgrounds into White City and Midway Plaisance seemed to emphasize the ostensible superiority of the west—epitomized by the United States and its western European counterparts—over conquered, less developed, and colored nations and peoples. Ultimately, the protesters focused their attention on the only two edifices representing black people at the Fair: the pavilion of the Republic of Haiti in the White City and the "hut" of the Dahomeans of West Africa on the Midway.

The Reason Why the Colored American Is Not in the World's Columbian Exposition, subtitled *The Afro-American's Contribution to Columbian Literature*, forcefully articulates the protesters' consternation over the exclusion of African-American representation. Ida B. Wells organized and oversaw the publication of the pamphlet. Wells aimed for as large and as varied an audience as possible. Like Douglass, Barnett, and Penn, she had extensive experience as a newspaper editor. As a pamphlet, *The Reason Why* could concisely convey information to its readers, and it could be reproduced less expensively than longer publications. Wells had mastered the form with her anti-lynching booklet, *Southern Horror: Lynch Law in All Its Phases* (1892). She perceived a direct relationship between informing the international community about the plight of blacks in America in *The Reason Why* and the success of her fledgling anti-lynching campaign. Like that anti-lynching work, *The Reason Why* consisted mainly of a compilation of previously published writings, speeches, and statistics by several authors. The preface was translated into French and German and addressed "To the Seeker after Truth." Wells stated that initially they had planned to translate the entire work into French and German, but a shortage of time and money made that infeasible. Situated strategically at a table in the Haiti Pavilion, Wells reported, she was able to distribute ten thousand pamphlets to visitors.[6]

The absence of African-American representation at the Fair was tied to Jim Crow politics, racial violence, and the declining political and economic status of black people and to the invisibility of the black middle classes whom the protesters represented. In full view of the international community at the Fair, Wells, Douglass, Barnett, and Penn hoped to symbolically situate black America in its rightful place in the economic, cultural, and political life of the nation.

In *The Reason Why* Ferdinand Barnett stated,

> The celebration of the four hundredth anniversary of America is acknowledged to be our greatest national enterprise. . . . The Negro wanted to show by his years of freedom that his industry did not need the incentive of a master's whip, and that his intelligence was capable of successful self direction. It had been said that he was improvident and devoid of ambition, and that he would gradually lapse into barbarism. He wanted to show that in a quarter of a century, he had accumulated property to the value of two hundred million dollars, that his ambition had led him into every field of industry, and that capable men of his race had served his nation well in the legislatures . . . and as national Representatives abroad.[7]

The activist nature of their concern is further suggested by the fact that in those economically lean days of the 1890s, the protesters did not refer to the money a black exhibition might have garnered for a black pavilion. Some concessions grossed revenues in six figures, only a small percentage of which went to the Exposition organizers.[8]

The Reason Why also documented the steps by which African-American representation was omitted from the Exposition, thus underscoring the racist nature of American race relations.

> Prominent colored men suggested the establishment of a Department of Colored Exhibits in the Exposition. It was argued by them that nothing would so well evidence the progress of colored people as an exhibit made entirely of the products of skill and industry of the race since emancipation. . . . [T]he National Directors . . . decided that no separate exhibit for colored people would be permitted.[9]

To a great extent *The Reason Why* was responding to the neglect that was behind the missing African-American exhibition—it was an alternative and defensive gesture, replete with illustrations, in lieu of a place in the White City. In the late nineteenth century, stereotypes and caricatures of black people depicted them as lazy, dumb, sexually aggressive, and brutish. Racists of the day charged that they were "beasts" who had to be controlled to protect the chastity and lives of white women. Douglass asserted that charges of rape were efforts "to divest the Negro of his friends" and "to make the world believe that freedom has changed the character of the Negro, and made of him a moral monster."[10]

Ida B. Wells, particularly, condemned lynching and other forms of violence as methods used to tarnish blacks' image and render them politically and economically powerless and socially isolated. She cited statistics indicating that in 1891 alone 169 African Americans were murdered by white mobs. She charged that accusations of rape and attempted rape were fabricated by owners of "the telegraph wires, newspapers, and all other communication with the outside world . . . [to] justify lynching by painting the Negro as black as possible." Wells also included two harrowing pictures of lynchings reprinted from her earlier pamphlets.[11]

Undeniably, there were exhibits by black Americans at several states' pavilions, but they were few in number and provided no single and unified representation. The protesters' pamphlet was their exhibition. As if to parallel other representations of blacks at the Fair, the booklet enumerated the many achievements of black people since the end of slavery and included statistics on the wealth black Americans had accumulated, state by state. It included names of important black educators and lists of inventions by blacks in various industries, with the dates of patents. The protesters also included the names of black artists and writers and illustrations of buildings erected by African Americans, including one from Booker T. Washington's Tuskegee Institute.

Exposition organizers divided the fairgrounds into two distinct parts. The irony of the main area's being called the White City, due to the color of the buildings and its clean and highly organized environment, could not be missed. The other was the Midway Plaisance. Contemporaneous photographs illustrate the grandeur of the White City. Its buildings were massive yet elegant, in the neoclassical design. They were dedicated to commerce, manufacturing, technology, and the arts. Spaced aesthetically amidst tranquil bodies of water, the buildings, connected by bridges and walkways, signified the power and splendor that the planners associated with western civilization. Pavilions dedicated to the United States government, individual states, foreign governments, and women were located there. All were a conspicuous contrast to the often makeshift edifices that characterized the villages of most of the eastern and African peoples on the Midway.[12]

The Midway was on a narrow strip of land adjacent to the main exhibition. It was the site of a variety of amusements, such as a Ferris wheel, a scaled-down version of the Eiffel Tower, restaurants, and shops selling souvenirs and demonstrating a variety of crafts. Dispersed amidst them stood mock ethnic villages. A few European cultures and ethnic groups were represented, but most were of third-world people and purported to display the lifestyles, artifacts, and products particular to the given society and culture. Official exposition photos of the Midway illustrate the placement of separate and distinct villages of Dahomeans, Algerians, and Tunisians. It also boasted a Bedouin camp, a Cairo street that aimed to reflect Egyptian culture, and Samoan Islanders and Eskimos in their "native" dress.[13]

Recent scholars of world's fairs, such as Robert Rydell, James Gilbert, and Burton Benedict, disagree on the extent to which the Midway was an ethnological "lesson" for fair-goers. Gilbert contends, in contrast to Rydell, that although Exposition organizers may have wanted the Midway Plaisance to serve as a hierarchically arranged ethnological exhibit, it quickly evolved into a moneymaking venture designed to entertain as well as inform. Independent but poor, Liberia sent a small exhibition of photographs and sample produce to the Fair. It was housed in the agricultural building in the White City. At the Fair, the Dahomean Village was the only freestanding exhibition representing a West African nation. Gilbert asserts that its remote location on the Midway, and the labels of barbarism and exoticism affixed to the Dahomean Village, could not have been unintentional.[14]

On the Midway, the display exhibitions often included living participants, arrayed in their native costume and represented as going about their daily routine. Benedict asserts that these "colonial exhibits" served several purposes. Along with their value as entertainment and instruction, he contends, they were meant to signify (and justify) the "trophies" or prizes of the colonizing western powers. "Savage" peoples, such as the Dahomeans, and their artifacts were designed to emphasize the "ethnic and cultural differences" between them and the fair-goers.[15]

In this age of imperialism, Social Darwinism, and Jim Crowism, visitors to the Fair were likely, whether by design or merely by impression, to have their existing prejudices and notions of cultural and racial hegemony reinforced. This was what concerned Douglass, Wells, and their fellow protesters about the Dahomean exhibition. The Dahomean Village was the only building representing people of West Africa, the ancestral home of most black Americans. Under French rule, in some areas they were still resisting French imperialism at the time of the Fair. The Dahomean Village was a thatched structure. A large poster above it advertised the exhibition and featured a scantily clothed "native"—who appeared to be female—brandishing a machete in one hand and holding what could have been the head of a European, probably French, in the other. A guidebook described the women as masculine Amazons, warriors, and the men as small and effeminate.[16] Contemporaneous photographs of the Dahomeans show them, seemingly without regard to sex, posed in leopardlike skins holding clubs and spears.

Douglass denounced the representation of the Dahomeans as a deliberate attempt to undermine black America. In the introduction to *The Reason Why* he asserted, "America has brought to her shores and given welcome to a greater variety of mankind than were ever assembled in one place since the day of Pentecost . . . and as if to shame the Negro, the Dahomians are also here to exhibit the Negro as a repulsive savage." In many speeches, during and after the Fair, he commented on the racist presentation of the Dahomeans. Similarly, in a lecture titled "The Lessons of the Hour" Douglass declared that all classes and conditions were at the Fair save the educated American Negro.[17]

Douglass's condemnation was well-founded. As historian Robert Rydell observed, "Visitors [to] the Fair were asked to note the Dahomeans' 'regretful absence of tailor-made clothes'." A vicious cartoon depicted an extremely obese Eskimo woman wearing heavy fur clothing and suffering from the heat, while a barely clothed, spear-bearing Dahomean man, with exaggeratedly broad features, shivers from the cold. The Eskimo gives her clothing to the African and a romance follows.[18] A satirical magazine titled *World's Fair Puck* combined racial stereotypes of Dahomeans and black Americans as "chicken thieves," intellectually stupid, and akin to the orangutan.[19] Such negative and racist stereotypes were companion pieces to the prevailing political, scientific, and popular views of West Africans and African Americans in the United States. They were employed to justify segregation and lynch law against black people in the South. From Douglass's perspective, and certainly that of his like-minded colleagues, the only manifestation of blacks' West African homeland at the Exposition was a source of racist insults.

The World's Congress Auxiliary provided protesters with another forum in which to voice their views. Conceived as "a parliament of nations," the congress conducted a series of meetings designed to "surpass all previous efforts to bring about a real fraternity of nations, and unite the enlightened people of the whole earth." The congresses consisted of twenty departments, among them Women's Progress, Medicine and Surgery, Temperance, Commerce and Finance, Music, Education, Literature, and Religion. Under the auspices of each department, organizers held open meetings to discuss issues and problems.[20] Many prominent black men and women addressed the congress. For example, Booker T. Washington addressed the Labor Congress on the need for industrial training.[21] Some black speakers took the opportunity to protest both the exclusion of African Americans from equal participation in the Exposition and the growing circumscription of blacks in American life.

Organizers of the Women's Building or Pavilion, as it was called, excluded black women from planning and administration. Clearly, they were not truly welcome even in the edifice dedicated to their gender. Distinguished African-American women such as Anna Julia Cooper, Fannie Barrier Williams, and Fannie Jackson Coppin—who addressed the World's Congress of Representative Women—took on the double task of celebrating the progress and promise of black women and denouncing the lower status of black Americans in society and at the Fair.[22]

The presence of African Americans at the Chicago Congress on Africa, as the series of meetings dedicated to discussing Africa was called, is particularly noteworthy because it illuminates the absence of a definitive site for African-American representation at the Exposition. A contemporary publication, *Our Day*, gave an account of the meetings, which focused on the need to end the slave trade and civilize, Christianize, and commercialize Africa. It reported that "the Chicago Congress [on Africa] consisted of one hundred experts and specialists." An assortment of individuals did attend the congress because they were concerned with uplifting what one speaker dubbed the "pariah of continents." These "friends of Africa" represented a variety of nations, professions, and interests. African colonization was a major concern. Among the prominent blacks attending the meetings were journalist and political and labor activist T. Thomas Fortune; Alexander Crummell, the black nationalist who fostered emigration to Liberia; the ardent black colonizationist and A.M.E. bishop Henry M. Turner; Frederick Douglass, whose longstanding opposition to colonization and emigration was no secret; and Ferdinand Barnett. Also present, according to *Our Day*, was Henry Osawa Tanner, an African-American artist who resided in Paris. The A.M.E. bishops Benjamin Tanner (the artist's equally prominent father) and Daniel A. Payne were among those who could not attend but sent papers to be read.

The list of so distinguished a group of black Americans—accomplished, educated, and of the middling classes—suggests what Douglass, Wells, and others meant by "acceptable" representation. At the congresses, whether on women or on Africa, blacks were not on their own ground. From time to time, *Our Day* reported, they had to contend with ex-Confederates and imperialists, some of whom praised slavery for "civilizing" blacks and colonization for uplifting Africa. It also reported that when the Congress on Africa considered "the relation of

American Negroes to Africa," a heated debate ensued among black Americans over the desirability and practicability of emigration to Africa. According to the editor of *Our Day,* "The debate proved that the American Negro will stay!" Issues related to the constitutional rights of African Americans, race relations in the South, and the status and future of Liberia were also discussed. One speaker concluded that Liberia "depended too little on herself."[23]

In Douglass's view, at least, West Africa had never been a viable source of cultural identification and pride for black Americans. In the 1850s Douglass, like David Walker three decades before him, drew upon contemporaneous ethnological and linguistic studies to admonish black Americans to be proud of their ancestral link to the "ancient, highly civilized and wonderfully endowed Egyptians." However, almost three decades later, Douglass asserted—apparently in response to new ethnological work—that the Egyptians belonged to neither the black nor the white race, but were descended from the Coptics.[24]

Moreover, representations of the Egyptians on the Midway did not reflect the builders of the pyramids. Egypt and other North African nations at the Fair, like Dahomey, were under the control of European imperialists. Consequently, a longstanding resource for identification with an ancient African civilization was no longer available. Now, in the late nineteenth century, the spread of colonialism and ideas that conflated "civilization" with nation status and technological advancement kept other nations and people of color from becoming a viable symbol for African Americans at the Fair.

In an 1883 address regarding black migration and emigration to Africa, Douglass stated,

> I do not look for colonization either in or out of the United States. Africa is too far off, even if we desired to go there. . . . There is but one destiny . . . and that is to make ourselves and be made by others a part of the American people in every sense of the word.

Douglass expressed similar sentiments in a speech in Detroit in 1893, while he was still on duty at the Haitian Pavilion in Chicago:

> I hold that the American negro owes no more to the Negroes of Africa than he owes to the negroes in America. . . . We have a fight on our hand right here, . . . and a blow struck for the negro in America is a blow struck for the negro in Africa. The native land of the American negro is America . . . , and millions of his posterity have inherited Caucasian blood.[25]

Thus, throughout most of his long career as a preeminent black leader and activist, Douglass stood in steadfast opposition to black emigration. Yet in 1861, two decades before his appointment as minister to Haiti, Douglass had briefly considered black emigration, to Haiti rather than Liberia. The problem was that not only was the African continent overrun with imperialists, it was also considered not yet fit for the march toward civilization. America was the only homeland for blacks, and for some blacks of both Euro-American and African-American parentage, such as Douglass, even racial identification with West Africa was difficult.[26]

However, not permitted to join the World's Columbian Exposition on an equal footing with other nations and peoples, and unable to identify with Dahomey, Liberia, and other African nations, many African Americans took the Haitian Pavilion in the White City as the locus of protest and racial and cultural identity at the Fair. Due to the largess of the Haitian government and its relationship to Douglass, the pavilion became a usable space for both protest and black American representation in the White City.

Douglass served as chargé d'affaires for Santo Domingo and minister to Haiti from 1889 to 1891. The Haitian government appointed Douglass, their acclaimed ex-minister, and Charles A. Preston, a native of Haiti and a former member of the Haitian legation to Washington, joint commissioners.[27] In assessing the "crowning honors" accorded him over the years, Douglass included his "unsought appointment by President Florvil Hyppolite to represent Haiti among all the civilized nations of the globe at the World's Columbian Exposition."[28]

As United States Minister to Haiti, Douglass had presented to Haiti's secretary of foreign affairs the United States' invitation to the Exposition.[29] In a diplomatic message to Douglass dated June 27, 1891 —which Douglass received at the end of his appointment, just before his departure for the States—President Hyppolite accepted the invitation. Hyppolite's letter underscored Haiti's hope to maintain amiable relations with the United States. It also reflected Hyppolite's awareness of the Fair as a significant symbolic site at which the fruit of western "civilization" was to be in full display, and in his view Haiti had a definite place in that parade of nations:

> It will be for us a happy occasion to show to the civilized world our rich natural products and the first efforts which [Haiti] has been able to realize in industrial endeavor and in the liberal arts. Our disastrous civil wars have without doubt greatly paralyzed our

march toward progress; nevertheless one will be able to see that we
are not lacking in elevated aspirations and that we are endeavoring
to figure worthily in the grand concert of American nations.[30]

Hyppolite's letter underscored the qualities that Douglass, Wells,
Barnett, and Penn attempted to demonstrate in *The Reason Why* on behalf of black people in the United States. Consequently, there was every
reason for Douglass and his fellow protesters to seize the opportunity that Haiti's generosity presented. The pavilion was a space where
African-American visitors to the Fair could feel at home. It also became
a site from which Wells, Douglass, and their associates could protest
black Americans' exclusion from the Exposition and identify them with
the march of civilization in the western world.

As Wells put it in her autobiography, "Had it not been for [the generosity of Haiti], Negroes of the United States would have no part . . .
in any official way in the World's Fair." Moreover, she asserted that

> Haiti's building was one of the gems of the World's Fair, and in it
> Mr. Douglass held high court. . . . Needless to say, the Haitian
> building was the chosen spot; for representative Negroes of the
> country who visited the Fair were to be found along with the
> Haitians and citizens of other foreign countries.[31]

The Haitian pavilion stood in the midst of the pavilions of Germany,
Spain, and New South Wales. An official guide to the Fair described it
as "in the Greco-Colonial style, surmounted by a gilded dome, which is
copied after the State capitol of Massachusetts. The structure has a
frontage of 126 feet, including piazzas 12 feet wide which surround
three sides of the building. In the center of the façade is the coat-of-
arms of the Republic of Haiti in a medallion surrounded by a scroll
bearing the following inscription: 'Republique Haitienne,' and the dates
1492 (the discovery), 1804 (date of Haytian national independence) and
1893 (the present anniversary)."

Besides a description of the building's structure and façade, the
guide summarized Haiti's exhibits and artifacts. They included "some
pre-Columbian relics and the authentic anchor of the caravel Santa
Maria, the mate to which was loaned by the Haytians to the Columbus collection in the Convent of La Rabida." Toussaint L'Ouverture's
sword, a symbol of Haiti's independence, was also among the artifacts.[32]

Another account notes the presence of the flag of Haiti, a marble
statue by a native sculptor, and paintings of President Hyppolite,
Frederick Douglass, and other prominent black men. To represent the
natural resources of the island and the industry of the Haitian people "a

choice collection of wood was displayed, including a huge block of mahogany. Among the many articles of manufactures were fine specimens of saddlery, laces, and embroidery; and fibers and minerals were exhibited." Haitian coffee and its various by-products, such as liqueurs, were prepared and sold by "native hands" in a restaurant at the southern end of the building.[33]

African-American cultural expression was not ignored. For example, the budding African-American poet Paul Laurence Dunbar, whom Douglass hired as a clerk at the pavilion, was also present with *Oak and Ivy,* his first volume of poems. Wells claims that Dunbar distributed his poems at the Haitian pavilion and came to the attention of the famous American literary critic William Dean Howells: "Mr. Howells reviewed that little volume a few months later in the columns of the *Atlantic Monthly,* and Paul Dunbar's fame as a poet was established in America."[34] The prominent persons whom Dunbar encountered in distributing his work, such as Angelina Grimké, Hallie Brown, Mary Church Terrell, and Alexander Crummell, as well as other black poets,[35] illustrate the extent to which the Haitian Pavilion was a haven for black people and their supporters.

The gatherings at the Haitian pavilion had an even wider impact. Wells attributed the Fair managers' decision to designate August 25 as a "Colored Peoples Day" or "Negro Day" to the popularity of the Haitian building with foreign visitors. She suggested that the managers were shamed into recognizing the presence of black Americans with a special day of speeches and festivities, at which Douglass presided. Wells also asserted that she and Douglass initially differed on whether blacks should participate in what was an afterthought by the Exposition directors. However, Douglass's speeches, Dunbar's poetry, and the music of the Fisk Jubilee Singers, along with other speeches and cultural events, changed the tone of the day from apologetic afterthought to honor.[36]

At the World's Columbian Exposition of 1893, the existence of a Haitian building in the White City filled a void for many black Americans that African and third-world exhibitions on the Midway could not. It was the age of Social Darwinism, and as Richard Hofstadter suggests, European and American imperialists adapted such ideologies to explain and justify their takeover of less economically developed peoples.[37] The spread of imperialism, and their internalization of prevailing ideas about nationhood, race, culture, and civilization, deprived black Americans of other viable sources of racial and cultural identity at the Exposition.

A black and independent nation that had fought for and won independence from one of the world's most powerful nations, Haiti was the bright and shining exception. Despite its bloody internal strife, it had won diplomatic recognition from the United States and other powerful nations, and had maintained its national sovereignty in the face of U.S. demands and veiled threats. Haiti had rudimentary industries that suggested future progress. Haiti was a beacon of black accomplishment and potential in a period in which, increasingly, nationhood was synonymous with progress and civilization.

Moreover, from the time of its independence in 1804 to the period of the World's Columbian Exposition, Haiti had been a symbol—an object of calumny for some but a source of pride for others. For the slaveholding South, Haiti had been its worst nightmare come true—a stronghold of barbaric ex-slaves who had overthrown civilization. At the same time, black Americans, and sometimes their white allies, looked to the small black republic with pride. It was evidence that black people would not remain in slavery eternally, that they would not be long-suffering forever, and that they were capable of self-government. Furthermore, Haiti was central to colonization schemes that began with Jefferson's plans to rid the nation of blacks. It was an important site of black American emigration at several points in the nineteenth century. It rivaled Liberia and Canada as a prospective homeland for U.S. blacks, and was also central in the emigrationist efforts of men such as the Reverend James Theodore Holly and James Redpath.[38]

At the dedication ceremonies for the Haitian pavilion on January 2, 1893, Douglass gave many speeches affirming Haiti's relationship to all people of African descent, but particularly those in the United States. He defended Haiti from its detractors, who labeled the black republic uncivilized due to its recent revolutions and, no doubt, to its refusal to capitulate to the United States's demands for a fueling station at the Môle St. Nicholas.

Douglass asserted, "[T]he people of Haiti, by reason of ancestral identity and color are more interesting to the colored people of the United States than to all others, for the Negro like the Jew, can never part with his identity of race. Color does for the one what religion does for the other."[39] In another speech, Douglass established a link between Haiti's successful revolution against France and the freedom of people of African descent throughout the diaspora:

> Civilized or savage, whatever the future may have in store for her, Haiti is a black man's country. . . . We should not forget that the freedom you and I enjoy to-day; that of . . . colored people in the British West Indies; the freedom that has come to the colored

people the world over is largely due to the brave stand taken by the black sons of Haiti ninety years ago. . . . It was her one brave example that first startled the Christian world into a sense of the Negro's manhood.[40]

Wells's and Douglass's decision to make their stand at the Haitian pavilion rather than identify with other peoples of African descent or of color illuminates far more than the problem of racism in late-nineteenth-century American society and culture. It also illustrates the problematic nature of ideas of racial, national, and ethnic identity in that period. Pavilions and villages at the Fair represented a variety of distinct nationalities and recognized ethnic groups. For example, some Indian (Native American) nations were represented. German nationals and German-Americans had a village on the Midway and a pavilion in the White City. Ireland was under British domination, but Irish Americans could look to a replica of Donegal Castle on the Midway.[41]

The Dahomeans, Arabs, Egyptians, and Laplanders were also associated with specific homelands. However, black Americans in the United States were in a nation that clearly viewed itself as a "white man's country." They were of West African descent but cut off from Africa by virtue of time, culture, and birth. Viewed as a distinct ethnic and cultural entity for the purposes of exclusion, and as part of the American collective in order to render them invisible, they were a people without a nation at a gathering of nations.

Yet when Wells and others used the Haitian pavilion as a place from which to distribute copies of *The Reason Why* and to greet African Americans and international visitors, they made it a symbolic site on which to protest the exclusion of African Americans from the Fair. Now, at the Fair, African Americans in the United States had a space in which to contest their invisibility and, paradoxically, both affirm and contest the racial and cultural distinctness of blacks as people of African and American descent in the world Columbus discovered.

Notes

1. *Report of the President to the Board of Directors of the World's Columbian Exposition: Chicago, 1892–1893* (Chicago: Rand McNally, 1898), 11, 155. The exposition began with thirty thousand subscribers or stockholders, who reportedly received 10 percent on their investments. Over $10 million was earned in ticket sales and almost $4 million netted from concession sales. According to the report, these amounts would have been more had it not been for the depression.

Barbara J. Ballard

122

2. Jeanne Madeline Weimann, *The Fair Women* (Chicago: Academy Chicago, 1981), 35–42.

3. David F. Burg, *Chicago's White City of 1893* (Lexington: University Press of Kentucky, 1976), 108–109.

4. Elliot Rudwick and August Meier, "Black Man in the White City: Negroes and the Columbia Exposition, 1893," in *Phylon: The Atlanta University Review of Race and Culture* 4 (1965): 354–361. See also Burg, *Chicago's White City*, 210; Robert W. Rydell, *All the World's a Fair: Visions of Empire at the American International Exposition, 1876–1916* (Chicago: University of Chicago Press, 1984), 53.

5. Frederick Douglass, "Inauguration of the World's Columbia Exposition," *World Columbian Exposition Illustrated* III:1 (March 1893): 300.

6. Ida B. Wells, "Southern Horrors: Lynch Law in All Its Phases" (1892), in *On Lynchings: Southern Horrors, A Red Record, Mob Rule in New Orleans* (New York: Arno Press and the New York Times, 1969); *Crusade for Justice: The Autobiography of Ida B. Wells*, edited by Alfreda M. Duster (Chicago: University of Chicago Press), 117.

7. F[erdinand] L. Barnett, "The Reason Why," in *The Reason Why the Colored American Is Not in the World's Columbian Exposition: The Afro-American's Contribution to Columbian Literature* (Chicago, 1893), 63–64; Papers of Frederick Douglass, Library of Congress, Manuscript Division.

8. See *Report of the President*, 474–483. A total of $16,583,051.53 was grossed from 370 concessions, of which $4,237,563.95 went to the Exposition. For example, the Irish village grossed $65,000; the Dahomean village, $113,152.50; and the German village, $622,500.30.

9. Barnett, in *The Reason Why*, 66.

10. Douglass, in ibid., 7–8.

11. Wells, in ibid., 26.

12. *Bird's Eye View of the World's Columbian Exposition in Chicago, 1893*, map (Chicago: Rand McNally, 1898); *Official Views of the World's Columbian Exposition Issued by the Department of Photography*, C. D. Arnold and H. D. Higinbotham, photographers (Chicago: Press Chicago Photo-Gravure, 1893).

13. See *Official Views of the World's Columbian Exposition*, plates 110–114.

14. Rydell, *All the World's a Fair*, 42–43; James Gilbert, *Perfect Cities: Chicago's Utopias of 1893* (Chicago: University of Chicago Press, 1991), 111–117.

15. Burton Benedict, "Rituals of Representation: Ethnic Stereotypes and Colonized Peoples at World's Fairs," in *Fair Representations: World's Fairs and the Modern World*, edited by Robert W. Rydell and Nancy E. Gwinn, 31–39 (Amsterdam: VU University Press, 1994).

16. *Official Views of the World's Columbian Exposition*, plate 110; Norman Bolotin and Christine Laing, *The Chicago World's Fair of 1893: The World's*

Columbian Exposition (Washington, D.C.: The Preservation Press, 1992), 130.

17. *The Reason Why,* 9; Frederick Douglass, "Lessons of the Hour: An Address Delivered in Washington, D.C. on 9 January, 1894," in *The Frederick Douglass Papers,* edited by John W. Blassingame, series 2, vol. 5 (New Haven: Yale University Press, 1992), 592–593.

18. Robert W. Rydell, "A Cultural Frankenstein? The Chicago World's Columbian Exposition of 1893," in Neil Harris, Wim de Wit, James Gilbert, and Robert W. Rydell, *Grand Illusions: Chicago's World Fair of 1893* (Chicago Historical Society, 1994), 145–146.

19. Benedict, "Rituals of Representation," 39.

20. *Report of the President,* 325–334. Also see Burg's chapter on the Congress Auxiliary in *Chicago's White City,* 235–285.

21. Rydell, *All the World's a Fair,* 41, 83.

22. See Weimann, *The Fair Women,* 117, 120–123, 525–530, 545; the speeches of Fannie Barrier Williams, Anna Julia Cooper, and Hallie Q. Brown in May Wright Sewall, ed., *The World's Congress of Representative Women: The World's Congress Auxiliary,* vol. 2 (Chicago: Rand McNally, 1893); Burg, *Chicago's White City,* 277–278; and Hazel V. Carby, *Reconstructing Womanhood: The Emergence of the Afro-American Woman Novelist* (New York: Oxford University Press, 1987), 4–6.

23. "The Chicago Congress on Africa," *Our Day: A Record of Reform* 10, no. 70 (October 1893): 284–286, 290–293.

24. Frederick Douglass, "The Negro Ethnologically Considered," in *The Frederick Douglass Papers,* series 1, vol. 2, ed. Blassingame (New Haven: Yale University Press, 1979), 517, vol. 5, ed. Blassingame and McKivigan (New Haven: Yale University Press, 1992), 305–306; Charles M. Wiltse, ed., *David Walker's Appeal, in Four Articles; Together with a Preamble, to the Coloured Citizens of the World, but in Particular, and Very Expressly, to Those of the United States of America* (1829; New York: Hill and Wang, 1965), 8.

25. Douglass, "Our Destiny Is in Our Own Hands: An Address Delivered . . . on 16 April, 1883" and "Lessons of the Hour: An Address Delivered in Washington D.C. on 9 January 1894," in *The Frederick Douglass Papers,* ed. Blassingame and McKivigan, series 1, vol. 5, 79–80, 598.

26. Waldo Martin, Jr., *The Mind of Frederick Douglass* (Chapel Hill: University of North Carolina Press, 1984), 74, 207.

27. *The Frederick Douglass Papers,* ed. Blassingame, series 1, vol. 2, 502 n.3.

28. Frederick Douglass, *The Life and Times of Frederick Douglass, Written by Himself* (1892; reprint, New York: Collier Books: 1962), 620.

29. Frederick Douglass, *A Black Diplomat in Haiti: The Diplomatic Correspondence of United States Minister Frederick Douglass from Haiti, 1889–1891,* vol. 2, edited and with an introduction by Norma Brown (Salisbury, N.C.: Documentary Publications, 1977), 81–87.

30. Douglass, *A Black Diplomat in Haiti*, 242.

31. Wells, *Crusade for Justice*, 116.

32. Moses P. Handy, ed., *The Official Directory of the World's Columbian Exposition: May 1st to October 30th, 1893: A Reference Book* (Chicago: W. B. Conkey, 1893), 127–128.

33. Rossiter Johnson, ed., *A History of the World's Columbian Exposition Held in Chicago in 1893* (New York: D. Appleton, 1897), 423; and Handy, *Official Directory*, 128.

34. Wells, *Crusade for Justice*, 117–118.

35. See Benjamin Brawley, *The Negro in Literature and Art in the United States* (New York: Duffield, 1930), 65; and Addison Gayle, Jr., *Oak and Ivy: A Biography of Paul Laurence Dunbar* (Garden City, N.Y.: Doubleday, 1971), 108–109.

36. Wells, *Crusade for Justice*, 118–119; and Rydell, *All the World's a Fair*, 53.

37. Richard Hofstadter, *Social Darwinism in American Thought, 1860–1910* (Philadelphia: University of Pennsylvania Press, 1944), 175. Hofstadter asserts that after 1880 individualist Social Darwinism began to wane as a more "collectivist" or nationalistic and racialist variety emerged.

38. Howard H. Bell, "Introduction," in James Theodore Holy and J. Dennis Harris, *Black Separatism and the Caribbean, 1860,* edited and with an introduction by Howard H. Bell (Ann Arbor: University of Michigan Press, 1970), 1–15; Alfred N. Hunt, *Haiti's Influence on Antebellum America: Slumbering Volcano in the Caribbean* (Baton Rouge: Louisiana State University Press, 1988), 147–188; Brenda Gayle Plummer, *Haiti and the United States: The Psychological Moment* (Athens: University of Georgia Press, 1992), 28.

39. Frederick Douglass, "Lecture on Haiti: Dedication Ceremonies Delivered at the World's Fair in Jackson Park, Chicago, January 2d, 1893," Papers of Frederick Douglass, Library of Congress, Manuscript Division, 26.

40. Ibid., 34–35.

41. *Official Views of the World's Columbian Exposition*, plates 72, 95, 99, 100.

Eight

Race, Womanhood, and the Tragic Mulatta
An Issue of Ambiguity

Christine Palumbo-DeSimone

> Black women are called, in the folklore that so aptly
> identifies one's status in society, "the mule of the world,"
> because we have been handed the burdens that everyone
> else—*everyone* else—refused to carry. We have also been
> called "Matriarchs," "Superwomen," and "Mean and Evil
> Bitches." Not to mention "Castraters" and "Sapphire's
> Mama."
>
> —Alice Walker, *In Search of Our Mothers' Gardens*

As Alice Walker keenly notes, black women's prescribed identity in American culture has at times proven powerfully deterministic. "Mules," "mammies," "bitches," "whores": the "folklore" of black womanhood has been used to legitimate and perpetuate the oppression of black women in the white patriarchy. In tracing and reclaiming her personal and cultural heritage, Walker knows that she must navigate a maze of images and caricatures that have represented black womanhood in America for generations. The character of the black woman has been distorted in American cultural mythology, primarily because her persona as someone who shoulders cultural "burdens" has served the mythology so well. *In Search of Our Mothers' Gardens*, then, is Walker's journey not merely to discover her "lost" mothers and grandmothers, but to confront and defeat the chimeras of black womanhood she will meet along her way. For indeed, as countless feminist writers have found, women's road to self-definition abounds with monstrous images of womanhood.

Twentieth-century writers such as Alice Walker resist the popular image of the black woman by exposing the "fable" in the "folklore" of black womanhood. But the effort to reveal the racist and sexist origins of the black female character in American mythology itself has roots stretching back generations. Several important nineteenth-century writers used their fiction to show how American ideology constructed the black woman to serve white America's social and political ends. Their work forms a revealing context not just for nineteenth-century representations of black womanhood, but for endeavors by contemporary writers to retrieve a truer picture of America's cultural past.

Among the images that pervade American folklore, the "tragic mulatta" was one of the more popular characters in nineteenth-century fiction about the South. In the hands of propagandists such as Thomas Nelson Page and Thomas Dixon, the mulatto came to represent unacceptable social disorder and a threat to dominant white culture. The majority of American writers in the nineteenth century portrayed the mulatta more sympathetically than did Page and Dixon; critics cite such works as William Wells Brown's *Clotel* (1853) and Harriet Beecher Stowe's *Uncle Tom's Cabin* (1852) as examples of fiction which present the mulatta more compassionately. Yet, even in these "sympathetic" portrayals, the mulatta is little more than the embodiment of what had become the standard literary representation of the mixed-raced character: female, "observably white" in all regards, and dazzlingly beautiful, the mulatta "suffers from a melancholy of the blood that inevitably leads to tragedy."[1] However, the standard rendering of the mulatta is not universal, even among Southern authors. A few notable exceptions not only present significantly different images of the mulatta, but deliberately subvert the expectations of the traditional character. In contrast to the pervasive archetype of the tragic mulatta, writers such as Charles W. Chesnutt, Kate Chopin, and Frances E. W. Harper offer representations of the mulatta which recognize and confront the battle of images surrounding her both as a member of nineteenth-century American society and as a literary device.

The mulatta is, by definition, a racially ambiguous figure. In a society which asserted inherent and irreconcilable racial disparity as a basis for white domination, the mulatta called into question absolute racial categories. In accordance with the Southern maxim "one drop of Negro blood makes a Negro,"[2] the mulatta was legally labeled "black," but the near-white as slave or servant was still a disturbing image which was not always so easily categorized. Many Southern writers endlessly pondered how varying percentages of white and black blood affected intelligence, physical stamina, and moral character. For example, one 1884 writer asserted that "certain scientists, assuming brain size as criteria," had found the mulatto to be nearest to whites in mental capacity, while the offspring of a mulatto and a pure black constituted "a breed decidedly below the negro . . . an inferior race."[3] The mulatto blurred the neat racial distinctions upon which white domination was founded, and thus threatened the theory of inherent racial superiority which justified white rule.

In addition to being racially ambiguous, the mulatta further complicated the complex set of codes and images defining womanhood in the antebellum South. As scholars such as Elizabeth Fox-Genovese and Barbara Welter have shown, white and black womanhood were characterized and defined through opposing sets of images and assumptions relating directly to each woman's function within Southern patriarchy.[4] Commenting on the nineteenth-century "cult of true womanhood," Catherine Clinton explains how gender stereotypes in the antebellum South reveal men's anxiety about women's sexuality:

> The cult of virtue was all the more fervent because men believed that the opposite sex possessed a dual and dangerous essence; femininity was rooted in vice, but women could be raised to a status of virtue.[5]

Southern culture sought to defuse the "dual and dangerous" nature of women through a convenient dichotomy: white women embodied the passionless Christian virtue which became the essence of femininity, while black women represented the sexually appealing yet largely "nonfeminine" antithesis to the desexualized white "lady."

Most significant in considering the tragic mulatta figure, the popular stereotypes of black women held that they were "loose" and incapable of virtue and that they, unlike their white counterparts, "craved sex inordinately."[6] Many popular depictions of black women in both Southern and Northern publications concurred with the 1882 *Atlantic Monthly* that "the prevalence of unchastity among the young colored women is . . . almost universal," and that the "development of domestic purity" was "entirely unknown" to black women.[7] Because her behavior and character were held to be antithetical to the mandates of "true womanhood," the black woman was broadly labeled "not woman" in Southern culture. The positioning of black women outside of the standard model of femininity both justified the physical and sexual exploitation of black women and reinforced the ideal of white womanhood. In the Southern mythology the virgin/whore dichotomy of white and black womanhood was absolute, for the value of these images rested primarily upon their ability to dictate unconditionally the expected behavior of women in both races. Of course, by refusing to be clearly categorized within the "true woman"/"not woman" dichotomy, the mulatta undermined the power of both stereotypes.[8]

As a literary figure, however, the racially ambiguous mulatta became for white writers the one "black" character with whom a white popular audience could identify and sympathize. As Barbara Christian observes,

> Undoubtedly many white women could identify with the beautiful woman who looked as white as they did, who was certainly more wealthy and privileged than they were, and who, despite all this, is instantly pummeled into the pit of servitude only because she has a few drops of black blood in her veins.[9]

Jules Zanger has accurately observed that the tragic mulatta convention often functioned as more than an appeal to racial affinity in a white audience. Abolitionist authors used the convention to attack the slave system and specifically the slave woman's "particular vulnerability to sexual outrage."[10]

Yet even taking into account the abolitionist uses of the convention, the tragic mulatta still largely remains a product of antebellum ideology; since the mulatta's tragic ending serves to resolve the contradictions she represents, the nineteenth-century literary tradition of the tragic mulatta (in both its pro-slavery and abolitionist forms) ultimately upholds white patriarchal order. Conversely, writers who break away from and subvert the archetype of the tragic mulatta voice a protest not merely against white patriarchy but against the literary tradition which served to uphold and perpetuate racial and gender roles.

One such writer is Charles W. Chesnutt.[11] Chesnutt's *The Marrow of Tradition* (1901) from the start introduces the mulatta as a disturbing figure who disrupts social order. The novel opens with Lily Carteret physically ill from the jolt of seeing her mulatta half-sister, a woman who resembles Lily so much that Mammy Jane says, "Folks sometimes takes 'em fer one ernudder."[12] Lily has refused to acknowledge in any way her relation to Janet, while Janet has longed all her life for "a kind word, a nod, a smile, the least thing that imagination might have twisted into a recognition of the tie between them" (*MT,* 65). Yet Lily's certainty that she is neither legally nor morally obligated to acknowledge her half-sister is shaken when she finds the marriage certificate that establishes Janet's legitimacy. With this discovery, all the racial distinctions which served as the basis for Lily's treatment of Janet are called into question, as is the very order upon which Lily's world is founded:

> If the woman had been white,—but the woman had not been white, and the same rule of moral conduct did not, *could* not, in the very nature of things, apply as between white people! For, if this

were so, slavery had been, not merely an economic mistake, but a great crime against humanity. (*MT*, 266)

Traditional social order and race relations are further confused in *The Marrow of Tradition* when, by the end of the novel, Lily must plead with her mulatta sister to save the life of her child, who has been critically wounded in a race riot.[13] "You are my sister," Lily implores, "—the child is your own near kin! . . . Sister! for our father's sake who did you no wrong, give me my child's life!" (*MT*, 327). Lily's sudden and dramatic recognition of her relation to Janet not only blurs traditional white/black distinctions but also emphasizes the arbitrary nature of such distinctions, as well as how racial categories are created and manipulated by whites for their convenience. Lily's appeal to Janet's sisterly compassion is presented in ironic contrast to Major Carteret's white-supremacy campaign, which vehemently argues that "the white and black races could never attain social and political harmony by commingling their blood" and that "no two unassimilable races could ever live together except in the relation of superior and inferior" (*MT*, 31). The mulatta in *The Marrow of Tradition* shows both of these assertions to be invalid.

Chesnutt's novel also explores the racial distinction within womanhood. In response to the stereotype of the sexually promiscuous black female, *The Marrow of Tradition* presents Julia, a black servant who refuses a physical relationship with Mr. Merkell until they are married. Far from merely attempting to avoid public scorn, Julia insists upon marriage so that their union will be blessed "in the sight of God" and then permits the marriage to be kept secret, since "for the opinion of men she did not care" (*MT*, 261). In contrast to Julia's goodness and devotion stands Polly Ochiltree, a woman who is almost witchlike in her treatment of Julia and her child. Polly steals and conceals important legal documents, she falsely accuses Julia of theft and turns her out penniless, she robs Janet of her inheritance and her legitimacy, and she tells Lily that she would have had Julia "whipped to death" had slavery still been in effect (*MT*, 138). As Polly is venting her wrath she says to Julia, "I am a lady, and you are—what?" (*MT*, 138) The cutting irony of Polly's status as "a lady" and Julia's apparent lack of status in the Southern social system is a direct attack on such distinctions and further underscores the mulatta's ambiguous position.

The traditional images of white and black womanhood are also undermined in Lily's treatment of Janet. Far from being the submissive and obedient "true woman," Lily follows in Polly's tradition by deliberately destroying legal documents in order to maintain the position of her son and hence her own position as a bearer of a legal heir. Yet the marriage certificate that Lily destroys also makes Julia the bearer of an heir, thus making the roles of white and black women ambiguous with regard to progeny. Unlike the traditional mulatta character, Janet does not owe her goodness to her white blood, and, in fact, she behaves strikingly unlike the "lily white" Lily and Polly. It is significant that the myths of white and black womanhood are undercut in part through the treatment of black women by white women, for it points to the relatedness and interdependence of racial and sexual stereotypes in a racist patriarchy.

Finally, *The Marrow of Tradition* subverts the "tragedy" of the tragic mulatta convention. Janet is not tragic in the traditional sense, for she does not tie her identity to the white race; she marries a successful man (in contrast to the conventional position of the mulatta as concubine), and she is educated, affluent, and happy. Of course Janet does suffer, for her little boy is killed by a stray bullet during a race riot. But she is never pathetic. In *The Marrow of Tradition* the mulatta suffers tragedy, not because of her ties to the black race, but because of her relationship to the white power structure. Catherine Juanita Starke has noted that the tragedy of the mulatta has often been a problem of identity for the individual who is neither white nor black—"the tragedy of the submerged self."[14] In Chesnutt's novel Janet finds her identity through her tragedy, for she is able to reject the claims of the white race which would categorize and thus oppress her. Janet tells Lily,

> For twenty-five years I, poor, despicable fool, would have kissed your feet for a word, a nod, a smile. Now, when this tardy recognition comes, for which I have waited so long, it is tainted with fraud and crime and blood, and I must pay for it with my child's life! . . . I throw you back your father's name, your father's wealth, your sisterly recognition. I want none of them,—they are bought too dear! (*MT,* 328–329)

In *The Marrow of Tradition* the mulatta gains pride in her race and herself, and thus turns tragedy into triumph.[15]

Like Chesnutt, Kate Chopin also subverts the mulatta convention to critique prescribed racial and gender roles.[16] In "Desiree's Baby" (1893) the mulatta again undercuts absolute racial distinctions, for nearly all the characters in the story are of "mixed blood" or "questionable" ancestry: there is a "yellow" maid, a "black" woman named "La Blanche," "yellow" slave children, and the foundling Desiree. Despite the obvious presence of racial mixing, Desiree's husband, Armand, insists upon a rigid interpretation of race, for when their child shows signs of mixed blood it means unconditionally to Armand "that the child is not white."[17] Proclaiming Desiree also to be "not white," Armand repudiates their marriage, for Desiree's "taint" is reason enough to disown her. His rejection of Desiree and their child is ironic, for the truth of Armand's own racial heritage is unknown to him.[18] When his own black ancestry is revealed through an old letter from his mother to his father, all of Armand's conscientiousness over racial purity becomes appallingly pathetic. "Desiree's Baby" employs such powerful images as a barefoot, half-naked quadroon boy fanning a "yellow" baby asleep on satin sheets to dramatize the real arbitrariness of "fixed" racial distinctions. Desiree's "true" race is never discovered, for it is ultimately meaningless—what matters in a system of racial discrimination is the label one receives from the group that has the power to label.

Desiree's tragedy is as much a tragedy of her sex as of her race.[19] Armand feels himself cheated and violated by Desiree's "taint," and believes that "Almighty God had dealt cruelly and unjustly with him" (DB, 244). Yet before the baby's race becomes an issue, Desiree comments that her husband has heard their child's cries "as far away as La Blanche's cabin," and her baby's "black" features first become apparent to Desiree when she observes the infant's likeness to one of La Blanche's little boys (DB, 241). Clearly Armand has had relations with La Blanche, and the quadroon boy who so closely resembles Desiree's baby is probably Armand's child as well. Armand's outrage is not because of his sexual union with Desiree but because he has married this woman who is now proved unfit to be his wife. The contrasting images of white and black womanhood are cruelly embodied in Armand's women, for the "black" La Blanche is only valuable as a servant and sexual partner and the "white" Desiree is of worth only if she can bear the child who will inherit the Aubigny name. When either woman fails in her role she is considered useless and is discarded; Desiree is cast off by Armand with as little compassion as is expressed when slave women are sold away. In "Desiree's Baby" the mulatta brings to light how restrictive and arbitrary are the roles assigned to white and black women, as well as how these roles are designed by white men to suit their social and sexual needs.

Ultimately it is Desiree's position as a woman in a male-dominated society which destroys her, for as a "true woman" she is both legally and personally powerless. When their child's race becomes unclear, Desiree turns to her husband to define her situation, saying, "What does it mean? tell me" (DB, 243). Armand's verdict that the child and Desiree are "not white" is final. His own status as a white is at no time questioned, even when Desiree tells him, "Look at my hand; whiter than yours, Armand" (DB, 243). As a white male, Armand is clearly in a position to accuse—Desiree is not. Desiree is indeed a tragic mulatta, for she is literally "lost" when Armand rejects her, and wanders off to die in the swamps. However, the source of Desiree's tragedy is not her assumed "taint"; it lies instead in the system of racial and sexual oppression which destroys her. The white patriarchal system is the "taint" in human relationships, and this rigid patriarchy is contrasted to the standards of love and human compassion which first compel Mrs. Valmonde to accept a "backgroundless" child. Armand is the truly tragic mulatto in "Desiree's Baby," for he has not only lost his family but has inculcated the racist values which must now lead him to self-loathing. Chopin manipulates the tragic mulatta convention in "Desiree's Baby" to reveal how concepts of race and gender are themselves conventions.

A third text worthy of note for its subversion of the tragic mulatta archetype is Frances E. W. Harper's *Iola Leroy* (1892).[20] In Harper's novel "inherent" racial differences are not merely obscured but are, in fact, obliterated; "black" characters are so indistinguishable from "white" that the main issue is whether they should "pass" as white or not. *Iola Leroy* denies the right of the white patriarchy to dictate racial categories, for in the novel individuals deliberately decide not to "pass" and instead to identify themselves through their black heritage. When trying to convince Iola to pass as a white woman and be his wife, Doctor Gresham says, "Iola, I see no use in your persisting that you are colored when your eyes are as blue and complexion as white as mine."[21] Iola's response reveals that she does not consider her black blood a shameful "taint" of her being:

> No, Doctor, I am not willing to live under a shadow of concealment which I thoroughly hate as if the blood in my veins were an undetected crime of my soul. (*IL*, 23)

Similarly, the fair-skinned Doctor Latimer belongs to the Negro race "both by blood and choice," for he has "nobly refused to forsake his mother's people and has cast his lot with them" (*IL*, 238). When Iola's "black" brother, Harry, is asked by another Negro to leave a black-only car, he comments, "It would be ludicrous, if it were not vexatious, to be too white to be black, and too black to be white" (*IL*, 245). The mulatto in Harper's novel emphasizes just how ludicrous such concerns are.

Like *The Marrow of Tradition*, *Iola Leroy* subverts the tragic mulatta convention by presenting blacks who gain pride through their black heritage.[22] Iola's story has all the markings of a tragic mulatta tale: observably white yet abruptly cast into slavery, Iola is separated from her family and hounded by the sexual advances of her owners. Yet unlike the traditional tragic mulatta, Iola is able to use the horrors of her slave experience to become a more caring and socially conscious person, and she comes to realize that her life has "much grander significance" now that her black ancestry is known (*IL*, 274). Similarly, Iola is like the conventional tragic mulatta in that her black blood prohibits her from marrying the white Doctor Gresham. However, it is not the "taint" of her blood but Iola's pride in her race which keeps her from forsaking her black family and "passing" as a white.[23] In *Iola Leroy* being black is not a tragedy but is, in fact, an asset in spiritual growth. Iola asserts that Harry "has greater advantages as a colored man" than if he had passed as white, since his will be the task of uplifting an oppressed people (*IL*, 219).

The mulatta in Chesnutt's and Chopin's fiction is ambiguous in her role as a woman because she is caught between two opposing images of womanhood. In *Iola Leroy*, Harper brings her critique of women's roles beyond a simple condemnation of stereotypes to a repudiation of any preconceived notions of what it means to be a woman. Iola is chaste, pious, and refined, but she is also strong, determined, career-oriented, and very much active in the advancement of her people. Thus Iola subverts not just the convention of the tragic mulatta, but the concept of the black "not woman" and the ideal of the white "true woman" as well. *Iola Leroy* asserts that the black people need "a union of women with the warmest hearts and clearest brains to help in the moral education of the race" (*IL*, 254), and Iola herself considers her life-work to be the uplifting of her people.[24] By rejecting standard images of womanhood, Harper's novel suggests that women, like blacks, must choose their own destinies and discard traditional limitations and labels. In taking pride in her black womanhood, Iola negates the "tragedy" of being black and being a woman in a white, male-dominated society.

Charles W. Chesnutt, Kate Chopin, and Frances E. W. Harper subvert the tragic mulatta archetype in an effort to show how literary conventions, like social conventions, are merely representations through which a dominant group maintains and perpetuates its power. The nineteenth-century Southern system of racial and sexual oppression relied as heavily upon absolute racial distinctions as it did upon unconditional stereotypes of womanhood. At one point in Harper's novel Iola Leroy comments, "Our enemies have the ear of the world, and they can depict us just as they please" (*IL*, 115). By undermining the tradition of the tragic mulatta Chesnutt, Chopin, and Harper emphasize the tragic mulatta's existence as a representation, and thus as a product and reflection of a particular version of reality. And in this sense, the works of these nineteenth-century writers are indeed tied to Alice Walker's search, generations later, to "know beyond all efforts to erase it from our minds, just exactly who, and of what, we black American women are."[25]

Notes

1. Barbara Christian, *Black Women Novelists: The Development of a Tradition, 1892–1976* (Westport, Conn.: Greenwood Press, 1980), 16.

2. Lawrence J. Friedman, *The White Savage: Racial Fantasies in the Postbellum South* (Englewood Cliffs, N.J.: Prentice-Hall, 1970), 105.

3. "The African Problem," *North American Review* 139 (1884): 418–419.

4. Elizabeth Fox-Genovese, *Within the Plantation Household: Black and White Women of the Old South* (Chapel Hill: University of North Carolina Press, 1988); Barbara Welter, *Dimity Convictions: The American Woman in the Nineteenth Century* (Athens: Ohio University Press, 1976).

5. Catherine Clinton, *The Plantation Mistress: Woman's World in the Old South* (New York: Pantheon Books, 1982), 93.

6. Christian, *Black Women Novelists*, 13.

7. "Studies in the South," *Atlantic Monthly* 49 (1882): 189–190.

8. For discussions of the "true woman"/"not woman" dichotomy, see Catherine Clinton, "The Sexual Dynamics of Slavery," in *The Plantation Mistress*, 199–222; Elizabeth Fox-Genovese, "Gender Conventions," in *Within the Plantation Household*, 192–241.

9. Christian, *Black Women Novelists*, 26.

10. Jules Zanger, "The 'Tragic Octoroon' in Pre-Civil War Fiction," *American Quarterly* 18 (1966): 65.

11. For studies of Chesnutt's life and works, see William L. Andrews, *The Literary Career of Charles W. Chesnutt* (Baton Rouge: Louisiana State University Press, 1980); J. Noel Heermance, *Charles W. Chesnutt* (Hamden, Conn.: Archon, 1974).

12. Charles W. Chesnutt, *The Marrow of Tradition* (Ann Arbor: University of Michigan Press, 1969), 8 (hereafter cited parenthetically in the text as *MT*).

13. For some insight into the Wilmington, North Carolina, race riot of 1898 and its relation to *The Marrow of Tradition*, see Frances Richardson Keller, *An American Crusade: The Life of Charles Waddell Chesnutt* (Provo: Brigham Young University Press, 1978).

14. Catherine Juanita Starke, *Black Portraiture in American Fiction: Stock Characters, Archetypes, and Individuals* (New York: Basic Books, 1971),

106. For a psychoanalytical approach to the themes of repression and racial identity in *The Marrow of Tradition*, see Marjorie George and Richard S. Pressman, "Confronting the Shadow: Psycho-political Repression in Chesnutt's *The Marrow of Tradition*," *Phylon* 48 (winter 1987): 287–298.

15. P. Jay Delmar focuses on the figures of Josh Green and Doctor Miller to assert that *The Marrow of Tradition* presents an ambiguous racial message because Chesnutt "could not effectively resolve the moral dilemma which he had created" (269). This reading fails to recognize the moral and racial dilemma that is confronted and resolved in Janet's relationship with Lily. "The Moral Dilemma in Charles W. Chesnutt's *The Marrow of Tradition*," *American Literary Realism* 14 (1981): 269–272.

16. For critical biographies of Kate Chopin, see Emily Toth, *Kate Chopin* (New York: William Morrow, 1990); Per Seyersted, *Kate Chopin: A Critical Biography* (Baton Rouge: Louisiana State University Press, 1969).

17. Kate Chopin, "Desiree's Baby," in *The Complete Works of Kate Chopin*, edited by Per Seyersted, vol. 1 (Baton Rouge: Louisiana State University Press, 1969), 243 (hereafter cited parenthetically in the text as DB).

18. Barbara C. Ewell discusses how Chopin carefully lays the groundwork for the "surprise" reversal in the story, as well as the mythical dimensions of the characters of Armand and Desiree. *Kate Chopin* (New York: Ungar, 1986), 69–72.

19. For a discussion of Chopin and gender issues in relation to Southern themes, see Anne Goodwyn Jones, "Kate Chopin: The Life behind the Mask," in *Tomorrow Is Another Day: The Woman Writer in the South, 1859–1936* (Baton Rouge: Louisiana State University Press, 1981), 135–182.

20. For a profile of Harper's life and works, see Elizabeth Ammons, "Frances Ellen Watkins Harper (1825–1911)," *Legacy* 2 (fall 1985): 61–66. For the literary and historical context of Harper's work, see Paul Lauter, "Is Frances Ellen Watkins Harper Good Enough to Teach?" *Legacy* 5 (spring 1988): 27–32.

21. Frances E. W. Harper, *Iola Leroy; or, Shadows Uplifted* (New York: Oxford University Press, 1988), 232 (hereafter cited parenthetically in the text as *IL*).

22. Blyden Jackson misses the subversion and largely dismisses Harper as a sentimental writer. Jackson categorizes *Iola Leroy* as a "plantation novel" akin to *Clotel*, holding that Harper's characters are "stock figures" and that "brooding over all is the tragic mulatto." *A History of Afro-American Literature*, vol. 1 (Baton Rouge: Louisiana State University Press, 1989), 396.

23. For a discussion of Iola's marriage to Doctor Frank Latimer in light of the symbolic function of marriage in nineteenth-century black women's fiction, see Claudia Tate, "Allegories of Black Female Desire; or, Rereading

Nineteenth-Century Sentimental Narratives of Black Female Authority," in *Changing Our Own Words,* edited by Cheryl A. Wall (New Brunswick: Rutgers University Press, 1989), 98–126.

24. See Marjorie Pryse's introduction to *Conjuring: Black Women, Fiction, and Literary Traditions,* edited by Marjorie Pryse and Hortense J. Spillers (Bloomington: Indiana University Press, 1985), 1–24, for a discussion of the role of the novel as genre in racial uplift and of the uplift theme as a means for black writers to break into fiction.

25. Alice Walker, *In Search of Our Mothers' Gardens* (New York: Harcourt Brace Jovanovich, 1983), 235.

PART III

IMAGES OF WOMEN

Nine

"My Sisters Toil"

Voice in Anti-Slavery Poetry by White Female Factory Workers

Susan Alves

The most compelling evidence of a complex white working-class wom-
en's poetic voice is found in the anti-slavery poetry of the Lowell, Massachusetts, factory workers. This is a heterogeneous subjectivity shared
by many of the female factory operatives. In their abolitionist poems,
these mid-nineteenth-century women negotiate their concerns over
hegemonic gender roles, upper-class expectations of lower-class people,
and their identity as laboring daughters of freemen. As powerful as
these voices may be, they often are not heard in traditional canons of
American literature.

Often written pseudonymously, the poetry of antebellum female
workers challenges not only the primacy of the identified individual author but critical reading practices as well. The poets' observation of
such nineteenth-century literary conventions as the apostrophe has
caused female factory poets to be dismissed as imitative, sentimental,
and derivative. By examining the complex poetic voice of the white
native-born female factory worker, I will show that critical literary definitions and valuations of the categories of poetry and poetic subjectivity
must be expanded.

As nineteenth-century women, many factory operatives attempt to
embrace the dominant middle-class "cult of true womanhood" by constructing a poetic voice which is pious, pure, submissive, domestic, and
silent in response to public matters (Welter 21). This tendency toward
"true womanhood" is found most pointedly in the editorials, short fiction, and verse of the *Lowell Offering*. In this magazine, daughters of
New Hampshire and Vermont farmers, now factory laborers, write as if

139

their current status in the mills is temporary, and indeed for many women it was.

As female laborers in industrial complexes, these writers exchange their time and labor for capital, and many embrace the identity of "wage slave."[1] Such an identity, put forward by labor activists like George Henry Evans and Orestes A. Brownson in the 1830s and 1840s, does not simply suggest a willingness on the part of some of these Anglo-American women to align themselves with the slaves of African descent; rather, the semantic operation of the word "slave" points to an anxiety of association among Northern female factory workers with those laboring against their will in the South. By employing "slave" comparatively as part of the rhetoric of the labor movement, women workers position their argument for a shorter work day and stable pay by posing the impossibility of an imbedded racial comparison of whites and blacks:

> Oh! isn't it a pity, such a pretty girl as I—
> Should be sent to the factory to pine away and die?
> Oh! I cannot be a slave,
> I will not be a slave,
> For I'm so fond of liberty
> That I cannot be a slave. (Robinson 51)

By exercising a term like "slave" in this context, the poet is not placing herself in solidarity with black slaves, but calling attention to the "inappropriate oppression of whites" (Roediger 68).

As Northerners, the female factory poets often adopt an impersonal tone in their poetic presentation of black men and women. This tone might suggest the geographical, or territorial, distance between most white operatives and blacks, but a thriving African-American community of several hundred people lived and worked in the mill city. No evidence that free blacks labored in the Lowell factories has been found. Still, because antebellum Lowell was not a segregated city, it is very likely that white female factory workers had regular contact with black women and men who were merchants or worked in such occupations as barbering. Many African-American men were in key positions in Lowell's commercial and civic community; some African-American women worked in such service professions as housekeeping; many African-American families were part of the city's growing middle-class population.[2] The observational tone taken toward blacks in poems by white female laborers may suggest the racist canceling-out of Lowell's black community and/or an inability on the part of these white working-class women to comprehend middle-class and merchant-class African Americans within the same populace as blacks in slavery. The objectified representation of black men and women as slaves by these northern, white, working-class poets in poems such as "The Slave's Revenge" and "The Slave Mother" implies that they perceived economic class significantly differently in relation to blacks.

The factory workers' position as white writers is marked in the linguistic configurations and contents of the text. The racial position of white female factory poets influences their depiction of enslaved black men and women as other, while producing their own racial identity, their whiteness, as an unwritten norm transcribed on the text.

Interrogation of the literary construction, representation, and function of whiteness is long overdue. Toni Morrison, in *Playing in the Dark: Whiteness and the Literary Imagination* (1992), outlines a critical project which stresses the "embedded assumptions of racial (not racist) language" (xii). She insists that American writers historically have constructed black figures as reflexive, as "an extraordinary meditation on the self; a powerful exploration of fears and desires that reside in the writerly conscious" (17). Morrison argues that an assumption of whiteness has continued to operate on the part of both the writers and the readers of American literature. When this assumption remains unwritten and unexamined, the critical gaze is averted from the subject to the object, thus eliding any investigation of the effect of "whiteness" on the text.

In her reading of twentieth-century North American white women's life histories, anthropologist Ruth Frankenberg systematically examines the construction and function of whiteness. Frankenberg identifies her project as an examination of the way white women are marked, or perceive their identity through race. Her study considers the effect of the social encoding of whiteness on the subjects' lives. Frankenberg maintains that

> [w]hiteness changes over time and space and is in no way a transhistorical essence. Rather, . . . it is a complexly constructed product of local, regional, national, and global relations, past and present. . . . And if whiteness varies spatially and temporally, it is also a relational category, one that is constructed with a range of other racial and cultural categories, with class and with gender. This construction is, however, fundamentally asymmetrical, for the term "whiteness" signals the production and reproduction of dominance rather than subordination, normativity rather than marginality, privilege rather than disadvantage. (Frankenberg 236–237)

Embedded in the invisibility of whiteness in the life histories of Frankenberg's twentieth-century subjects as well as in the diction, semantics, and poetics of nineteenth-century white female factory workers' poetry is a complex repertoire of relationships, ideology, and culture.

To get a sense of the complexity of the white working-class female poetic subjectivity developed by these workers, we must examine specific poems dealing with the issue of slavery. Of the hundreds of poems published in New England antebellum labor periodicals, approximately fourteen address the issue of race or the slavery of blacks. Among these are "What Is It to Be a Slave?" by the pseudonymous "Ellen," "The Slave's Revenge" by "Sarah W.," and "Weaving" by Lucy Larcom, which she published under her own name. In these works a multifaceted poetic voice is foregrounded, thereby providing a site for exploring the effect of whiteness on literary texts.

As a topic, the slavery of blacks in antebellum America merges a nexus of concern for the female factory poet. In an era of Christian revivalism, both radical and conservative, many of these women participated in various Protestant missions for social change as these were put forth by such institutional communities as the Episcopalians, Presbyterians, Methodists, and Unitarians. With this participation came a sense of personal and pious responsibility for social problems. While most of the Lowell poets encountered the slavery of blacks as an abstract evil, a spiritual blight on the country, many female factory workers did not know that, in the contemporary rhetoric of labor activism, wage labor was compared to the oppression of black women and men in slavery. Yet for many female workers, slavery either consciously or subconsciously provoked a conflict among the convictions of Christian humanism, their social role as women, and their status as workers.

Reflecting back thirty years to her first meeting with poet and abolitionist John Greenleaf Whittier in July 1844, native-born factory operative Lucy Larcom recalls that

> Mr. Whittier's visit to Lowell had some political bearing upon the antislavery cause. It is strange now to think that a cause like that should not always have been our country's cause,—our country,— our own free nation! But antislavery sentiments were then regarded by many as traitorous heresies; and those who held them did not expect to win popularity. If the vote of the millgirls had been taken, it would doubtless have been unanimous on the antislavery side. But those were also the days when a woman was not expected to give, or even to have, an opinion on subjects of public interest. (Larcom, *Girlhood*, 255)

If Larcom's recollection is any indication, then many New England mill girls were caught between an idealized view of American democracy, an internalized acceptance of the middle-class Cult of True Womanhood, and the experience of being female wage laborers in such factory systems as those in Lowell, Massachusetts, during the "speedup" and "stretch-out" periods.[3]

Ironically, Whittier's visit to the factory operatives' improvement circle came through an invitation from Harriet Farley. In her role as editor of the *Lowell Offering* Farley purposefully refrained from public commentary on social issues. In a November 1843 editorial she attempts to appease her middle-class patrons and subscribers:

> With regard to politics we, as females should do, remain entirely neutral. . . .
>
> The Abolition of Intemperance, Slavery, and War, is now discussed in the different publications dedicated to those subjects; neither are we capable of assisting in their discussion. (Farley 24)

While Larcom, a frequent contributor to the *Lowell Offering*, hints that Whittier's presence may have been a catalyst for self-examination and militancy among her female colleagues, Larcom, like other mill girls, waited until after she had left the mills to publish her own anti-slavery poetry, in the late 1840s.

Although the poetry published in the *Lowell Offering* and the *Voice of Industry* had similar subjects and poetic styles, the two bodies of work developed separately. In 1845, Sarah Bagley, the editor of the *Voice of Industry* and a poet herself, issued a public attack on Harriet Farley, accusing her of being unwilling to take up key topics of political concern to the female operatives. This break between two prominent women editors is reflected in the tone and poetic subject matter of both Lowell periodicals.

Only the radical labor newspaper *Voice of Industry* solicited articles and poems by male and female workers who spoke out directly on such subjects as labor reform and slavery. Such anti-slavery poems as "North and South" and "What Is It to Be a Slave?" participate in an ongoing public dialogue concerning the slavery of blacks in the South and the effect of wage labor on freemen of the North.

Although terms such as "white slavery" and "the slavery of wages" were common metaphors in the popular rhetoric of nineteenth-century America, especially during the boom industrial years of the 1830s and early 1840s, women workers did not employ these terms in their poetry. Still, the poets' use of the word "slavery" in their works occurs at a time when comparisons between the lot of the white wage laborers in the North and the black slaves in the South dominated public debate. The need for and the growth of a laboring class challenged the notion that the American republic was a society of independent men. White industrial workers exchange physical labor for income, and thus their situation, unlike that of the artisans of a previous era, attracts comparisons with that of blacks enslaved in the South. For example, in "The Laboring Classes" (1840), Orestes Brownson argues that

> [i]f the slave has never been a free man, we think, as a general rule, his sufferings are less than those of the free laborer at wages. As to actual freedom one has just about as much as the other. The laborer at wages has all the disadvantages of freedom and none of its blessings, while the slave, if denied the blessings, is freed from the disadvantages. (Brownson 366)

The idea that white wage laborers were "enslaved" in the North became part of the rhetoric of such labor movements as the Lowell Strike of 1834 and the Ten Hour Movement of the 1840s. Antebellum analogies made between black slaves and white wage laborers by Northern workers and labor activists are not necessarily based in empathic connections between these two groups. Instead, David Roediger argues,

> it should be obvious that for all but a handful of committed abolitionists/labor reformers, use of a term like "white slavery" was not an act of solidarity with the slave but rather a call to arms to end the inappropriate oppression of whites. (Roediger 68)

The paternalistic system of the textile mills in cities such as Lowell enhanced workers' fears that they were becoming bound and oppressed by their overseers and the owners of the factories. In the Lowell Strike of 1834, the female workers expressed their resistance to wage slavery, even as they claimed their identity as the daughters of freemen.

As native New Englanders, many of the women who came to work in the Lowell factories were steeped in the Whig tradition of John Locke, Thomas Paine, and Daniel Webster, a legacy of natural rights, civil liberty, and the constitutional alliance of society and government. For these New England women, then, the language of slavery has its roots in a Whig heritage out of which came the American Revolution and the contradictions of the anti-slavery struggle.

The subject, syntax, and diction of the poem "What Is It to Be a Slave?" participate in the moral problem of slavery in antebellum America as well as in the debate over the status of the wage laborer. The poem's appearance in a commanding location, at the top of the first column of the first page in the January 23, 1846, issue of the *Voice of Industry,* suggests not only the respected role of women poets such as the pseudonymous Ellen, but also the way these poets negotiate their relationship to a reading audience they construct as male and female, Yankee, working-class and bourgeois. Consideration of this audience was important in 1845 and 1846, for during these years the Ten Hour Movement shifted from public protest to political petition campaigns which called on the Massachusetts state legislature to limit the hours of labor in the mills (Dublin, *Women at Work,* 90). The move to a political arena limited women's involvement in the forefront of the labor movement. Female labor leaders instead took up a variety of roles in the infrastructure of the Ten Hour Movement. The *Voice of Industry* became an "important educational and organizing tool of the Lowell Female Labor Reform Association" (90).

Using a question in the title and in the first stanza of her poem, Ellen constructs a poetic voice which is conversational, thereby drawing the reader into personal consideration of slavery:

Hast thou ever asked thyself
   What is it to be a slave?
Bought and sold for sordid pelf,
   From the cradle to the grave! (ll. 1–4)

The initial question extends the female poet's True Woman role of empathetic and moral mediator into the public sphere by assuming that the audience is receptive to her message. An assumption of readerly compassion bridges the geographical distance which separates both speaker and listener from first-hand experience of people who are actually enslaved. Ellen's choice of the informal second-person pronoun form, "thou," as a referent for the poetic audience implies her assumption of their similar class standing and her address to the reader's "higher" moral self. In line four, the standard metaphor used to illustrate the span of human life, "the cradle to the grave," works to further produce an audience fundamentally sympathetic to the figure of the slave, with whom the reader shares a common humanity.

In the stanzas that follow, Ellen does not portray specific scenes of slavery; rather, the poetic voice transmits emotionally sentimental knowledge of a slave's experience. The speaker is positioned as an omniscient observer who regards the moral dilemma of slavery for those in the North and South, and as a judge who renders her opinion of the participants in this institution. Although the poem appears to be addressing a Northern male middle- to upper-class audience at its beginning, in the last stanza the poetic voice collapses the distinction between silent Northerners and Southerners of the slaveholding class:

Such is slavery! Couldst thou bear
    Its vile bondage? Oh! my brother,
How, then, canst thou, wilt thou dare
    To inflict it on another! (ll. 41–44)

By erasing the boundaries between these two groups, Ellen not only
calls her audience to embrace a higher moral standard by rejecting whatever role they play in the structure of slavery, but also privileges her
status as a non-participant in this codified institution.

This last stanza should be read not only in the context of New England antebellum anti-slavery discourse, but in the rhetoric of labor activism as well. For the denunciation of slavery's "vile bondage" and
the moralistic plea against its infliction imply an immediacy of concern
as well as the ability of members of the constructed audience to directly
act against this wrong. With the assumption of such an urgency the
poet erases the boundaries between the social classes in her audience
and eliminates distinctions between the bondage of Africans and the
enslavement of white factory workers.

Significantly, the black figure of the slave is an objectified presence
in the poem. Ellen represents the slave indirectly by using the infinitive verb forms "to know," "to learn," and "to feel" as a means of cate-
gorizing aspects of slave life. Because infinitive verbs express a verbal
notion unrelated to a particular subject, they obscure the concept of a
specific person who is a slave, thus positioning the black figure as an
object in, rather than a subject of, the poem. As an objectified presence,
the slave functions as a reflexive construct allowing this white working-
class female poet to explore the "fears and desires that reside in [her]
writerly conscious" (Morrison 17).

The infinitive verbs also suggest aspects of the life of female factory
operatives during speedup periods in the Lowell mills. For example, the
indirect description of the slave's experience implies the requirement to
increase productivity that many white factory workers faced, as well as
the sexual demands often made on female operatives by male inspectors
and bosses:

'Tis to know the transient powers
    E'en of muscle, flesh and bone,
Cannot in thy happiest hour,
    Be considered as thine own! (ll. 5–8)

Similarly, Ellen may be proposing that twelve-and-a-half-hour factory
days, shrinking pay, and declining factory conditions produced by bad

ventilation and the density of cotton fibers in the air cause many women workers to despair of their lot and resonate, at least temporarily, with the "hopeless slave!" (l. 40).

Turning on the poet's elusive representation of the black figure in this poem is an unwritten reflexive construction of a female white working-class speaker. The poem queries the parameters of this poetic subjectivity. The poet's use of a pseudonym, common among middle-class women writers in the nineteenth century, is significant because it suggests one of the ways working-class women attempt to position themselves in relation to women of a higher class. The pseudonym gives this female working-class poet space to address concerns outside the domestic sphere while maintaining a certain anonymity. Just as the slave's identity is obscured by his remaining unnamed, so too is the female poet's actual identity concealed by the use of a pseudonym. The poetic voice occupies an indeterminate position, claiming multiple contradictory alliances with female and male working-class peers, with Northern and Southern bourgeois men, and with the figure of the male slave of the poem. Such an ambiguous subjectivity reflects the conflicted mutability of white female native-born factory workers, while the poet's relatively privileged social status as a white female engenders a view of other persons which blurs important distinctions such as those of race, class, or gender.

A poetic voice similar to that of "What Is It to Be a Slave?" is found in Sarah W.'s "The Slave's Revenge." In "The Slave's Revenge," the speaker occupies a transmutable omniscient space from which moral judgments are made and empirical knowledge is imparted. Published in the *Voice of Industry* a year after "What Is It to Be a Slave?" Sarah W.'s poem also emphasizes the personal toll slavery exacts of black Americans, but unlike that in the earlier poem, the black male figure of this poem has agency and a voice that speaks in the first person.

With the story-telling convention of calling forth the power of imagination in the audience, the speaker of Sarah W.'s poem is positioned in the specifically female nineteenth-century middle-class role of cultural conveyor, while the audience is constructed as geographically removed from firsthand experience of slavery, of personally knowing people who are slaves:

Lend, lend imagination wings,
    While yonder sun in beauty wanes; —
    Soar far away to southern clime,
    Where souls in cruel bondage pine. (ll. 1–4)

While slavery is distanced physically, the poet proposes an emotional closeness shared by the Northern working-class and bourgeois readership of the *Voice of Industry* and the figure of a male slave.

The link between the reader and the poem's black figure is spiritual as well as material. By representing the male slave as a soul, a convention of anti-slavery writing, the poet references the rhetoric of Judeo-Christianity, which posits the soul as a person's true self, and thus suggests a profound similarity between a white reader (who is familiar with the rhetoric) and the black figure. By presenting the central conflict of the poem's narrative as slavery's effect on the family unit, Sarah W. reduces the ills of slavery to a single aspect of life that is understandable to her white Northern readers regardless of their economic class or gender. The spiritual and material connection between the poem's speaking black figure and a silent audience imagining slavery's "cruel bondage" advanced by this working-class white female poet allows her to claim a space within the conventions of the socially dominant norm of the Cult of True Womanhood, and thus the connection as well as the poet's pseudonym perform a pious, pure, submissive, and domestic poetic voice, a working-class voice mediated through the hegemonic standards of middle-class society.

The black male figure of "The Slave's Revenge" functions not only as a representation of human suffering, but as a literary appropriation through which the white writer displaces her own anxieties and reproduces white dominance over black subordination. For instance, the black figure articulates a concern of both wage labor and slave when he cries out, "Must I in bondage always sigh?" (l. 8). If this black character, as Toni Morrison suggests, is "an extraordinary meditation on the self; a powerful exploration of fears and desires that reside in the writerly conscious" (Morrison 17), then any reading of the poem must take into account the problematic double value of this figure. The poet's whiteness operates within a complex repertoire of relationships, ideologies, and assumptions. The blackness, maleness, and servitude of the unnamed figure provide this white, female, and wage-earning poet with a distance across which she may transfer concerns regarding the uncertain meaning of her racial identity, gender, and economic status in antebellum industrial America.

Representations of black men and women in works such as "What Is It to Be a Slave?" and "The Slave's Revenge" are common in anti-slavery and women's rights rhetoric of the 1830s and 1840s. On January 1, 1831, William Lloyd Garrison published the first issue of his fiery and widely distributed anti-slavery newspaper, the *Liberator*. Other periodicals, such as the *Congregationalist*, edited by Sarah Knowles Bolton, the *National Era*, co-edited by Margaret L. Shands Bailey and John Greenleaf Whittier, and the *Voice of Industry*, under Sarah G. Bagley's guidance, merged a variety of social concerns into their publishing mission, thus contributing to the spread of debate on these issues among the American public. In *Touching Liberty: Abolition, Feminism, and the Politics of the Body*, Karen Sanchez-Eppler maintains that texts such as these insert blacks and women into a contemporary political arena that excludes them from governmental power and call attention to the unnamed and unwritten juridical person who is implicitly white and male (Sanchez-Eppler 3).

Both white working-class women and black slaves are thrust into public view by white working-class women writing poems about black slaves and by white male editors of prominent presses publishing and prominently featuring these works. This is a public view which doubles the otherness of these figures, thereby representing the political unrepresentability of black male and female slaves and white working-class women even as these figures locate the whiteness, maleness, and middle-class independence of the normative American.

The poetic voice in "The Slave's Revenge" recedes into an omniscient narrative juxtaposing the behavior of the slave in his home with the events of the slave market. Comparatively few lines are given to his voice:

> In yonder cabin kneels a form
> That slavery's galling yoke hath worn;
> In broken accents hear him cry,
> "Must I in bondage always sigh?" (ll. 5–8)

Such positioning allows the writer to contrast the slave's quiet and faithful heart with that of the loud, cruel slave-trader. Implicit in this contrast are the differences not only of the skin colors of the bound and the free men, but of their moral caliber as well. Further, by locating the male slave in a familial milieu and the male slave-trader in the marketplace, the poet attributes gendered positions usually associated with women and men to these two male figures as well.

When the white trader ignores the black man's plea to keep his family together, and instead rends the family, the figure of the black slave asserts his autonomy, thereby declaring his masculinity:

> "You cast my lot far far away;
> Me never work for you a day." (ll. 35–36)

While Sarah W. attempts to personalize the experience of slavery by giving the character speech, this white poet appropriates a black dialect to meet her end. With the speech act of the black slave, Sarah W. reduces the category of black man to an essential identity of slave, which is marked by a configuration of language usage. In this way, the poet reproduces her racial dominance over the subordinated black figure. The speech action of this black figure, although standard in lines eight and twenty-five, is in dialect form in the most emotionally charged lines of the poem (ll. 27–28, 35–36, 47–48). In these lines, the poet calls attention to the ideological differences between her representative figures and implies a hegemonic distinction, signified by linguistic patterns, between blacks and herself as a white person.

The representations of antebellum black dialects of English by white writers of this period raise a number of contradictory questions. Among these are, Is the poet using an "Africanist idiom . . . to establish difference?" (Morrison 52). Does Sarah W.'s "reinscription of white imaginings of black speech, her orthographic display of racial difference, simply fall back upon itself, 'othering' itself while at the same time further immuring black speaking subjectivities in the tar baby of white discourse?" (Nielsen 7)

In the poem's climatic narrative, the character dramatically claims agency over his own capital, in an act that titillates the audience with the possible horror of a slave killing his master, a horror deflected instantly:

With frantic yell he leaped the stand,
Seized fast an axe—cut off his hand.

Then he raised his bleeding arm to him
Who vainly thought the prize to win —
"Remember sir, again me say,
Me never work for you a day." (ll. 43–48)

The poem ends with this ennobling and self-destructive act by which the poet asserts that within the industry of slavery there is no room for an articulation of unmutilated, undamaged masculine agency.

In representing a figure of a black female slave in her poem "Weaving," white working-class poet Lucy Larcom suppresses an "Africanist idiom" in her text, thereby engaging an ideology of race similar to that at work in Ellen's and Sarah W.'s anti-slavery poems. Although Larcom writes this poem in her own name and after leaving the Lowell mills, the use of a poetic persona allows her to foreground similarities between the figures of a black female slave and a white female factory worker, while also providing the poet a public space to address the issue of slavery. Unlike Ellen and Sarah W., Larcom employs such poetic devices as a controlling image to fuse gender and labor in her reflexive representation of a black female figure.

Larcom reworks Tennyson's "Lady of Shalott" by privileging the female narrating persona in a variety of ways. Among these are the speaker's race-free identity and the depiction of this figure within a literary tradition which equates the image of a woman weaving with the qualities of insight and fidelity:

All day she stands before her loom;
    The flying shuttles come and go . . .

Is she entangled in her dreams,
    Like that fair weaver of Shalott . . .

Her heart, a mirror sadly true,
    Brings gloomier visions into view. (ll. 1-2, 7-8, 11-12)

Through speech, the poet empowers the figure of the female factory worker. The presence of a silent black female limns the persona's whiteness by forming a literary contrast between a voiced subject and a silent other.

The flowing river provides a context for labor as well as a metaphoric connection between the female figures:

Wind on, by willow and by pine,
    Thou blue, untroubled Merrimack!
Afar, by sunnier streams than thine,
    My sisters toil, with foreheads black (ll. 37-40)

Larcom's choice of the word "sisters" implies a female familial relationship dispersing the experiential power of race, while stressing the characters' shared gender and life of labor. Ending the stanza in the rhymed couplet, the poet posits a socioeconomic alliance of black and white women laboring in the cotton industry:

And water with their blood this root,
    Whereof we gather bounteous fruit. (ll. 41-42)

While the form of the rhymed couplet emphasizes the poetic lines and enacts the union of black and white women, these lines also call attention to such idealized benefits of the cotton industry as a reliable income, a means of economic improvement, and the freedom to leave the work at will. From each of these advantages black female and male slaves were excluded and from each of these many female factory workers profited. Because key differences in the speaker's and slaves' racial identities as well as in the specific terms of the labor of white free women and black slave women are unwritten, Larcom leaves ambiguous the terms of this sisterhood. The poet's whiteness makes her assume that femaleness and laboring status are essential similarities, and this assumption underlies her use of the word "sisters."

In Larcom's description of the black figure in "Weaving," the poet's syntax operates within the boundaries of Christian humanism. The indeterminate quality of Larcom's language suggests contradictory meanings:

I think of women sad and poor;
    Women who walk in garments soiled:
Their shame, their sorrow, I endure;
    By their defect my hope is foiled:
The blot they bear is on my name;
Who sins, and I am not to blame? (ll. 43–48)

In this religious and historical framework suffering is a punishment for sin. The poet appears to blame the lot of blacks under slavery on their own sinfulness, while suggesting that the participants in the community of faith also bear responsibility for the transgressions and afflictions among their population. If these lines posit a faith community which joins the white female persona and the black female slave, then the voiced persona is claiming accountability for the condition of the other woman's life. If, on the other hand, the poet is suggesting that "shame," "sorrow," and "defect" have been foisted upon the black female figure by whites of the slaveholding class, then Larcom's white female speaker is claiming the burden of this white community's sins, while restricting her sisterly alliance with the figure of the enslaved black woman.

Other middle-class white poets, such as John Greenleaf Whittier (in "Toussaint L'Ouverture") and Maria White Lowell (in "The Slave-Mother"), shared the factory workers' inability to address their own racialized position. This inability obscures the root issue of racism in the institution of slavery and its role in the white anti-slavery movement. In *Writing Between the Lines: Race and Intertextuality*, Aldon L. Nielsen asserts that

[t]he mistake in the thought of many abolitionists of the past . . . has been to believe that racism was a special case of prejudice that would eventually yield to empirical experience; that if white people really got to know black people, racism would vanish. Africanist discourse exists so that white people will not have to get to know black people. Africanist discourse tells white Americans that they

already know black people and black culture. It exists so that white
people may be white. (Nielsen 14)

The position of the figure of the black female slave in Larcom's "Weaving" underscores the problematics of literary representations of blacks
by whites in abolition poetry and other texts.

When read as a "meditation on the self," the construction of black
figures in "What Is It to Be a Slave?" "The Slave's Revenge," and
"Weaving" reveals a writerly conscious that is produced in a tension
between the desire to participate in hegemonic racial and gender roles
and the fear of exclusion from that society due to the writer's gender
and class status. These three poems are representative of the way female
factory operatives posit empathy for black slaves, while the poets render
these black male and female figures indistinct, unnamed, and silent. By
emphasizing labor as a tie which binds working-class white women to
black men and women enslaved, these white labor poets depict their
own anxieties about the permanence and invisibility of their status as
wage workers in a changing American economy. While empathetic connections between white female factory workers and black slaves may
elide their key differences, the poets' unexamined and uncritical assumptions about shared similarities between the people of these two
groups foreground the poetic appropriation of black slave experience by
white working-class women.

This multifaceted poetic subjectivity of nineteenth-century, white,
native-born, working-class female poets reflects and refracts the patterns of the lives and concerns of mid-nineteenth-century female factory workers. Because these poets produce a subjectivity which circumvents critical standards of originality, their omission from literary
histories not only is a great loss but also calls attention to the inadequacy of literary histories in contextualizing difference within categories such as authorial identity, voice, and the genre of poetry.

Notes

1. David R. Roediger, in *The Wages of Whiteness: Race and the Making of the
   American Working Class,* presents an extensive discussion of the use and
   function of such terms as "wage slavery," "white slavery," and the "slavery
   of wages" in the rhetoric of United States labor-management struggles
   during the 1830s and 1840s (65–92).
2. Archivist Martha Mayo of the Mogan Center for Labor History in Lowell,
   Massachusetts, detailed the lives of this mostly middle-class community
   in a 1994–1995 museum exhibit. I am particularly grateful to Martha

Mayo for her time and generous willingness to answer my numerous questions about the African-American population in Lowell before the Civil War. Brad Parker's *Black and Antislavery History in Early Lowell* also traces the history of African Americans in Lowell.

3. According to labor historian Thomas Dublin, "[t]he specific terms *speedup* and *stretch-out* were not used in contemporary Lowell, but have come into common usage since that time, particularly with reference to the textile industry" (*Women at Work*, 271 n. 4).

Works Cited

Brownson, Orestes A. "The Laboring Classes." *Boston Quarterly Review*, July and October 1840.

Dublin, Thomas. *Women at Work: The Transformation of Work and Community in Lowell, Massachusetts, 1826–1860* (New York: Columbia University Press, 1979).

———. "Women, Work, and Protest in the Early Lowell Mills: *The Oppressing Hand of Avarice Would Enslave Us.*" In *The Continuing Revolution: A History of Lowell, Massachusetts*, edited by Robert Weible (Lowell: Lowell Historical Society, 1991), 77–95.

Ellen. "What Is It to Be a Slave?" *The Voice of Industry*, January 23, 1846, 1.

Farley, Harriet. Editorial. *Lowell Offering*, November 1843, 24.

Frankenberg, Ruth. *White Women, Race Matters: The Social Construction of Whiteness*. Minneapolis: University of Minnesota Press, 1993.

Larcom, Lucy. *A New England Girlhood*. Boston: Houghton Mifflin, 1889.

———. "Weaving." In *Larcom's Poetical Works*, 93–94. Boston: Houghton Mifflin, 1884.

Morrison, Toni. *Playing in the Dark: Whiteness and the Literary Imagination*. Cambridge: Harvard University Press, 1992.

Nielsen, Aldon L. *Writing Between the Lines: Race and Intertextuality*. Athens: University of Georgia Press, 1994.

Parker, Brad. *Black and Antislavery History in Early Lowell*. Lowell, Mass.: Landmark, 1986.

Robinson, Harriet H. *Loom and Spindle: or, Life among the Early Mill Girls*. 1898. Rev. ed., Kailua, Hawaii: Press Pacifica, 1976.

Roediger, David R. *The Wages of Whiteness: Race and the Making of the American Working Class*. London and New York: Verso, 1991.

Sanchez-Eppler, Karen. *Touching Liberty: Abolition, Feminism, and the Politics of the Body*. Berkley: University of California Press, 1993.

Sarah W. "The Slave's Revenge." *Voice of Industry*, June 18, 1847, 1.

Welter, Barbara. "The Cult of True Womanhood: 1820–1860." In *Dimity Convictions: The American Woman in the Nineteenth Century*, 21–41. Athens: Ohio University Press, 1976.

Ten

Enacting Culture
Zora Neale Hurston, Joel Chandler Harris, and Literary Anthropology

Juniper Ellis

In their respective collections of African-American oral tales, Joel Chandler Harris and Zora Neale Hurston both use literary techniques to present the tales they collect. In quite different ways, each author thus anticipates recent practices in literature and anthropology, by considering culture across disciplinary boundaries. Zora Neale Hurston's *Mules and Men* (1935) confronts popularized versions of African-American "folklore" such as those presented by Joel Chandler Harris in his *Uncle Remus* tales (1880, 1883). Hurston situates the oral tales in a social context and examines the ways in which race, class, and gender affect their gathering and narration, in contrast to Harris, who sanitizes the tales by placing them in an idealized plantation context. Novelistic collections of oral traditions, then, can be employed to present the conditions of culture, as Hurston does, or to occlude them, as Harris does. These very different fictional frames allow for an analysis of the crossing of cultures and disciplines. Namely, writing down these oral traditions registers trans-cultural exchanges—or, in today's popular terminology, the multicultural bases of U.S. literature and ethnography.

Among the first so-called native anthropologists to collect African-American oral tales were Arthur Huff Fauset and Zora Neale Hurston, in the 1920s (Hemenway, *Hurston*, 87, 90). Prior to that, Joel Chandler Harris had been hailed by the *New York Times* as collecting "the first real book of American folklore" (Hemenway, "Author," 14). This first collection of tales was originally titled *Uncle Remus's Folk-Lore* but was renamed *Uncle Remus: His Songs and His Sayings* to appeal to the popular market at Christmas (Baer, "Harris," 189). My goal in this essay is

155

not merely to identify the precedents set by Harris and by Hurston in the field of folklore, but to examine how each author anticipates, to varying degrees, recent efforts to acknowledge intersections of anthropological and literary narratives.[1] An analysis of their rhetorical and social stances makes explicit the extent to which recognizing that culture and history are comprised of texts, as theorized in postmodern reformulations of literary and anthropological studies, is not of itself cause for celebration and can preserve intact the very boundaries ostensibly in question.

In this context, Harris retains interest beyond the critical paradigms that have denounced him for his blatant racism or attempted to redeem him by arguing that he subverts racism.[2] Another, as yet unexamined facet of his work is his use of both literature and anthropology, one of the most important ways in which he presents race and culture in the South. Harris conveys his collection of African-American tales partly by establishing multiple frames around them. He provides a scholarly introduction, which appears in his first two collections, greatly expanded from eleven pages in *Uncle Remus: His Songs and His Sayings* to thirty-two pages in *Nights with Uncle Remus*. The collections develop the character of Uncle Remus from newspaper character sketches Harris had published in the Atlanta *Constitution*, beginning in the late 1870s. In his extended introduction, Harris focuses increasingly upon a comparativist examination of various bodies of oral tradition, including Native North and South American. His additions attempt to grant more authority to the ethnological value of his collection. To this end, he includes a glossary of terms to explicate tales given to the character of Daddy Jack, who speaks a Gullah dialect, and he also reprints a tale told in the creole of Louisiana.[3]

Harris makes a number of provocative statements in the introduction, centering on issues of race and the context of the tales. He apparently recognizes that the tales may be read as a response to slavery, claiming, "[I]t needs no scientific investigation to show why he selects as his hero the weakest and most harmless of all animals, and brings him out victorious in contests with the bear, the wolf, and the fox" (Harris, *Nights*, xiv). If he grants the tales a kind of subversive power here, in other statements he claims that the narrator he creates "has nothing but pleasant memories of the discipline of slavery" (xvii). Other contradictions fracture his scholarship. His estimate that the tales originated in Africa (xiv) has been borne out by folklorists' research that traces over two-thirds of the tales to African analogues (Baer, *Sources*, 168–169). But he also suggests that the tales are "plantation lore" told to a young white boy who is the product of the reconstruction of the South (xvii). Given his attempt to preserve the dialect and the tales, which he perceives to be disappearing (xvii), and his claim that the white child represents the New South, his nostalgic reconstruction of antebellum plantation life effectively places the dialect, the tales, and the people who tell them in the agrarian past, while anticipating a white, industrial future.

But most prominent in his collection is the fictional frame that introduces, and is central to, the collection proper. The fictional frame opens with the white boy's mother, who misses her son and finds him in Uncle Remus's cabin, sitting on Uncle Remus's lap. As she looks through the window at them, she listens to the story that Uncle Remus tells the boy. Harris introduces the tale by writing, "This is what she heard," placing the reader in the position of Miss Sally, overhearing what the seventy-year-old black man tells the seven-year-old white boy. The reader is implicitly white, and the narrative also conveys the desires of Uncle Remus's white auditor. In the tales themselves, in which Brer Rabbit trounces Brer Fox in nineteen of twenty encounters, the little boy wants a linear progression of tales, tracing animal protagonists from one episode to another.

Uncle Remus insists upon telling the tales his way, but in the final portions of the book, Harris leaves Uncle Remus, the plantation story-teller, behind and begins to present linear catalogues of material. The enumeration of different African-American sayings, like the other final sections of the book, serves to impose a sense of closure that writes history with a bias for the Old Plantation as it is revisited by the New South. Harris lists "Plantation Proverbs and Songs" and tells "A Story of the War," in which Uncle Remus describes how he shot a Union soldier who was threatening one of his white owners. As if this Confederate War story served as a transition to the New South, the book ends with a series of character sketches, with Uncle Remus in postwar Atlanta. Harris makes no attempt to reconcile the two different Uncle Remus characters, except in the loyalty to authority that they both express. Indeed, the collection ends with a sketch titled "The Fourth of July." In later presentations of Uncle Remus tales, such as in *Nights with Uncle Remus: Myths and Legends of the Old Plantation*, Harris emphasizes that the telling of the tales takes place on a plantation before the war, a contrast from his first collection, in which Harris had Uncle Remus refer to the war. The later works, through eight subsequent volumes, emphasize the re-creation of a romanticized view of the Old Plantation and an evasion of the war and the Reconstruction that changed its nature and meaning. Thus Harris's fictional frame is grafted onto the African-American tales he presents, creating his version of a renascent South, one in which black people, ironically, play little part.

To acquire these tales, Harris relied on the memory of his time as a printer's apprentice on Turnwold Plantation from 1862 to 1866, and on tales he solicited. He took out a newspaper ad to request tales, explaining, "The purpose is to preserve these . . . myths in permanent form" (Wiggins 149). Harris wishes to preserve tales insofar as they fit the frame he establishes. The statement betrays a belief that cultural forms can be fixed or preserved, and does not allow for improvisation and transmission of cultural practices in different social and political contexts. As Talal Asad suggests, the assumption that cultures can be labeled and made into museum exhibits helped to propel anthropology as well as colonization. Harris attempts to fix African-American cultures in the past, and to align white American cultures with the present and future. This move exemplifies a fallacy that Johannes Fabian identifies in his book *Time and the Other* (1983): Harris denies the coeval existence of the differing cultures, using the flawed logic of cultural evolution. These teleological conceptions of culture contend that other people remain at a stage analogous to the European and white U.S. past, positing an inevitable delay in cultural development. The denial of coeval existence of cultures, such as Harris's, is one that postmodern anthropology explicitly attempts to revise, through emphasizing the literary qualities of anthropological narrative. Literary techniques, however, such as Harris's use of a fictional frame, may still support claims that one culture is more evolved than another.

On the other hand, recognizing the literary aspects of cultures or ethnologies allows us, as Hurston did, to emphasize the material conditions of cultures' coeval productions. Hurston uses literary and ethnological techniques quite differently from others, and this difference revises previous conceptions of black culture and serves to modify postmodern anthropology's embrace of playful narratives. Hurston, like Arthur Huff Fauset, presents works that critique "the Harris variety of the Negro folk tale [which] assumes to interpret Negro character instead of simply telling his stories" (Fauset quoted in Hemenway, *Hurston*, 90). Hurston's works reconsider not just Harris's collections but the very conceptions of culture and character—black and white—presupposed by "the Harris variety" of black oral narratives.[4] That is, Hurston's works revise the approach of a single author and re-evaluate the methods of an entire field.[5] She emphasizes the material conditions encountered by teller and listener, and insists upon depicting the means by which living oral traditions are transmitted to the writer.

In contrast to Harris, who removes himself from the tales he presents, Hurston introduces herself into her work—both *Mules and Men,* her collection of African-American oral tales, and *Tell My Horse,* her account of her research in Jamaica and Haiti—by specifying the nature of her fieldwork. Rather than presenting classifications and analysis, she describes how various factors shape the way the collection is formed, including her patronage, her education, her position in relation to intersections of race, gender, and class, and her allegiance to African-American culture as well as to her training in anthropology.

Hurston opens her narrative with an introduction that itself is framed by acknowledgments of her position. Her first statement conveys an implicit recognition of the way in which her research was sanctioned by others: "I was glad," she writes, "when somebody told me, 'You may go and collect Negro folklore'" (Hurston, *Mules and Men,* 1). Her opening words register the way in which her research proceeds at the behest of an as yet unnamed person. Hurston waits until the closing lines of her introduction to explicitly identify the person to whom she is indebted. Poised outside of the body of the collection, and holding her readers with her at the outskirts of her hometown of Eatonville, Florida, Hurston writes, "Before I enter the township, I wish to make acknowledgements to Mrs. R. Osgood Mason of New York City. She backed my calling in a hearty way, in a spiritual way, and in addition, financed the whole expedition in the manner of the Great Soul that she is. The world's most gallant woman" (4). The introduction opens and closes by placing Hurston as a recorder and transmitter of African-American culture.

But Hurston introduces her readers to more than this frame might at first suggest. Indeed, her introduction urges readers to recognize the difficulties involved in gathering oral traditions. She suggests that African Americans have perfected a means of fooling outsiders, particularly whites. In a passage that appears in quotation marks but is not attributed to any person or character, Hurston conveys the voice of an individual who speaks for the community:

The theory behind our tactics: "The white man is always trying to know into somebody else's business. All right, I'll set something outside the door of my mind for him to play with and handle. He can read my writing but he sho' can't read my mind. I'll put this play toy in his hand, and he will seize it and go away. Then I'll say my say and sing my song." (3)

The passage conveys the difficulty of getting access to African-American oral narratives, identifying a specific tactic and theory that complicate matters for the white interlocutor.

But the passage also questions the ability of written narratives—even those set forth by African Americans—to capture the "business" of African-American culture. Hurston's own narrative, by extension, poses a subtle challenge. Readers can read her writing, but we cannot read her mind. Hurston thus exploits her simultaneous status as insider and outsider to the oral communities in question, and ruptures the very frame of white audience that she identifies in her own introduction.

Hurston continues to emphasize her own role in making contact with people of the three communities she enters and in collecting the tales in the American South. She describes how she listens, prays, argues, sings, dances, and laughs with her interlocutors. This feature of her book allows a revised reading of her narrative's politics. Hazel Carby has remarked that in *Their Eyes Were Watching God* Hurston creates an idealized rural folk community, eliding the urban migrations of that period, and the same criticism could be extended to *Mules and Men*. Nevertheless, Hurston depicts her own position within the rural community, describing herself in Eatonville's terms as "just Lucy Hurston's daughter, Zora" (2).[6] While her statement could be an authorizing gesture, suggesting that she has access to the people, Hurston also acknowledges the potential dangers of the anthropological quest, choosing to return to Eatonville because she could get material there "without hurt, harm or danger" (2). The communities she conveys are rural, but they are not idealized.

Hurston thus calls attention to her own role in producing the collection. She places the conventions of literary and anthropological narrative at the forefront of her work, emphasizing the ways in which she gathers and connects the tales to one another. The persona she creates is instrumental to the entire book. Far from presenting what Hemenway called a "self-effacing narrator" (*Hurston* 164) in *Mules and Men*, Hurston predicates her narrative upon the position of her narrator in relation to the subjects she interviews.

Hurston emphasizes her own physical presence in Eatonville, in Polk County, and in the Hoodoo community in New Orleans. She acknowledges her sexuality and the appeal she presents to various men she meets along the way, a feature of the power relationship between ethnographer and subject that complicates claims of objectivity. In the Polk County lumbermill camp, for instance, she moves from social badinage with men to identifying her primary purpose of gathering oral tales or "lies." Hurston's passage registers the function of power created by gender, sexuality, and money:

"Miss, you know uh heap uh dese hard heads wants to woof at you but dey skeered."

"How come, Mr. Pitts? Do I look like a bear or panther?"

"Naw, but dey say youse rich and dey ain't got de nerve to open dey mouf." (Hurston, *Mules and Men*, 63)

Hurston manages to assuage this anxiety by proffering the explanation that her expensive dress and car were bought with bootlegging money. The lie not only enables her to enter the community and take part in their singing and dancing, but gains her access to their "lies," in this case the oral stories that Hurston seeks.

But Hurston's position remains a bit precarious: although the men find her appealing and respond to the "lying contest" that she initiates, some women view her as a threat. Men compete for the prizes Hurston offers in the lying contest, and gendered power is at issue in Hurston's reception in the community. In one passage, Hurston conveys the ways in which black women present themselves and are interpreted by observers. Her narrative both calls attention to the image of heterosexual desire and participates in it. In fact, the woman's walk interrupts Hurston's gathering of tales:

Tookie Allen passed by the mill all dressed up in a tight shake-baby [a dress]. She must have thought she looked good because she was walking that way. All the men stopped talking for a while. Joe Willard hollered at her.

"Hey, Tookie, how do you like your new dress?"

Tookie made out she didn't hear, but anybody could tell that she had. That was why she had put on her new dress, and come past the mill a wringing and twisting—so she could hear the men talking about her in the dress. (91)

The tale-telling stops, while the men, and, later, Hurston's readers, encounter the figure of the woman. Tookie stages her own identity through her physical presentation of herself. In this scene, men break off from speaking about oral traditions and articulate desire. Tookie, meanwhile, remains silent. Hurston complicates this presentation of gender, though, through the creation of her own narrative. Her account is informed by both the written and the oral, the word and the body.

Hurston's own body becomes a focus of attention when she is threatened by Ella and Lucy. Hurston escapes Lucy's open knife with the aid of a woman and a few men from the camp. The camp's turmoil, though, continues to rage, even as Hurston and her narrative leave the community. Hurston and her readers escape the fight catalyzed by the outsider's presence in the community:

Slim stuck out the guitar to keep two struggling men from blocking my way. Lucy was screaming. Crip had hold of Big Sweet's clothes in the back and Joe was slugging him loose. Curses, oaths, cries and the whole place was in motion. Blood was on the floor. I fell out of the door over a man lying on the steps, who either fell himself trying to run or got knocked down. I don't know. I was in the car in a second and in high just too quick. (179)

Hurston employs the mobility afforded by her car to escape a violent situation.

As Graciela Hernández remarks in her essay on Hurston's experimental ethnographies, "those trapped in the dance hall experience the bloodshed and chaos precipitated by her presence" (Hernández 161). While Hurston does "destabilize her own interpretive authority," as Hernández suggests (161), this scene extends a more complicated power exchange. In this scene, Hurston's interpretive authority is not really questioned, for she is able to leave behind the chaos of the dance hall and to impose closure. That particular narrative strategy recurs in ethnography, and reinforces rather than challenges the observer's authority. Hurston calls attention to the effort that founds ethnographic or literary narratives, conveying the Hoodoo practitioners' initial suspicion of her in the next section. But she also relies upon her ability to escape the community she has been observing, and to create a meaningful narrative even out of chaos.

In the history of anthropology, Hurston's importance is becoming increasingly evident. She was one of the earliest trained scholars of the emerging discipline, and one of the first "native" anthropologists. St. Clair Drake provides a history of African-American involvement in anthropology, identifying how devastatingly consistent were efforts to steer African Americans away from the discipline. Hurston's efforts went beyond even anthropologist Franz Boas's challenge to theories of cultural evolution, protesting against caricatured, popularized presentation of African-American characters, and depicting her interlocutors in varied interactions with one another and her.[7] Boas writes, in his often mentioned but rarely analyzed three-paragraph introduction to *Mules and Men*, that Hurston presents "the intimate setting in the social life of the Negro," which has been missing in most accounts of tales, songs, and sayings. She does so, Boas claims, because she "entered into the homely life of the southern Negro as one of them." This formulation does not take into account Hurston's own presentation of her double vision and double voice, where she breaks down any ostensible stability or opposition between cultural insider and outsider. But in addition, Boas's presentation of the way in which Hurston's account contributes to "our knowledge of the true inner life of the Negro" fails to acknowledge the challenges Hurston makes to the supposedly stable position of those whose knowledge is increased (Boas xiii).[8]

Her challenge lies in her rupturing concepts of cultural purity and essence, without leveling cultural differences. In her introduction to *Mules and Men,* she presents her culture as a garment, something extrinsic, in her description of how "it was fitting me like a tight chemise. I couldn't see it for wearing it. It was only when I was off in college, away from my native surroundings, that I could see myself like somebody else and stand off and look at my garment. Then I had to have the spy-glass of Anthropology to look through at that" (1). The spyglass of anthropology does not clarify matters, however, but reveals "peculiar amalgamations" of cultures, languages, clothes, and technology. The spyglass may be turned in any number of directions, including upon oneself, and Hurston does precisely this throughout the narrative. Hurston's image of the ways in which culture's garment may be seen radically anticipates and amplifies postmodern practices in anthropology and claims about the invented nature of culture and science.[9]

Scholars of the history of anthropology, such as the contributors to Eric Hobsbawm and Terence Ranger's *The Invention of Tradition,* suggest that much of what has been defined in various contexts—nativist, nationalist, and anthropological—as traditional or pure culture was in fact invented during the colonial period. Both imperial and resistance forces attempted to create and codify "pure" cultures to achieve their divergent agendas. These forces, however, created something that had not existed before. Hurston anticipates the recognition that there is no static or essential culture in her refusal to simplify the meeting between divergent cultural practices.[10]

Her use of literary and ethnological conventions to narrate her own return home conveys a reflexive awareness of new forms created by cultures' meetings. In two tales at different points in Hurston's *Mules and Men,* tellers of tales present the difficulty of transcribing or translating verbal or oral traditions after formal education has provided distance from those traditions.[11] The first occurs in Hurston's transcription of tales told in Eatonville. A daughter, having been educated for seven years, returns home and attempts to write a letter for her father, but cannot convey in writing a clucking sound he makes. The father asks,

"How come you ain't got it?"
"Cause Ah can't spell (clucking sound)."
"You mean to tell me you been off to school seben years and can't spell (clucking sound)? Why Ah could spell dat myself and

Ah ain't been to school a day in mah life. Well jes' say (clucking
sound) he'll know what yo' mean and go on wid de letter. (41)

Hurston marks the points in her narrative at which oral sounds cannot
be translated directly or completely into writing. She emphasizes the
act of translation: from uttering to inscribing words, from one set of
narrative conventions to another, from one community to another. Her
own text is predicated upon bringing oral speech within the compass of
writing, but she by no means elevates one tradition over another. In fact,
part of the challenge of her text is to acknowledge the ways in which
narrative traditions inform and interrupt one another.

The second tale is one of those told in Polk County. A boy was educated at college for seven years, until he "schooled out" and came home,
only to find himself unable to help his parents milk an unruly cow (125–
127).[12] The disruptive animal illustrates the gulf between the boy's
book learning and practical experience. But it also exemplifies, according to its teller, the saying "'a man can cackerlate his life till he git
mixed up wid a woman or git straddle of a cow'" (124). Despite the
teller's protestations to the contrary, the unruly cow is compared to the
woman, Big Sweet, who speaks and "signifies" when she wishes, con-
founding expectations. In Hurston's narrative, the authorial persona
and other women work within and beyond the positions assigned to
them.

Hurston's *Tell My Horse* conveys a similar awareness of how her own
position structures her research experience. In that narrative, however,
Hurston feminizes the landscape of the Caribbean countries, as in references to Jamaica's "sensuous bosom." This feminization threatens to
replicate the tradition of imperialistic imagery associated with the Caribbean, and her image of "peeping in" on the Caribbean peoples implies eavesdropping rather than personal engagement. This implication
is carried through to Hurston's decreased focus on her own structuring
of the cultural texts produced in her fieldwork and in her narrative.

In presenting oral tales, both Joel Chandler Harris and Zora Neale
Hurston create a return to a childhood home, but their different degrees
of acknowledgment of how, why, and for whom the collector gathers the
tales produce disparate narratives. Harris encloses the tales in a plantation setting and pretends that they are immediately accessible to him,
while Hurston acknowledges the difficulty of gathering them. Their
narratives suggest that the practice of postmodern anthropology, which
has the benefit of recognizing cultures as being composed of texts,
needs to be further revised. Current models too often simply allow the
anthropologist to ironize his or her position without accounting for the
material conditions surrounding it. The blurred boundaries that are so

touted in prominent literary and anthropological postmodernism occur in conditions that are repressive as well as generative or productive, across and within each constituent and changing boundary. Hurston exposes the process of speaking and writing cultures into being through asymmetrical interactions within and among peoples. Her work thus anticipates current recognition of the need for trans-disciplinary and trans-cultural scholarship. She refuses to retain unexamined assumptions of cultural isolation or self-sufficiency. Her work thus establishes the undeniable multicultural bases of U.S. written and oral literatures.

Notes

1. Joel Chandler Harris repeatedly characterized himself as a mere journalist or "compiler" of folktales, although his self-description may have been part of the public image he wished to present (Bickley 39). Zora Neale Hurston's work, in particular, has drawn criticism from both literary critics and anthropologists. An anthropologist who has assessed her anthropological work rationalizes her "fluctuations" as resulting from economic contingencies: "Her fluctuations between literature and anthropology caused some to consider her an anthropological dilettante. The fluctuations may have reflected, not choice, but a movement in the changing directions of that which was necessary to earn a living" (Mikell 164). Similarly, her challenge to boundaries is criticized by a literary scholar who suggests that "there is no evidence of the scholarly procedures which would be expected from a formally trained anthropologist or researcher in folklore." Furthermore, "[i]t cannot be said in her defense that Miss Hurston regarded the folklore with the eye of a novelist rather than a scholar" (Turner 117). Thus, it is reductive to classify Hurston's texts as either literature or anthropology, as some have done. One recent commentator on Hurston's folklore claims, "*Mules and Men* is literature rather than ethnography through the clear intention of its author" (Dolby-Stahl 54). Rather, Hurston's text is both, regardless of her intention.

2. Wayne Mixon provides a brief acknowledgment of the critical tradition that recognizes Harris's obvious racism, including statements by W. E. B. Du Bois, but then tries to argue that Harris presents the "ultimate irrelevance of race."

3. Linguists and folklorists long denied the influence of African language and culture on African-American speech, including speech in English and Gullah. Shelley Fisher Fishkin, tracing the influence of African Americans on Mark Twain's work, notes that one of the first scholars familiar with African languages was Lorenzo Turner, whose 1949 *Africanisms in the Gullah Dialect* examined the substantive linguistic presence of Africa in the U.S.

4. In his article "That Which the Soul Lives By," Hemenway points to the

significant way in which Hurston's collections of tales modified Harris's: "Black identity receives expression in Afro-American folklore because folklore permits the presentation of emotions so deeply felt that they often cannot be openly articulated. Hurston understood this process in a way Joel Chandler Harris did not. The Uncle Remus tales are always told from within the plantation tradition; the context is always a serene, kindly old darky relating animal tales to pre-adolescents—the mask is never dropped" (Hemenway, "That Which the Soul," 90). Hemenway's article, which was originally his introduction to a 1978 edition of Hurston's *Mules and Men,* introduces briefly in these sentences the important ways in which she modifies Harris. Another note on Hurston's revision of Harris is offered by Dana McKinnon Preu in "A Literary Reading of *Mules and Men,* Part I" (1991), when she quotes Hemenway: "Hemenway contrasts the 'heuristic function' of the animal tales of black culture with the tales' reduction to 'pediatric literature' in either Joel Chandler Harris's or Walt Disney's literate Uncle Remus setting" (Preu 55). An extended examination of both writers' works reveals the distinct methods they use to present their differing views of black oral literature and culture.

5. More is at issue here than establishing an intentionalist reading of Hurston. Such an approach would suggest her deliberate return to Harris's presentation of folklore, and to some degree would lock her into a response to the earlier writer's works. Rather, Hurston modifies the entire field of folklore, offering as she does an innovative presentation of black oral literature and culture that accounts for the circumstances of narrative production and transmission.

6. Hurston's identifying herself as a daughter and acknowledging the role that position plays in creating her narrative anticipates a later attempt on Alice Walker's part to claim Hurston as a foremother, in what has been termed a collaborative relationship (Smith-Wright 21). Walker aligns herself with Hurston in essays like "Looking for Zora" and her account of Hurston as a "cultural revolutionary" in "Zora Neale Hurston: A Cautionary Tale and a Partisan View," both included in her *In Search of Our Mothers' Gardens.*

7. Hurston presents cultures as coeval, and sometimes even moves toward depicting culture as universal. As Lynda Hill points out in *Social Rituals and the Verbal Art of Zora Neale Hurston,* Hurston had noted, in a draft of an essay titled "Folklore," that folklore is "a world and an ageless thing." The revised version of the essay, later published as "Go Gator, and Muddy the Water," proclaims, "Folklore is the boiled-down juice of human living. It does not belong to any special time, place nor people" (Hill 78).

8. Hurston's own preface to her work mentions another problematic figure in her life, her patron, Mrs. R. Osgood Mason, who attempted to control Hurston's collections of folklore, forbidding Hurston to publish her work without Mason's prior consent. Hurston is placed in a position, financially and institutionally, where she is considered by her "godmother" (Hemen-

way, *Zora Neale Hurston,* 104) to be a native informant, a representative of a race and culture that is supposedly at an earlier stage, according to the model of cultural evolution.

9. Among the ethnographies that attempt to openly acknowledge the elements of biography, autobiography, story-telling, and even invention as important constituents of their narratives are Marjorie Shostak's *Nisa,* Loring Danforth's *Firewalking and Religious Healing,* and Barbara Myerhoff's *Number Our Days.* Renato Rosaldo, James Clifford, George Marcus, and Michael Fischer are some of the contemporary anthropological theorists who have focused on such attempts at revising methods of social analysis.

10. In both of her collections, Hurston closes the narrative with a folktale before moving on to an appendix. She refuses to provide categories or limit interpretations, simply presenting the songs in *Tell My Horse* with their musical notations. The songs appear in an appendix divided into two sections, "Songs of Worship to the Voodoo Gods" and "Miscellaneous Songs."

11. Hurston's presentation of black speech is important in the history of both literature and anthropology. In *"Their Eyes Were Watching God:* Hurston and the Speakerly Text," Henry Louis Gates, Jr., notes the differing presentations of dialect in Hurston and in Harris: "Dialect signified both 'black difference' and that the figure of the black in literature existed primarily as object, not subject; and even sympathetic characterizations of the black, such as Uncle Remus by Joel Chandler Harris, were far more related to a racist textual tradition that stemmed from minstrelsy, the plantation novel, and vaudeville than to representations of spoken language" (Gates 160).

12. In her short story collection *Spunk,* for example, Hurston follows "Story in Harlem Slang," with a "Glossary of Harlem Slang" that is of almost equal length. Hurston portrays the ways in which speech and slang translate partially into formal writing. She emphasizes that speech and slang exceed even the glossaries and supplements she provides.

Works Consulted

Abrahams, Roger D., ed. *Afro-American Folktales.* New York: Pantheon Books, 1985.

Asad, Talal, ed. *Anthropology and the Colonial Encounter.* New York: Humanities Press, 1973.

Baer, Florence E. "Joel Chandler Harris: An 'Accidental' Folklorist." In *Critical Essays on Joel Chandler Harris,* edited by R. Bruce Bickley, Jr., 185–195. Boston: G. K. Hall, 1981.

———. *Sources and Analogues of the Uncle Remus Tales.* Helsinki: Academia Scientiarum Fennica, 1980.

Bickley, R. Bruce, Jr. *Joel Chandler Harris.* 1978. Athens: University of Georgia Press, 1987.

Boas, Franz. Introduction to *Mules and Men,* by Zora Neale Hurston. 1935. Reprint, New York: Harper Perennial, 1990.

Carby, Hazel. "The Politics of Fiction, Anthropology, and the Folk: Zora Neale Hurston." In *New Essays on* Their Eyes Were Watching God, edited by Michael Awkward, 71–93. New York: Cambridge University Press, 1990.

Clifford, James. *The Predicament of Culture.* Cambridge: Harvard University Press, 1988.

Clifford, James, and George E. Marcus, eds. *Writing Culture.* Berkeley: University of California Press, 1986.

Dolby-Stahl, Sandra. "Literary Objectives: Hurston's Use of Personal Narrative in *Mules and Men.*" *Western Folklore* 51, no. 1 (1992): 51–63.

Drake, St. Clair. "Anthropology and the Black Experience." *The Black Scholar* 11, no. 7 (1980): 2–31.

Fabian, Johannes. *Time and the Other: How Anthropology Makes Its Object.* New York: Columbia University Press, 1983.

Fishkin, Shelley Fisher. *Was Huck Black? Mark Twain and African-American Voices.* New York: Oxford University Press, 1993.

Gates, Henry Louis, Jr. "*Their Eyes Were Watching God:* Hurston and the Speakerly Text." In *Zora Neale Hurston: Critical Perspectives Past and Present,* edited by Henry Louis Gates, Jr., and K. A. Appiah, 154–203. New York: Amistad, 1993.

Glassman, Steve, and Kathryn Lee Seidel, eds. *Zora in Florida.* Orlando: University of Central Florida Press, 1991.

Harris, Joel Chandler. *Nights with Uncle Remus: Myths and Legends of the Old Plantation.* Boston and New York: Houghton Mifflin, 1883.

———. *Uncle Remus: His Songs and His Sayings.* 1880. Reprint, New York: Hawthorn, 1921.

Hemenway, Robert E. "Author, Teller, and Hero." Introduction to *Uncle Remus: His Songs and His Sayings,* by Joel Chandler Harris, 7–47. New York: Penguin, 1982.

———. "That Which the Soul Lives By." In *Modern Critical Views on Zora Neale Hurston,* edited by Harold Bloom, 83–95. New York: Chelsea House, 1986.

———. *Zora Neale Hurston: A Literary Biography.* Chicago: University of Illinois Press, 1977.

Hernández, Graciela. "Multiple Subjectivities and Strategic Positionality: Zora Neale Hurston's Experimental Ethnographies." In *Women Writing Culture,* edited by Ruth Behar and Deborah A. Gordon, 148–165. Berkeley: University of California Press, 1995.

Hill, Lynda Marion. *Social Rituals and the Verbal Art of Zora Neale Hurston.* Washington, D.C.: Howard University Press, 1996.

Hobsbawm, Eric, and Terence Ranger, eds. *The Invention of Tradition.* Cambridge: Cambridge University Press, 1983.

Hurston, Zora Neale. *Mules and Men*. With an introduction by Franz Boas. 1935. Reprint, New York: Harper Perennial, 1990.

———. *Spunk*. Berkeley: Turtle Island Foundation, 1985.

———. *Tell My Horse: Voodoo and Life in Haiti and Jamaica*. 1938. Reprint, New York: Harper and Row, 1990.

Johnson, Barbara. "Thresholds of Difference: Structures of Address in Zora Neale Hurston." In *Zora Neale Hurston: Critical Perspectives*, edited by Henry Louis Gates, Jr., and K. A. Appiah, 130–140. New York: Amistad, 1993.

Marcus, George E., and Michael M. J. Fischer. *Anthropology as Cultural Critique*. Chicago: University of Chicago Press, 1986.

Mikell, Gwendolyn. "Zora Neale Hurston." In *Women Anthropologists: A Biographical Dictionary*, edited by Ute Gacs et al., 160–166. New York: Greenwood Press, 1988.

Mixon, Wayne. "The Ultimate Irrelevance of Race: Joel Chandler Harris and Uncle Remus in Their Time." *Journal of Southern History* 56, no. 3 (1990): 457–480.

Preu, Dana McKinnon. "A Literary Reading of *Mules and Men*, Part I." In *Zora in Florida*, edited by Steve Glassman and Kathryn Lee Seidel, 46–61. Orlando: University of Central Florida Press, 1991.

Smith-Wright, Geraldine. "Revision as Collaboration: Zora Neale Hurston's *Their Eyes Were Watching God* as Source for Alice Walker's *The Color Purple*." *Sage* 4, no. 2 (1987): 20–25.

Turner, Darwin T. *In a Minor Chord*. Carbondale: Southern Illinois University Press, 1971.

Wainwright, Mary Katherine. "Subversive Female Folk Tellers in *Mules and Men*." In *Zora in Florida*, edited by Steve Glassman and Kathryn Lee Seidel, 62–75. Orlando: University of Central Florida Press, 1991.

Walker, Alice. *In Search of Our Mothers' Gardens*. Orlando: Harcourt Brace, 1983.

Wiggins, Robert Lemuel. *The Life of Joel Chandler Harris*. Nashville: Methodist Publishing House, Smith and Lamar, 1918.

Wolfe, Bernard. "Uncle Remus and the Malevolent Rabbit: 'Takes a Limber-Toe Gemmun fer ter Jump Jim Crow.'" In *Critical Essays on Joel Chandler Harris*, edited by R. Bruce Bickley, Jr., 70–84. Boston: G. K. Hall, 1981.

Eleven

Abby Kelley Foster
A Feminist Voice Reconsidered, 1810–1887

Richard E. Greene

On Friday, April 12, 1861, a telegram was read at the regular session of
the Ohio State Senate announcing that Fort Sumter, South Carolina,
had been fired upon by Southern troops. The news was greeted in
stunned silence by the members, including a future American president, James A. Garfield. Suddenly that silence was broken by a strident
scream from the visitor's gallery. Abby Kelley Foster, a radical member
of the most militant segment of the anti-slavery crusade, cried out,
"Glory to God!" The good people of Ohio and the Oberlin College
faculty and administration, where Abby Kelley Foster had been debating slavery issues, had not much in common with her, but most of them,
like her, now seemed to welcome the impending conflict.[1]

The story of the decade that ended with the firing on Fort Sumter
reveals the role of the abolitionists in making the nation face the issue
of slavery. America thought it could contain slavery, but could not. The
radical abolitionists had finally reached a point in their crusade where
they advocated disunion from the South as the only logical way to rid
the country of this moral evil. However, it was the South that decided
to leave the Union, and the unavoidable conflict had become reality.
Many of the abolitionists had known that their moral agitation would
ultimately lead to a conflict between slavery and the United States'
democratic ideals. They had upset the ill-founded alliance between the
North and South. Their moral agitation had not caused the Civil War,
but it had played an indispensable part in precipitating the crisis that
led to war.

The story of the struggle against the inhuman system of slavery, the rise of abolitionism, and the pursuit of equal rights for African Americans and women is the story of Abby Kelley Foster. Several of her contemporaries, especially Lucy Stone, stated that America's women's rights movement began with Abby Kelley Foster.

She became the most famous—or notorious, according to her critics—woman abolitionist in America. For forty years as a moral agitator, this volatile Quaker led the fight to break down the barriers that forbade women to speak publicly before mixed audiences, to vote, and to own property. Equally as important, she was a leader in the anti-slavery movement and the postwar struggle to secure civil rights for all African Americans. She was determined, in Frederick Douglass's words, "to have a nation live up to its creed."[2]

Initially, she was a lonely, marginalized voice in this struggle for equality, but over five decades (1830–1880) she recruited hundreds of women to join her as active participants in the cause, and she converted thousands of Americans throughout the Northeast and the West to the principles of anti-slavery and equal rights for women. Several of her women recruits, such as Lucy Stone and Susan B. Anthony, assumed leadership roles in the women's rights movement.

In an outstanding example of early multiculturalism, Kelley[3] worked closely with African-American men and women in the anti-slavery effort. Frederick Douglass had been a free man for only three months when he joined Kelley in Rhode Island during Dorr's Rebellion in 1841–42. Sojourner Truth made her first extended anti-slavery tour with Kelley in 1851, and both she and Douglass traveled many times with Kelley through New York and the western states. Other prominent African-American women, such as Sarah Parker Remond and Frances Ellen Watkins Harper, accompanied Kelley on lecture tours throughout the country.

Abby Kelley Foster was America's first woman universal reformer, embracing every major reform movement of her social milieu, including temperance, peace and pacifism, anti-clericalism, disunionism, and the beginnings of trade unions. But this has never been fully recognized by historians. One of the major reasons for this oversight is that, during the post–Civil War period, she made the unpopular decision to actively support black suffrage over women's suffrage even though she considered equal rights for women to be an issue with broader social implications than black suffrage. But for her, it was a question of which one should take precedence. She had correctly determined that the country was ready to give the ballot to the freedmen but was not yet ready to extend it to women. Neither Elizabeth Cady Stanton nor Susan B. Anthony ever forgave Abby Kelley Foster for taking such a position, and in their later writings on the women's movement they refused to acknowledge her major contributions to the cause.

Converted to abolitionism by William Lloyd Garrison in 1829, she was one of his closest friends for the next four decades and had a profound influence on his thinking on issues such as the rights of women, anti-clericalism, and the anti-slavery secessionist movements of come-outerism and disunionism. Garrison, not given to compliments, told her, "Of all the women who have appeared upon the historic stage, I have always regarded you as peerless—the moral Joan of Arc of the world."[4]

During the second quarter of the nineteenth century a large number of humanitarian reform movements appeared, all motivated by a passionate desire to improve American society. The people of that era looked ahead to the day when an ideal society would exist in a perfect state. They were determined to reshape society in their image, to make it conform to their standards of morality, and to bring to fulfillment the promise of the American Revolution. "What is a man born for," Emerson once asked, "but to be a Reformer, a Remaker of what man has made?"[5]

The attempts to remake American society had many tangential aspects and covered a wide area of reform. They included, for example, the establishment of utopian communities, a temperance movement, pacifism, transcendentalism, support for women's rights, and a host of other reforms. But the noblest of all of these was the crusade to free the American slave.

The anti-slavery reformers of this generation went forth with an evangelical fury, an uncompromising spirit, and a belief that through their efforts they were advancing humankind closer to the ideal society. These apostles carried their message to every village hamlet of the North, to the vast western frontier, and even to the South. They appealed to the emotions and consciences of men, and openly denounced the United States government, the Constitution, and the established churches of the time. Finally, these agitators willingly exposed themselves to incredible hardships and sufferings in order to bring an end to the "peculiar institution."

Abby Kelley Foster was one of these reformers. Born in Pelham, Massachusetts, on January 15, 1810, she was the seventh of nine children fathered by Wing Kelley, an independent Irish Quaker farmer.[6] Wing Kelley's Quaker beliefs, which he passed to his daughter, led Abby to a concern about slavery and into the ranks of reform. She was typical of many of the earliest abolitionists of New England, especially Massachusetts. For these abolitionists, religion and freedom from slavery were rooted in the same belief system. Almost every one of them came from strong Puritan stock and the concern with sin was deep in their souls. "A sin against God," Garrison called slavery over and over again.[7] Sin, guilt, purification, and a gnawing conscience echoed ceaselessly in Kelley's mind.

The young reformer felt she had a divine call "to engage in the abolitionist movement"; it gave purpose and direction to her life. Abolition was the clarion call to action. The origin of her mission was explained in the only document that she ever wrote concerning her experiences.

> In order that you may understand certain peculiarities in my case, I must say a few words about my earlier anti-slavery life. I heard Mr. Garrison in Lynn in 1829 or 1830 on Colonization as no remedy for slavery. Next Arnold Buffum . . . the first agent of our first Society, the New England. From this time I did whatever I could to carry forward the work; distributing our publications, soliciting subscriptions to our journals, and raising funds for our societies . . . at length my whole soul was so filled with the subject that it would not leave me, even during my school hours.[8]

Thereupon Kelley began a crusade for reform that would span a period of fifty years, from 1830 to 1880. Her career paralleled William L. Garrison's in its intensities, trials, and persecutions.[9]

She entered into the fray with all the fight and vigor at her command. Spurred on by an evangelistic conscience, the quest for Christian perfection, and her strong belief in the equality of men and women, this young Quaker epitomized the religious struggle against slavery that was above politics and compromise. Slavery was totally evil and had to be obliterated immediately and forever. The "conspiracy of silence" about it was broken which had prevailed among Congress, government leaders, and churches since the Missouri Compromise, and she was ready to play a significant role in the anti-slavery movement.

However, a raging, bitter argument over women's role in the movement developed and ultimately resulted in a schism in the ranks of the abolitionists. In 1837 Kelley wrote to her brother Albert, "If you have read the *Liberators* I have sent you, you see what a change is going forward in public sentiment in relation to the rights and duties of women. Those who go in the forefront of this as well as all other reforms must inevitably bear all manner of censure, scorn, contempt, reproach and severe persecution. . . . the more persecution a good cause meets, the stronger of course is the evidence that there is the greater cause for its persecution."[10] Kelley was referring not only to herself but also to the Grimké sisters, who had now burst on the New England scene and helped to create a division in the anti-slavery forces.

The Grimké sisters were the first American women to lecture before mixed audiences, and men came in droves to hear "the thrilling tale of Carolina's high soul'd daughters."[11] Women's public role as speakers threatened a long-standing social structure perpetuated by religious organizations. It's not surprising, then, that the churches decided to take drastic action to curtail them. The Orthodox Congregational Churches issued an "Appeal of Clerical Abolitionists on Anti-Slavery Measures" which spoke out against public lectures by females and closed their churches to them. However, it was exhaustion, not the orthodox clergy, that stopped the sisters. In addition, Angelina Grimké, at the height of her career, was courted by and married Theodore Weld, the most dynamic abolitionist in the West, who feared that she had fallen under the "ultra" influences of the Garrisonians.[12] All three then retired to a farm at Fort Lee, New Jersey, and continued to write against slavery.

These Southern women "had pricked the conscience of the New Englanders with fire" in their short but spectacular career.[13] The torch was now passed to Abby Kelley Foster, who, inspired by the Grimké sisters, began to speak publicly against slavery. She was the first New England woman to speak before mixed audiences. Sara Moore Grimké wrote to her, "It seems to be very important to me that some New England women should practically assert the right to speak in public. . . . what thou hast done will do more towards establishing the rights of women on this point than a dozen books."[14]

The fact that she was one of the first American women to be heard on the public platform unavoidably linked anti-slavery with another cause. While speaking in defense of the slave, she was defending the right of a woman to speak in public. William L. Garrison had involuntarily become a pioneer of women's rights.[15] His newspaper *The Liberator* would now carry an additional department—a section called "Equal Rights"—devoted to the new crusade for women's rights.

During the late 1830s and 1840s, Kelley developed her skills in fundraising, organizing, and speaking. She launched an anti-slavery speaking campaign that took her through howling mobs, carried her up and down the Atlantic seaboard, and brought her crusade to the far reaches of the western frontier. In town after town, she was ridiculed and abused severely, yet she became one of the best-known women abolitionists of the time. Throughout the years, she recruited many women to both the anti-slavery and women's rights movements: Susan B. Anthony, Lucy Stone, Sallie H. Day, and hundreds of women who called themselves Abby Kelleyites.

More significantly, Kelley became the unquenchable feminine abolitionist, "the flying wedge of Garrisonian policy" that would split the American Anti-Slavery Society wide apart.[16] The events of the American Anti-Slavery Society's annual meeting in 1840 made Kelley a national figure. The movement, although committed to the abolition of slavery, was divided over women's rights, the roles of political parties and the church, and non-resistance. All the tensions and issues culminated in the question of whether a woman could be a full member of the Society. A majority thought yes: Abby Kelley Foster was nominated and elected to serve as a committee member. The vote split the Society into two camps, with many clergy and others walking out of the meeting, ceding control to the Garrisonians. The American Anti-Slavery Society was now ready to confront the American conservative tradition on the high road of moral idealism, a strategy that would eventually lead the states to secession and civil war.

In 1841–42, Kelley joined in Dorr's Rebellion in Rhode Island. Thomas Dorr led a party that had met as the People's Constitutional Convention, an assembly of no legitimate authority, and tried to influence the legislature to move toward broader suffrage. However, the delegates to the extra-legal People's Constitutional Convention ratified a clause of "whites only" suffrage, over the opposition of Dorr and his abolitionist backers. Kelley and others therefore opposed the proposed constitution, fighting the established church and the Rhode Island political establishment.[17]

The Rhode Island conflict brought together a number of anti-slavery speakers and agents from other parts of New England, including Frederick Douglass, who had escaped from slavery three years earlier but had been an active anti-slavery speaker for only a few months. He was joined by Stephen Foster, Kelley's future husband, and Parker Pillsbury, a well-known abolitionist, both of whom Kelley had met and worked with in New Hampshire in early 1841. Frederick Douglass wrote that Kelley "was perhaps the most successful of any of us. Her youth and simple Quaker beauty, combined with her wonderful earnestness, her large knowledge . . . bore down all opposition."[18]

In one of her many letters to *The Liberator*, Kelley described her attempts to support the right of all adults to be free and to vote:

I was there for six weeks since and held three meetings, the last of which was broken up by a mob of between 500 and 1000 which followed myself and friends to our lodging; rending the heavens with their fiendish shouts and pelting us with decayed apples, eggs, etc. Another time a meeting was closed by a mob. . . . While in Providence, the Mayor and the police officers were needed to restore order, but I spoke anyway.[19]

Despite the abuse heaped upon Kelley and Douglass, the results of their work in Rhode Island were impressive. Human rights had been expanded in a conservative state by the establishment of a more liberal constitution that omitted the word "white" and thus gave free black men the right to vote, while a woman (Lucinda Wilmarth) was to be appointed as an agent for the Rhode Island Anti-Slavery Society, and an African American (Frederick Douglass) was requested to become general agent for the whole state of Rhode Island.[20]

After the successful Rhode Island campaign, Douglass and Kelley continued to campaign together throughout the decade, especially in Massachusetts and the upper part of New York, where the population had increased dramatically since the Erie Canal's opening in 1825. Their goal in western New York was to rebuild the anti-slavery societies that had fallen apart after the 1840 split. They planned a series of both small and large conventions in Rochester, Syracuse, and Utica. "In court houses, town halls and picnic groves in good weather, Abby and Frederick held two conventions a week, each lasting two or three days. It was a punishing schedule, but they were rewarded by enthusiastic audiences almost everywhere."[21] Both believed in the power of newspapers to aid their cause. Kelley was a founder of the Ohio *Anti-Slavery Bugle* and maintained the New York *National Anti-Slavery Standard* through her fund-raising efforts. This latter paper eventually came in conflict with Frederick Douglass's New York paper, *The North Star.*

Frederick Douglass's successful British tour had helped him to raise funds to buy a new printing press. He was determined to publish his own newspaper as a sign of the equality of African Americans. Kelley, who had founded the Ohio *Anti-Slavery Bugle* and raised thousands of dollars for the *Standard,* was clearly upset by Douglass's plans to start his own newspaper. Writing to her husband Stephen, the unforgiving, uncompromising, and competitive Kelley noted, "I, for one, am not willing to trust the anti-slavery cause in the West to Douglass. I always have been and am still fearful of [him]. Do, I pray you, enforce on all the duty of sustaining the *Bugle.* Maybe we shall have to go out there next year to keep it afloat."[22]

Frederick Douglass broke away from Kelley and the Garrisonians in the 1850s on ideological grounds, but Kelley and Douglass reconciled after the war and remained friends until her death. In 1881 he wrote to Kelley, "I love to think of all who stand in our rapidly thinning ranks as well as the dear ones gone before us."[23]

During her campaign with Frederick Douglass, Kelley was requested by George Blackburn, a prominent Boston abolitionist, to write to Richard D. Webb of Dublin, Ireland, who was sympathetic to their struggle in Rhode Island—another significant step by the Garrisonians to promote the cause. Ireland was in revolt against England, demanding independence, and the Irish looked upon the abolitionists' fight as similar to their own. Correspondence between the two groups, such as the Kelley-Webb letters, resulted in a petition signed by the famed Daniel O'Connell and seventy thousand Irish men, urging their American brethren to support the abolitionists.[24] The Garrisonians also received funds from supporters in Great Britain who were opposed to slavery.

The Irish petition led Garrison to remark that he was "both an Irish Repealer and an American Repealer. I go for the repeal of the union between the North and the South."[25] The institution now marked for destruction was the American union. The radical Garrisonians, including Kelley, became convinced that Northern secession was necessary, which became known as "the doctrine of disunionism."

As Kelley preached the doctrine of disunionism, she also took up the cause of another secessionist movement, called "come-outerism" because its believers advocated "coming out" of corrupt churches that either maintained silence on slavery or supported the right of whites to own slaves. One of the leading figures of this movement was Stephen Foster, who had convinced Kelley and Garrison that the people of the North needed to develop a moral conscience over slavery, and that it was not going to develop within the Northern churches. One could not seek perfectionism by staying in a church that did not take a stand against slavery and for women's rights. However, before Kelley was to spread these two doctrines through the West, marriage awaited her.

Kelley and Stephen Foster planned to be married in December of 1845 in Pennsylvania, since a marriage ceremony there did not require a minister or magistrate to officiate. In the Quaker tradition, they had drawn up their own wedding certificate.[26] It was addressed "To whom it may concern" and certified that Stephen S. Foster and Abby Kelley had that day "consummated a matrimonial connection . . . by a public declaration of our mutual affection." There was no vow of obedience, but a simple promise "to perform faithfully all the relative duties of husband and wife."[27] Their marriage was based on equality, and both were committed to continuing their reform careers, though Abby did assume the married name of Foster. They raised their daughter, Alla, according to the latest child-rearing ideas, actually reversing traditional lifestyles, for after the birth of their daughter Kelley resumed her abolitionist work and Stephen raised Alla and ran their home in Worcester, Massachusetts. They named it "Liberty Farm" and made it a station on the Underground Railroad; it sheltered many fugitive slaves on their flight to Canada.

During the late 1840s and 1850s, one of the most significant areas where their efforts were rewarded was the West. With Sojourner Truth (who made her first extended anti-slavery tour with Kelley in 1851),

Sallie Holley, and Francis Wright as companions, the volatile Kelley headed into Michigan, Minnesota, and Wisconsin, spreading the anti-slavery gospel of disunionism—a peaceful separation of North and South. Kelley brought to the West an uncompromising faith in Garrisonian moral standards, a sharp, biting tongue that knifed through any opposition, and an amazing ability to spellbind great masses of people and convert them to her ideals. Stephen Foster joined her on the western frontier, and together they also fought for other leading reform movements, including the peace and temperance movements.

After several years of campaigning throughout the West, Stephen Foster wrote to his wife, "There is nothing that can be done here in the West to save the Disunion Movement—unless the question is carried to the ballot box."[28] Kelley agreed that the disunionism doctrine was not being accepted in the West, and therefore she attempted to spur Garrison and his followers to political action by advocating the creation of a new political party. The Garrisonians, however, chose to become supporters of the Republican party, which led to the successful campaign of Abraham Lincoln and brought the South to secession.

During the Civil War, Kelley fought for the Emancipation Proclamation and the Thirteenth Amendment, which abolished slavery throughout the nation. With the amendment's passage, Garrison and his followers were convinced their work was done and moved to have the Massachusetts Anti-Slavery Society dissolved, but Kelley, with the fire still flashing in her eyes, protested strongly that their work was not done until the freed slaves were guaranteed full civil rights.[29] Kelley continued the fight for the rights of African Americans. Although tired and worn down by ill health, she continued to campaign unceasingly with the Radical Republicans until the passage of the Fourteenth Amendment in 1868, which gave African Americans civil rights. After nearly forty years of campaigning, that cause had finally been won.

The civil rights protests of the 1960s, however, clearly substantiated Kelley's argument that the civil rights granted by the amendment needed to be protected. It took America nearly one hundred years to do so, with the passage of the Civil Rights Act of 1964.

As important as her crusade against slavery was, Kelley's impact on women's rights was equally significant. As she organized campaigns, raised thousands of dollars for the cause, and became one of the first women to speak out across America, her commitment, courage, and determination aroused many other women to follow her. She recruited everywhere she went, and trained women such as Lucy Stone, Susan B. Anthony, and countless others to work first for the anti-slavery cause and then for women's rights. Lucy Stone reflected on Kelley's commitment by stating, "Abby Kelley earned for us the right of free speech. The movement for equal rights of women began directly and emphatically with her."[30]

During Kelley's New York tour in the 1840s she went several times to Seneca Falls, a small village in upstate New York, "to shake up" the people and especially to involve the women in her anti-slavery "revivals"[31] This excitement eventually led a number of anti-slavery women who were also interested in women's rights to hold the first women's rights convention there, in 1848. Frederick Douglass, Elizabeth Stanton, and Lucretia Mott all spoke at great length on this issue. The 1848 Seneca Falls convention was followed by two more regional women's rights conventions, in Rochester, New York, and Salem, Ohio. Abby Kelley and her friends now believed it was time to hold a national women's rights convention.

At the conclusion of the annual meeting of the New England Anti-Slavery Society in May of 1850, Abby Kelley, Lucy Stone, Paulina Wright, and a number of other women came together. They wanted to call a national meeting of all those interested in promoting equal rights for women. The first National Woman's Rights Convention was held in Kelley's hometown of Worcester, Massachusetts, on October 26, 1850. Paulina Wright prepared a call that was signed by eighty-nine prominent citizens, including Ralph Waldo Emerson, Abby Kelley, Lucy Stone, and Wendell Phillips. The convention was an overwhelming success. Every seat in the auditorium was taken and thousands more surrounded the hall. Although men outnumbered women inside, the women were determined to run the meeting. Sojourner Truth, Abby Kelley, Dr. Harriot Hunt (one of America's first female medical doctors), Lucy Stone, William Lloyd Garrison, Frederick Douglass, and Stephen Foster all spoke in favor of women's rights. The proceedings of the convention were printed in the press, and for the first time people throughout the country became aware of a new national cause. Kelley attended nearly every national convention that was held on women's suffrage in the next thirty years. She was actively engaged in the women's rights movement through committees, correspondence, and speeches. At the thirtieth anniversary of the National Woman's Rights Convention in 1880, she was introduced as one of the few remaining pioneers of the movement.

In addition to women's rights, Kelley and Foster were active in the temperance movement, peace movements, and the beginning of trade unions. Their last public protest took place between the years of 1874 and 1879. They refused to pay taxes on Liberty Farm because Abby did not have the right to vote. Their property was repeatedly sold at public auction for non-payment of taxes, but their friends bought it back for them each time.

On September 8, 1881, Stephen Foster died peacefully at Liberty Farm. Just over five years later, on January 14, 1887, Abby Kelley Foster died, as her health could no longer bear up under the tremendous pressure she had endured so long. Her remarkable career had spanned the entire length of the major reform movements of the nineteenth century. She was the first woman universal reformer of her generation. Her uncompromising principles and courage placed her in the vanguard of the reform movements that would shape the course of American history by returning the nation to the principles of freedom, justice, and equality upon which it had been founded.

Yet where does Kelley fit into our overall view of nineteenth-century reformers? Why have her stature and fifty years' commitment to reform gone unrecorded by historians? One of her biographers, Dorothy Sterling, claimed that Kelley herself had a Quaker distaste for personal publicity and interviews, and added that the neglect of Kelley may be traced to the bias of male historians. Finally, she stated that her female contemporaries, such as Susan B. Anthony and Elizabeth Stanton, were still smarting over Kelley's support of the Fourteenth Amendment, which gave African-American males their civil rights but did not give women the same rights.[32] Though Kelley influenced and was influenced by the male reformers of her day, the power of her own voice and her commitment to both the anti-slavery crusade and women's equality demonstrate compellingly the potential power of a marginalized voice in effecting political and social change.

Notes

1. Robert S. Fletcher, *A History of Oberlin College from Its Foundation through the Civil War* (Oberlin, Ohio: Oberlin College, 1943), 2:844.

2. Philip S. Foner, *The Life and Writings of Frederick Douglass*, vol. 3 (New York: International Publishers, 1950), 245.

3. For the sake of simplicity and consistency, and to acknowledge that much of her activism predated her marriage to Stephen Foster, I refer to Abby Kelley Foster by her family name, Kelley, throughout this chapter.

4. *The Woman's Journal* (Boston), January 22, 1887, p. 4. Garrison said this in 1859.

5. Ralph Waldo Emerson, *Nature: Addresses and Lectures* (Boston: Houghton, Mifflin, 1883). Emerson gave the lecture entitled "Man the Reformer" in 1841.

6. From the genealogical data compiled by the American Antiquarian Society and kept with the Abby Kelley Foster and Stephen S. Foster Papers.

7. Arthur Young Lloyd, *The Slavery Controversy, 1831–1860* (New York: University of North Carolina Press, 1939), 52.

8. Kelley to Thomas Collier, Jan. 26, 1885, Abby Kelley and Stephen S. Foster Papers, Worcester Historical Society. Kelley was responding to a request from Collier, a Boston publisher, that she write a brief statement of some of her early experiences. However, none of this manuscript was published.

9. Abby Kelley was committed to anti-slavery as early as 1830 and was not Theodore Weld's "convert" a few years later, as alleged by Benjamin P. Thomas in *Theodore Weld: Crusader for Freedom* (New Brunswick, N.J.: Rutgers University Press, 1950), 175–176, 187.

10. Kelley to Albert Kelley, July 7, 1837, Abby Kelley and Stephen S. Foster Papers, Worcester Historical Society.

11. John Greenleaf Whittier, *Poems* (Philadelphia, 1838), 76.

12. Sara M. Grimké to Kelley, April 21, 1838, Abby Kelley Foster and Stephen S. Foster Papers, American Antiquarian Society, Worcester, Massachusetts (hereafter AAS). See also Angelina Grimké to Kelley, May 7, 1838, which is a wedding invitation to Abby signed by Angelina and Theodore Weld.

13. Lawrence Lader, *The Bold Brahmins: New England's War against Slavery 1831–1863* (New York: Dutton, 1961), 69.

14. Sara M. Grimké to Kelley, June 15, 1838, Abby Kelley Foster and Stephen S. Foster Papers, AAS.

15. Louis Filler, *The Crusade against Slavery, 1830–1860* (New York: Harper, 1960), 129.

16. Ibid., 134.

17. Dorothy Sterling, *Ahead of Her Time: Abby Kelley and the Politics of Anti-Slavery* (New York: W. W. Norton, 1991), 140.

18. Ibid., 142.

19. *The Liberator*, January 5, 1842.

20. S. Session to Kelley, March 15, 1842, Abby Kelley Foster and Stephen S. Foster Papers, AAS.

21. Sterling, *Ahead of Her Time*, p. 152.

22. Kelley to Foster, September 28, 1847, Abby Kelley Foster and Stephen S. Foster Papers, AAS.

23. Frederick Douglass to Kelley, October 13, 1881, ibid.

24. George Bradburn to Francis Jackson, January 15, 1842, Francis Jackson Papers, Boston Public Library, Boston, Massachusetts (hereafter BPL).

25. W. L. Garrison to G. W. Benson, March 22, 1842, William Lloyd Garrison Papers, BPL.

26. Sterling, *Ahead of Her Time*, 220.

27. Nancy H. Burkett, *Abby Kelley Foster and Stephen Foster* (Worcester, Mass.: Worcester Bicentennial Commission, 1976), 5.

28. Foster to Kelley, September 14, 1855, Abby Kelley Foster and Stephen S. Foster Papers, AAS.

29. *The Liberator*, February 3, 1865.

30. *Woman's Journal*, January 22, 1887.

31. Kelley to Foster, September 4, 1843, Abby Kelley Foster and Stephen S. Foster Papers, AAS.

32. Sterling, *Ahead of Her Time*, 4–5.

Bibliography

Bacon, Margaret. *Valiant Friend: The Life of Lucretia Mott*. New York: Walker, 1980.

Chadwick, John White, ed. *A Life for Liberty: Anti-Slavery and Other Letters of Sallie Holley*. New York: G. P. Putnam's Sons, 1899.

Commager, Henry S. *Theodore Parker*. Boston: Little, Brown, 1936.

Douglass, Frederick. *Life and Times of Frederick Douglass*. Hartford, Conn.: Park Publishing, 1884.

DuBois, Ellen C., ed. *Elizabeth Cady Stanton, Susan B. Anthony, Correspondence, Writings, Speeches*. New York: Schocken Books, 1981.

Emerson, Ralph Waldo. *Nature: Addresses and Lectures*. Boston: Houghton, Mifflin, 1883.

Filler, Louis. *The Crusade against Slavery, 1830–1860*. New York: Harper & Row, 1960.

Fletcher, Robert Samuel. *A History of Oberlin College from Its Foundation through the Civil War*. 2 vols. Oberlin, Ohio: Oberlin College, 1943.

Foner, Philip S. *The Life and Writings of Frederick Douglass*. 4 vols. New York: International Publishers, 1950.

Foster, Stephen S. *The Brotherhood of Thieves: A True Picture of the American Church and Clergy*. Boston: privately published, 1843.

Garrison, Wendell Phillips, and Francis Garrison. *William Lloyd Garrison, 1805–1879: The Story of His Life Told by His Children*. 4 vols. New York: Houghton, Mifflin, 1885–89.

Greene, Richard E. "Abby Kelley Foster: Ultra Abolitionist." Master's thesis, Clark University, Worcester, Mass., 1964.

Hofstadter, Richard. *The American Political Tradition and the Men Who Made It*. 1948. Reprint, New York: Vintage, 1954.

Nye, Russel B. *William Lloyd Garrison and the Humanitarian Reformers*. Boston: Little, Brown, 1955.

Stanton, Elizabeth C., ed. *History of Woman Suffrage*. 4 vols. New York: Ayer, 1881.

Sterling, Dorothy. *Ahead of Her Time: Abby Kelley and the Politics of Anti-Slavery*. New York: W. W. Norton, 1991.
Sweet, William W. *The American Churches: An Interpretation*. New York: Epworth Press, 1947.

Manuscript Collections

Boston, Massachusetts. Boston Public Library. Francis Jackson Papers.
Boston, Massachusetts. Boston Public Library. Samuel May Papers.
Boston, Massachusetts. Boston Public Library. Weston Family Papers.
Boston, Massachusetts. Boston Public Library. William Lloyd Garrison Papers.
Worcester, Massachusetts. American Antiquarian Society. Abby Kelley Foster and Stephen S. Foster Papers.
Worcester, Massachusetts. Worcester Historical Society. Abby Kelley and Stephen S. Foster Papers.

Newspapers and Convention Proceedings

Massachusetts Anti-Slavery Society, annual reports, 1836–1853.
New England Anti-Slavery Society, annual reports, 1838–1860.
Daily Spy. Worcester, Massachusetts.
Herald of Freedom. Concord, New Hampshire.
The Liberator. Boston, Massachusetts.
Massachusetts State Disunion Convention, proceedings, 1857.
New England Anti-Slavery Convention, proceedings, 1838–1860.
The Woman's Journal. Boston, Massachusetts.

PART IV
EXPLORING THE CANON

Twelve

African-American Childhood in Early Philadelphia

Janet Harrison Shannon

A child is not something you pass on from one to the other like a dog you no longer want. A child must know one home.

—Dalene Matthee, *Fiela's Child*

When young Frederick Douglass was in Talbot County, Maryland, in the 1830s and planning his escape to the North, he little realized the number of young people who had made that journey as early as 1780. For at that time, according to one historian, "there arose a considerable traffic in young negroes [from] Delaware, Maryland, and Virginia,"[1] caused by the tariff imposed on slaves entering Pennsylvania. To avoid taxation, slaves were brought into Delaware and Maryland and then into Pennsylvania.[2] What happened then to some of those "young negroes" is the subject of this paper.

The Pennsylvania Gradual Abolition Act, passed in 1780, freed no slaves immediately and, in fact, created a system of indenture which utilized the labor of blacks "for the greater part of their productive lives."[3] Its stipulation that indentures last to age twenty-eight "set the standard by which owners retained the labor of freed blacks through the prime of their lives."[4] For example, Liberty, a thirteen-year-old Malay boy, "in consideration of being set free from slavery for life," bound himself for a term of fifteen years.[5] And thirteen-year-old Samuel Patterson, a mulatto, was indentured to Robert R. Cross of Philadelphia for a term of fourteen years and four months.[6] Ten years after the passage of the Act there were approximately 240 black children indentured in Philadelphia.[7] We learn from *The Diary of Elizabeth Drinker* that Warner Mifflin, a Delaware Quaker and abolitionist, regularly sent young African-American children to work for the Drinkers, their relatives, and friends as domestic servants or laborers, depending upon their ages.[8]

187

Voluntary migration and the Act of 1780 not only swelled the ranks of available servants, but also provided a steady supply of cheap, unskilled laborers, many of whom were under the age of eighteen. Although indenture freed some from slavery, their labor was utilized for an extended period of time. As a result of the Act of 1780 and the influx of young African Americans from Delaware, Maryland, and Virginia, from 1779 to 1785 indentures increased in Philadelphia from one per year to an average of twenty-one.[9]

Indenture was a formal, legal process whereby individuals were required to work a specified number of years, in exchange for certain benefits during and at the expiration of the contracted period. The practice began in the colonies early in their history and lasted into the 1840s. Usually, indenture contracts were entered into under the auspices of one of several agencies: the Acting Committee of the Pennsylvania Abolition Society (PAS), the Committee of Guardians, the Philadelphia House of Employment, or the Overseers of the Poor. However, private arrangements were often made between individuals. The formal contracts stipulated that those indentured would have "sufficient meat, drink, apparel, washing, and lodging." Further, the child would be taught a trade or to read and write. At the expiration of the term those indentured often received two sets of clothing and a sum of money referred to as "freedom dues."[10] The amount of freedom dues varied from as little as two dollars to as much as forty dollars. Contractual terms varied, depending on the child's age and race and the mother's status. For some who came under the purview of the Pennsylvania Gradual Abolition Act, the indenture was until the age of twenty-eight. For others, the expiration date varied. Among other things, the practice of indenture promoted the employment of children, legally sanctioned their removal from the household, and encouraged their early entry into the labor force.[11]

Thus, in the span of one hundred years, Pennsylvania's labor system went from indenture in the 1680s, to slavery, and back to indenture in the 1780s. Although undoubtedly many members of the Society of Friends, the group most involved in abolition and indenture, believed their actions were aiding blacks, it would have been beneficial to those indentured if the members of this influential group had considered the issues of race, class, and the legacy of slavery before returning to the indenture system. For whereas most whites who had been indentured managed to climb the ladder of mobility, blacks who had been indentured were not so fortunate.

Although this paper examines the lives of several indentured children in Philadelphia, its specific focus is on African-American children, because the effect of indenture on their lives has not been considered. In fact, most of our knowledge of the history and sociology of black childhood focuses on children in the South during slavery, after emancipation, and in migration. We know little of the lives of black children in the North during the same periods of time. Philadelphia is a particularly interesting place to explore and reconstruct the history of childhood because there, beginning in 1780, were many children who were not slaves, not free, and not living with their parents—in short, not part of a family unit.

Sociologically, we argue that the family is the most important group to which individuals belong. It provides interaction, mediation, socialization, and transmission of culture. Thus, in this Northern urban setting in which men and women were enslaved and their children were indentured and sent away to other households, new social and cultural forms and new institutions were developing. Sidney Mintz and Richard Price found that "[i]n any social system, human interaction takes on its orderly character from the formalized expectations involved in playing out the roles attached to any particular status."[12] The status of an indentured child was that of a domestic worker or a common laborer. Considering that the family provides mutual support, nurturing, and socialization, I will explore how children developed who were not reared in this institution.

Both white and black parents indentured their children for a price or for employment training. The opinion of the day was that children were the property of their parents and obligated to them. The status of black children was unique, for not only were they indebted to their parents as their property, but the laws of Pennsylvania decreed that "a free black man has the same rights over his children as a white man has."[13] African-American males, who had few other legal rights, could enter into contracts to indenture their children. In the absence of the father, a mother could also indenture a child or authorize another to do so. Thus, Joanna Smith empowered Thomas Harrison to bind her daughter Sophia, age eleven, "to a suitable family, until she arrives at the age of eighteen years." Many indenture contracts were signed by children, who had no other legal rights but could bind themselves to adults for a period of service. The records of many indentures are preserved in the Pennsylvania Abolition Society Indenture Books at the Historical Society of Pennsylvania. Analyzing the data from the contracts along with ledgers, diaries, and other pertinent writings adds considerably to our knowledge of the indenture system. However, a significant amount of information comes from the published diaries of Elizabeth Drinker.

Elizabeth Sandwith Drinker (1735-1807) and her husband, Henry

Drinker (1743–1809), were wealthy white Quakers living in Clearfield County and in the city of Philadelphia. Henry was an ironmaster, a merchant, and the owner of a Philadelphia countinghouse, as well as a member of the Pennsylvania Abolition Society. Elizabeth came in contact with many children, and her diary provides invaluable information about them before, during, and after they were employed in her household. When it is supplemented by census data, newspaper articles, indenture records, and other documents, a compelling portrait of children's lives during this period is revealed.

Many children passed through the Drinker household. Often she mentions the presence of Indian children in her home or with others. An indenture contract dated July 17, 1784, indicates that Lette, an Indian girl aged fifteen, was apprenticed to William Stephenson for nine years.[14] Honduran children were supervised by Henry Drinker: "My husband has seven of *those Hondoras Children,* in some measure under his care" (2:815).[15] These contracts were probably business arrangements because of Henry's involvement in trade. European children were also mentioned.

When Patrick Dowling, a seventeen-year-old Irish youth, arrived at the port of Philadelphia, his labor was purchased by Henry Drinker before the lad left the vessel. Patrick remained at the Drinkers' home briefly and was sent to work at a shallop shop. Unfortunately, Patrick drowned shortly thereafter. Eight-year-old Ned Fifer was taken to the Drinkers by his mother. He was to work until the age of sixteen, if he proved to be satisfactory, but he was returned "because he was too small" (1:478). A Dutch child, Peter Wallover, twelve years old, was "purchased [by Henry] from on board a ship" (1:478). Six months later, there was a "rumpus" between his mother and the Drinkers, and Peter went to work at a paper mill. Sally Dawson was only nine and a half when her recently widowed father took her to the Drinkers. Described by Elizabeth as "a pretty looking child," Sally remained in the Drinker home until "out of her time" of indenture, a period of seven years (1:533). Tragically, before her eighteenth birthday, "in the bloom of youth . . . [she was] taken off the stage of life" (3:1691). Elizabeth's entries attest to the hardships endured by most children. Of Patrick, Ned, Peter, and Sally, two were dead before the age of eighteen. Children often died as a result of smallpox, yellow fever, influenza, or other diseases. African-American children, in addition to confronting poverty and illness, were often kidnapped and sold into slavery.[16] And indentured children often ran away from cruel masters. Even in the Drinker household, which might be considered a good one, children were beaten. However, it appears that most who were in the Drinker home had a good stay, considering the conditions.

The life of Scipio Drake, as recounted by Elizabeth, allows us to see how life was in early Philadelphia for one African-American child. Scipio Hollock Drake was born on February 23, 1783. By the time he was eleven he had run away from his indenture several times, always returning to the home of Miers Fischer, where his mother worked. The ultimate punishment for his behavior was jail. He was released into the custody of Henry Drinker on October 8, 1794, and a month later bound himself to Henry. The length of indenture was nine years and three months, freeing Scipio on February 22, 1804, at the age of twenty-one.[17]

Elizabeth found Scipio "very sulkey." His brooding is understandable, considering what had happened to him during his first eleven years of life: separation from his mother, different households, beatings, and incarceration, during which he had contracted lice (1:606, 612). Staying at the Drinkers' did not alter his behavior: when ordered to clean the knives, he took them to the yard, left them, and ran away. His father, "a good looking Negro man," brought him back and "advis'd and threatened him, wishd us to keep him" (1:607). Reluctantly, the Drinkers acquiesced. Even though Elizabeth thought well of Scipio's father, of his child she wrote, "if he goes off tomorrow, I hope he will not come back to us—a good servant is a valuable acquisition, the want of such is at present a general complaint" (1:615). Her thoughts about African-American children as servants were further revealed when she wrote, "so much for Negros, who are usefull to us, when they behave well" (2:1239). For a while Scipio behaved well; however, in less than a month he "took up hot ashes and threw them behind the Stable, near the barn, several hours after a Smoke was seen, some combustibles had taken fire" (1:615). The fire was sufficient to warrant Scipio's permanent removal from Elizabeth Drinker's household and his subsequent sale to her son-in-law, George Emlen.[18] Much relieved, Elizabeth wrote, "if he had liv'd longer with me, he would have known that I suffer not such as he to undertake a business of that nature" (1:615). It is interesting that Elizabeth did not consider the cruelty of a child's incarceration, nor from her writings are we able to discern any attempt on her part to understand Scipio's desire to be with his mother. Even though we learn from Elizabeth that her children had resided with her, and her grandchildren with their parents, there is scant indication in her writings that she considered the emotional condition and stability of children, especially African-American children, who remained apart from their families.

Another African-American child arrived from Virginia in November. Other than appearing "weakly" and not having had smallpox, seven-year-old Peter Savage seemed healthy. That he had not had smallpox was a concern, for it meant that he might die if he contracted the disease, thereby causing a financial loss. However, the Drinkers agreed that if he was found acceptable after the customary probationary period, they would pay fifteen pounds for his time. That afternoon Peter was washed ceremoniously in warm, soapy water, shampooed "with larkspur and rum" (2:995), and given clean clothes, and began his time of service. However, he was "but little worth at present" and in December, hoping "that he would be a good boy," the Drinkers gave him to Emlen, to whom the troubled, bothersome Scipio had been sold (1:758, 755).

On April 28, 1795, an African-American woman named Rebecca Gibbs and her twelve-year-old daughter, Patience, came north from the "lower counties," aided by Warner Mifflin. Patience worked for John and Nancy Drinker Skyrin, Elizabeth's son-in-law and daughter, for nearly six years, until her father, Absalom Gibbs, a "descent and sensible negro man," came for her (2:1385).[19] Eighteen-year-old Patience had served well, and Elizabeth lamented the difficulty the Skyrins would have finding a suitable replacement. The day after her father's arrival, Patience went to the Drinkers to say goodbye. Her father, who took "her home, [was] highly pleased with her education" (1:337). Patience's story demonstrates the familial use of indenture. Rebecca and Absalom Gibbs wanted their daughter educated and trained in the "mystery of housewifery." Therefore, this was an apprenticeship, formalized by an indenture contract that was beneficial for both the Gibbs family and the Skyrins, but not necessarily for Patience and her sweetheart; he was found hiding in the "necessary," trying to see Patience before her departure from Philadelphia.

Another child, whose case is crucial to the analysis of childhood in early Philadelphia, arrived after Peter Savage and before Patience Gibbs. His time with the Drinkers allows us to follow the life of someone indentured for many years. He is the child most mentioned by Elizabeth and the one who remained within her household longer than any other. On December 1, 1794, ten-year-old Peter Woodward[20] came from Kent County, Maryland, sent by boat by Warner Mifflin at an indenture cost of fifteen pounds. He arrived after more than a week at sea, unclean and unhealthy: "his appearance at first was rather formidable; being as I thought, hard favoured" (1:624). He was scrubbed, deloused, shampooed with the usual mixture of rum and larkspur, and given some of Scipio's clothing. And here Elizabeth described not only what happened to black children, but also her feelings about them: "One of our Daughters is to have one of the three little blacks that has lately come under our care. I feel much for the poor little fellows, little Peter has no parents here" (1:624). The "three little blacks" were Scipio Drake, Peter

Savage, and Peter Woodward; "little Peter" was Peter Savage. Indeed, apparently unknown to Elizabeth, Peter Woodward did have parents and other relatives in Philadelphia, though he had not seen his father for eight years.[21] But soon after Peter's arrival his father, Anthony Woodward, came to see him and took him to visit his mother, Alice. Peter also had a sister named Alice, who died at the age of sixteen of consumption.

Peter's parents formally bound him to Henry Drinker on March 30, 1796, two years after his arrival in Philadelphia. The term of the indenture was nine years, after which Peter would have reached the age of twenty-one, having lived eleven years in the Drinker home. Throughout the years the Drinkers maintained contact with Peter's family, many of whom sought character references for employment, notes to the dispensary for health care, and other forms of help. For example, Peter's brother, John Woodward, "came to ask for an order to the Despensary, as he has a sore tongue. . . . [Henry Drinker] gave him an order" (3:2032). Anthony Woodward went to the Drinker household for a winding sheet and cap for his daughter's burial (2:1400). In 1804, Peter's mother died, having been in the Philadelphia Almshouse "measurably deranged for some time past." Again, the Drinkers contributed the winding sheet (3:1784). Three years later, Anthony died "of a cramp in his stomach." That morning his second wife went to the Drinker house "for a shirt to lay him out in." Elizabeth sympathized: "poor old Anthony! I believe he was a sufferer in some respects" (3:2015). Not only were the Woodwards connected to the Drinkers through Peter, but a relationship existed among other members of both families. For example, Elizabeth's son-in-law hired Peter's nephew, Anthony, age twelve, at the rate of four dollars per month. Elizabeth thought her daughter and son-in-law would "have help enough, if it was of the right sort" (3:2042). These and other incidents noted in Elizabeth's diary, when taken together, weave a tale not only of race and domestic relations, but also of black family and community life. Most importantly, the lives of African-American children during this period of time are revealed.

Both Peter Savage and Peter Woodward experienced the usual illnesses and were attended by Elizabeth herself, by paid nurses,[22] and often by the eminent Dr. Benjamin Rush.[23] Treatment for pleurisy consisted of bleeding, purging, fever powders, and a poultice. On one occasion, for an upset stomach resulting from eating too many blueberries, a dose of catnip tea was administered immediately, and a purge of senna and manna in the morning. The children responded to these cures and were valued servants to the Drinkers, their children, other relatives, and friends.

Servant children in the household kept Elizabeth busy. "I have had much to do for the little black boys also, those small foulk ought to be of service when they grow bigger, for they are very troublesome when young, to those who have their good at heart" (1:634). Young Peter's duties included visiting different households to inquire after the residents' health, delivering messages, cleaning, washing dishes, removing ashes, and moving items. One such chore for Henry Drinker resulted in Peter's falling into the hold of a vessel. Immediate treatment consisted of a compress of Steer's Opodeldoc, with castor oil administered the next day. Medical care was not the only benefit of being with the Drinkers. When Henry Drinker went to Meeting, Peter, together with Peter Savage, frequently attended the separate service the Drinkers held for blacks, and he was taught to read and write.

As Peter grew older, his duties changed. When Henry Drinker was away, he slept in the passage to guard the house. At the age of nineteen, he was made a hostler. Finally, on March 20, 1805, Peter was free—"if being 21 years of age and [out] of his time will make him so." Elizabeth makes no reference to a celebration of freedom on his reaching adulthood. Her comment is telling because it is clear that even though he was "free," his status was dubious. Neither were immediate plans made; there was "no talk of parting yet." Still Elizabeth felt kindly toward him, writing, "poor fellow I sencerly wish him well" (3:1818). Her poignant phrases indicate Peter's lot as a free black man with no special training.

In spite of being "[out] of his time," Peter continued in the employ of the Drinkers. On November 20, 1805, perhaps overly confident of his new status, he had an altercation with a neighbor. Warrants were issued for both parties. Henry Drinker admonished the neighbor that he should have come to him with his complaint against Peter instead of engaging in a physical attack (3:1879).

The new year brought a new adventure for Peter. Despite Elizabeth's protestations, he

> made up his mind to go a voyage to sea, and has engaged to go in a sloop belonging to Cope and Thomas, to St. Domingo. A Son of John Thomas and another of Henry Drinker junr. are going in the same vessel as Supercargos: We knew not of Peters intention 'till he had engaged himself: We have said all that is proper to discourage him, laying before him the risks he will run, not only in winters passage, but the danger of his being taken and made a slave of, being black, but all will not do, —he has long wished to go to sea; poor fellow! (3:1897)

Her opposition to the voyage was rooted in more than the loss of a valued servant; her concern was almost motherly. Her concern was justified; black seamen were often kidnapped and sold into slavery or killed. Her anguish continued: "the river is not Navagable, so that we know not when Peter will leave us. . . . Peter has got from C. Biddle what is called a protection, I wish it may prove one" (3:1898). The "protection" to which she referred was a seaman's Protection Certificate, an official document certifying that its bearer was free. Unfortunately, it was not always sufficient protection against kidnapping. Peter's January 13th departure date was postponed because the ship filled with water and sank. While waiting for another vessel, he continued working at the Drinkers' and one evening worked as a waiter for a neighbor.

Finally, on February 5, 1806, Peter announced that he was leaving the next day and would sail soon thereafter. Elizabeth's worries resurfaced: "James Wood says that if the French takes them, Peter being a Negro, . . . they will hang him, the idea has given me pain, to tell him such a thought just now, as he seems determined, would be hard perhaps, yet I hardly know how to forbare" (3:1903). Peter left the next day as scheduled, even though Sally Downing, Elizabeth's daughter, had told him what Wood had said to her mother. Disregarding these warnings, and with the promise of sixteen dollars a month in wages, Peter left the Drinkers, dressed in a sailor's uniform (3:1905).

The ship was to sail on the ninth, at nine o'clock in the morning. Peter returned to the Drinkers on the eighth to bid them farewell. Henry Drinker cautioned him "to keep clear of strong drink and profane language," echoing advice that Elizabeth had offered previously in addition to other warnings she "thought necessary." He took a chest with him aboard the "small old vessel," the *Rising Sun*, bound for Santiago de Cuba (3:1904). An unfavorable wind on the ninth delayed the departure of the *Rising Sun*, and Peter visited the Drinkers twice that day. Finally, on the tenth, the *Rising Sun* cleared the port of Philadelphia. The crew list describes him as Peter Woodward, "a native of Kent County in the state of Delaware, a free black man." The master of the vessel was Jacob Sulger, and there were six crew members. Peter, the only black man on board, is described as aged twenty-one, five feet six inches in height, with "black woolly" hair, "square built" with a scar on his right arm.[24]

Elizabeth received a letter from Peter on April 2. Unfortunately that letter has not been located. He wrote that the voyage had not been as bad as he had anticipated. He had been seasick once, and expected to return to Philadelphia in April or May. On April 9, 1806, *Poulson's American Daily* reported that the *Rising Sun* had arrived at what Elizabeth called Cape Franioes (3:1918).[25] Elizabeth reported all news of the *Rising Sun* in her diary and noted when it docked at the Lazaretto.[26] Not seeing Peter as soon as expected, she suspected that he might have

remained at the Cape with John Thomas and Henry Drinker, Jr. However, on July 15, she wrote with apparent relief, "Our Peter Woodward
came this Afternoon, he is well, and if he can get a good place wishes
to stay on Shore, if not he will go to sea again" (3:1947). John Moore,
who was bound to Jacob Downing, had replaced Peter at the Drinkers',
and Peter did not return there, because John had performed satisfacto-
rily and "it would not do to turn him off" (3:1947).[27] It is significant
that in spite of having known him for twelve years and realizing the
hazards of the sea, the Drinkers did not employ Peter upon his return.
Instead, he worked for a month for Manuel Eyres, who lived in Ken-
sington, an area outside the city.[28]

Although no longer working for the Drinkers nor living in their
house, Peter remained in close contact. On one occasion he took them
a dozen "Read birds that he has shot" (3:1961). Additionally, Elizabeth
continued to include news about him in her diary. One such entry, dated
September 23, 1806, shows her continued concern for his well-being:
"Our Peter, a foolish Blockhead, is married on first Day last, to a girl of
Hazelhursts, who is not free—and by accounts not so good as she ought
to be—I am sorry for Peter!" (3:1967). This is provocative for a number
of reasons. First, because of the status of blacks in Philadelphia, "not
free" might indicate that Peter's wife was a slave. Slaves were still being
held in the city and county of Philadelphia; the censuses of 1800 and
1810 show 85 and 8, respectively, in the city. However, "not free" more
likely meant that she was still indentured. Indeed, Elizabeth's dismay is
apparent in that she never mentions Peter's wife's name. There was no
offer to host a wedding supper, as she had offered to do for other servants, nor did she enter any particulars of the nuptials in her diary.

Even though free, out of his time, hiring himself out, and married,
Peter still sought Henry Drinker's advice. Elizabeth's choice of words
informs us that, at least in her mind, the master/servant relationship
was still maintained: "Peter Woodward came this evening to talk with
his Master and JD. he seems inclined to go to Atsion to work there,
as he is about leaving John Hearts service" (3:2091). Peter did leave
Hearts's employ, and a few weeks later a note arrived from the manager
of the Iron Works in Atsion, New Jersey, stating that Peter and his wife
"behave well, and are very serviceable and handy" (3:2095). It is not
clear whether Peter was employed in the foundry or in the household;
in any case, Elizabeth was "pleased to hear it" (3:2095). That entry was
made on November 17, 1807. She made only one more entry before her
death on November 24. It is significant that a child who had spent so
much of his life with her is mentioned so very close to the end of her
days.

We do not know what became of the other children mentioned by Elizabeth Drinker. However, because of what extant historical records and sociological analysis tell us, we can make certain assumptions. African-American children in early Philadelphia experienced a different type of family life than did white children, being raised in the households of others. And although many of them knew where their parents were, they were more dependent on those to whom they were indentured than they were on their own parents. The dependency persisted into adulthood.

Although no information has been found which allows an analysis of Peter's adult life, we can speculate. He and his wife may have remained in New Jersey. His wife may have been employed as a domestic servant. For extra money, the couple may have done whitewashing. If Peter was unable to support his family, he may have returned to the sea. Peter's wife may have been able to live in her home and work outside the home only during the day, rather than living in space provided by her employer. Certainly we can assume that Peter would never have been in a position to earn enough that his wife could remain at home, doing only her own domestic work, as a few did. Any male children born of the union would probably have worked in the foundry as laborers when old enough to do so. Female children would have worked in the home helping their mother with washing, ironing, and sewing, or in the households of others. The children might have been indentured.

Thirty-three years after the Gradual Emancipation Act, a number of articles in various newspapers revealed the nature of the continued treatment of black children in Philadelphia. In 1813 several Philadelphia newspapers advertised the sales of indentured black children.[29] Indenture continued because it was one of the few ways in which families could obtain extra income and children could be trained. For a long period of time, everyone's income was needed for the family to survive. Children needed to work to supplement the family's income, and indenture enabled children to be cared for, educated, and trained, if placed with good families. The practice continued into the 1830s and its effects were felt for many years.

As late as 1847, when the Pennsylvania Abolition Society conducted a census of blacks in the city and county, black children were still being employed outside the home. Young females washed, made mantuas, cooked, cleaned, and sewed. Young males were employed as laborers in brickyards and lumberyards. They worked as hod carriers, waiters, and sweeps, and in barber shops and grog shops. Two boys working in a brickyard increased the family's monthly income by $26.00. Two other male children reportedly doing the same work earned $57.00

per month. Wages were presumably dependent upon age, physical stature, and what work the child was able to perform. Those who analyzed the census and the condition of African Americans at that time were cognizant of the effect of the menial occupations and concluded, "But here as in many other particulars, they are met by the prejudices with which they have to contend, which renders it difficult for them to find places for their sons as apprentices, to learn mechanical trades."[30]

During the period covered by this essay there is no indication that black male children were apprenticed directly to Henry Drinker, even though the record is clear that Honduran and some white male children were. It would seem that most black male children were not apprenticed in merchant houses or in the mechanical trades, even though many of them had learned to read and write. This discrimination relegated them to a lifetime of labor in unskilled occupations from which it was difficult, almost impossible, to escape. For example, Elizabeth mentioned that a black minister wanted his nephew to accompany the Drinkers' son aboard the vessel as an apprentice in order to become a supercargo. This request was denied. Even though Peter Woodward sailed with supercargoes Henry Drinker, Jr., and John Thomas, a cousin of the Drinkers, he went as a seaman. It is clear that many whites wanted only laborers and domestic servants, and this ensured the continued existence of a cheap labor pool, which prevented upward mobility for African Americans. Although the indenture system provided children with education, employment, clothing, medical care, and money (at the end of the indenture), we cannot ignore the fact that it was exploitative and one of the reasons that the African-American population of Philadelphia had difficulty maintaining stable family structures. Therefore, any attempt to explain childhood in the North must also consider economic exploitation and familial separation.

African Americans in early Philadelphia responded to the indenture system by establishing and maintaining family and community. First, the augmented family was established. Members of the augmented family cared for one another when the nuclear or extended family was not present to do so. Other blacks aided, nurtured, and cared for those who were alone in this strange new region. For example, Alice Wright, who nursed the children in the Drinker home, took Africans from the Congo into her own. Similarly, the Drinkers' servant Joseph was nursed by African Americans in their home in the city when he fell ill, and he eventually went to relatives in New Jersey to recover further. Although servants worked and lived in white households, many had rooms in the homes of other African Americans. The emotional and economic importance of boarders in nineteenth-century Boston is detailed by James

Oliver Horton and Lois E. Horton.[31] This situation, which persisted in Philadelphia well into the middle of the twentieth century, was the beginning of the augmented black family.

Secondly, many African Americans in early Philadelphia tried to maintain existing familial relations. Regardless of the distance, they sought out family members. For example, Joseph, mentioned above, traveled to Trenton, New Jersey, to be cared for by his extended family after leaving his augmented family. Peter Savage, Sr., traveled to Boardingtown, Pennsylvania, to visit with his son. Likewise, Peter Woodward's uncle, Soloman, traveled a great distance to see his nephew. These are but a few examples of the many blacks who sought out their relatives in order to maintain the family connection. Finally, we can surmise that Peter Woodward and others like him kept in contact with their relatives in Philadelphia and elsewhere, visited them and hosted them, and established a system of friendship and kinship with other blacks in New Jersey. However, as one of Frederick Douglass's biographers astutely notes, "even frequent visits would have been a poor substitute for the constancy of a daily life together."[32]

But what of the children? In spite of the fact that they were raised in the households of others, there is evidence that many attempted, in their marriages, to establish the nuclear family as they had observed it. We can speculate that economic conditions forced them to require their children to work outside the home, and even parents might be separated, not only from one another, but from the children. What of the socialization and nurturing that scholars argue the family provides? Socialization and nurturing were provided by some whites and many blacks in the community. Therefore, in spite of the hardships endured by many black children, upon reaching adulthood they established nuclear families, many of which endured, but they were and continue to be strengthened by extended and augmented families.

The literature which focuses on children in the eighteenth and nineteenth centuries does not give sufficient insight into the diversity of the history of family life, because much of what is written pays scant attention to the lives of children. Even though we still lack sufficient information about the intimate details of family life, we can piece together and surmise what it must have been like in certain circumstances. Particularly, we know something of the lives of some individuals, and by adding to the little we have learned we can develop a clearer picture of childhood in early Philadelphia, a topic which needs further investigation.

The removal of children from one place to another continued. For example, in New York in the twentieth century, children were sent on trains to the West.[33] There some were adopted, but more often than not they were employed as farm laborers. As late as the 1950s, children were sent from England to Australia as laborers. In the United States, it was not until 1978 that the Indian Child Welfare Act banned the removal of Native American children from their homes. These conditions, along with crimes against children and their high rate of mortality, continue to call our attention to the need to focus on ways in which children have not been and are not now protected by society. Are there historical patterns that we can discern in an attempt to understand the mistreatment and neglect of children in general, and minority children specifically? What has caused this mistreatment of children to continue? What has been the extent of this neglect, and how has it affected children and our treatment of them? An analysis of the life of some children in the eighteenth and nineteenth centuries in Philadelphia and elsewhere might help us understand and respond to these questions.

Notes

I am indebted to the editor and publisher of *The Diary of Elizabeth Drinker* for permission to cite therefrom; to Jennifer Holladay for research assistance with the indenture records; and, for insightful comments and suggestions for revision, to Nancy Fairley, Grant Jones, Isaac Jack Lévy, Lakshaman Sabaratnam, and Rosemary Lévy Zumwalt. My research was supported by the generosity of the Davidson College Committee on Faculty Study and Research.

1. Edward Raymond Turner, *The Negro in Pennsylvania: Slavery—Servitude —Freedom* (New York: Negro Universities Press, 1969), 93.

2. Gary B. Nash and Jean R. Soderlund, *Freedom by Degrees: Emancipation in Pennsylvania and Its Aftermath* (New York: Oxford University Press, 1991), 54.

3. Ibid., 165.

4. Ibid., 165.

5. Indenture books of the Pennsylvania Abolition Society, Historical Society of Pennsylvania (hereafter PAS), indenture book C, reel 22.

6. Ibid., reel 23.

7. Gary B. Nash, *Forging Freedom: The Formation of Philadelphia's Black Community, 1720–1840* (Cambridge: Harvard University Press, 1988), 77.

8. Elizabeth Drinker, *The Diary of Elizabeth Drinker*, edited by Elaine Forman Crane, 3 vols. (Boston: Northeastern University Press, 1991). Further references to the *Diary* are given in the text. Warner Mifflin was born in Virginia and later resided in Kent County, Delaware. Inspired by "an inner light," he prepared petitions against slavery for the Delaware General As-

sembly and the United States Congress. He was one of the founders of the Delaware Society for Promoting the Abolition of Slavery. Mifflin transported blacks from the Lower Counties to Philadelphia, offering them freedom in return for a period of indentured servitude (John A. Munroe, *Colonial Delaware: A History* [Millwood, N.Y.: KTO Press, 1978]; John A. Munroe, *History of Delaware* [Newark: University of Delaware Press, 1979]; Carol E. Hoffecker, *Delaware: A Bicentennial History* [New York: W. W. Norton, 1977]).

9. Nash and Soderlund, *Freedom by Degrees,* 54.

10. Freedom dues were not always money; they might be a set of tools of the trade.

11. See Edward Shorter, *The Making of the Modern Family* (New York: Basic Books, 1977).

12. Sidney W. Mintz and Richard Price, *The Birth of African-American Culture* (Boston: Beacon Press, 1992), 33–34.

13. PAS, reel 24.

14. PAS, reel 23.

15. Many of Henry's business associates in the Bay of Honduras wanted their sons educated in Philadelphia. Henry placed these children with his associates in Philadelphia and even, on occasion, in his own business (Drinker, *Diary,* 1:768).

16. Julie Winch, "Philadelphia and the Other Underground Railroad," *Pennsylvania Magazine of History and Biography* 111, no. 1 (January 1987): 3–24.

17. PAS Indenture Book C, 1758–1795, p. 72.

18. George Emlen had married Elizabeth's daughter Anne. Against the dictates of the Meeting, George was a slave holder at least until 1790 (Nash and Soderlund, *Freedom by Degrees,* 144).

19. Patience's undated indenture to John Skyrin is in PAS Indenture Book D, reel 22, page 16; it does not specify the length of the contract. In 1790 Absalom Gibbs lived in Queen Anne's County, Maryland. There were six in the family, all free black people. An Abram Gibbs is also listed, with three in his family. Both Kent County, where Mifflin lived, and Queen Anne's County are located on the eastern shore of Maryland. *Heads of Families at the First Census of the United States,* Maryland (Washington, D.C.: Government Printing Office, 1907), 100.

20. Elizabeth also spells the surname "Woodard."

21. Peter's uncle, Soloman (or Solomon) Tant, raised him. Soloman, along with Peter's father, visited in 1796 (Drinker, *Diary,* 2:837).

22. One such nurse was a black woman named Alice Wright. She often recommended black people to the Drinkers, and her endorsement was valued by them. Moreover, Alice apparently employed servants herself. When the ship *Ganges* arrived in Philadelphia, she told Elizabeth that "she wants one

of the blacks that are still down the river, to be bound to her" (Drinker, *Diary*, 2:1329). Alice died on February 25, 1803. Elizabeth offered a "Windingsheet and other things to bury her in." She was buried the next day at the Methodists Ground. Peter attended the funeral; Elizabeth did not (ibid., 3:1630).

23. As well as a physician, Benjamin Rush was an abolitionist and a member of the board of the House of Employment.

24. Crew Lists, Historical Society of Pennsylvania, p. 29.

25. She may have been referring to Cabo Frances Viejo, in what is now the Dominican Republic.

26. The Lazaretto was the quarantine house erected on Fisher's Island, later known as Province Island, "purchased and owned by the Province, for the use of sick persons arriving from sea." John F. Watson, *Annals of Philadelphia and Pennsylvania* (Philadelphia, 1845), 461.

27. John Moore, also known as Sam Moore, was indentured to Jacob Downing on December 6, 1802, for a period of five years (PAS Indenture Book D, 76).

28. Emanuel Eyres, also known as Manuel Eyres, was a shipwright and a Presbyterian (Drinker, *Diary*, 3:2147). In 1790 he headed a household in Northern Liberties of two free white males over the age of sixteen, three free white males under the age of fifteen, eight free white females, one other free person, and four slaves (*Heads of Families at the First Census of the United States*, Pennsylvania [Washington, D.C.: Government Printing Office, 1907], 204).

29. See *Relf's Philadelphia Gazette*, April 8 and October 26, 1813; *Poulson's American Daily Advertiser*, August 9, 1813, and December 6, 1813.

30. Henry M. Minton, *Early History of Negroes in Business in Philadelphia* (Nashville: AME Sunday School Union, 1913), 8.

31. James Oliver Horton and Lois E. Horton, *Black Bostonians* (New York: Homes and Meier, 1979).

32. William S. McFeely, *Frederick Douglass* (New York: W. W. Norton, 1991).

33. Marilyn Irvin Holt, *The Orphan Trains: Placing Out in America* (Lincoln: University of Nebraska Press, 1992).

Thirteen

Border Controls of Race and Gender
Crane's The Monster *and Chesnutt's* The Conjure Woman

Matthew Wilson

Eighteen ninety-nine saw the publication of both *The Monster,* by Stephen Crane, and *The Conjure Woman,* by Charles W. Chesnutt. Although these writers are contemporaries, they seem hardly to exist within the same national or literary narratives. Crane has been thought of as central to the narrative we tell ourselves about our literature: the naturalist writer pushing the envelope in works like *Maggie, A Girl of the Streets* and *The Red Badge of Courage,*[1] and the writer who gave us the figure of the journalist as a cultural paradigm for certain male American writers in this century. Chesnutt, conversely, has until very recently been marginal to our national literary narrative: a writer who produced tales based on the African-American vernacular tradition, who wrote a tragic mulatto novel and two other novels which are a curious mixture of realism and melodrama, a man who fell silent as a writer and who, unlike Crane, for many years hardly seemed to belong to any literary tradition. In this essay, I want to link Crane and Chesnutt as contemporaries and to explore the ways in which both writers deploy the discourses of race and gender in these two texts of 1899 in an effort to reinsert these works into the historical and cultural context of late-nineteenth-century America.

Elaine Showalter has written that in "periods of cultural insecurity . . . the longing for strict border control around the definition of gender, as well as race, class, and nationality, becomes especially intense" (4). The 1890s were such a period of heightened cultural anxiety, one which linked, as never before, the discourses of race and gender. The historian Joel Williamson has argued, for instance, that before 1889

[t]here had been a great fear of blacks . . . but the older fear was that they would rise massively and kill whites, or do them bodily injury, or destroy their property—not that they would rise individually and sporadically and rape white women. In and after 1889, however, that crime and its punishment commanded a new and tremendously magnified attention. (Williamson 84)

The statistics are horrific: in America from 1889 to 1899 "one person was lynched every other day, and two out of three were black" (85). What drove this epidemic of violence was the conviction on the part of what Williamson terms "racial radicalists" that blacks, deprived of the "civilizing" effect of slavery, were quickly "'retrogressing' toward their natural state of bestiality" (78). The contemporary "experts" who were often cited to bolster this conclusion were Frederick L. Hoffman and Philip Alexander Bruce. Hoffman's *Race Traits of the American Negro* (1896), published by the prestigious American Economic Association, claimed that blacks had been degenerating since at least 1810, but that the degeneration had dramatically accelerated since the Civil War, and as a result of this degeneration, Hoffman predicted the "'gradual extinction of the race'" (Williamson 89). The book of the other "expert," *The Plantation Negro as Freeman* (1899), was issued by Putnam, another highly regarded publisher, and as early as 1884 a version of this argument appeared in the New York *Evening Post*. Bruce writes in the book (and here I need to quote an extended passage),

There is something strangely alluring and seductive to . . . [black men] in the appearance of a white woman; they are aroused and stimulated by its foreignness to their experience of sexual pleasure, and it moves them to gratify their lust at any cost and in spite of every obstacle. This proneness of the negro is so well understood that the white women of every class, from the highest to the lowest are afraid to venture to any distance alone, or even to wander unprotected in the immediate vicinity of their homes. . . . rape, indescribably beastly and loathsome always, is marked in the instance of its perpetration by a negro, by a diabolical persistence and a malignant atrocity of detail that have no reflection in the whole extent of the natural history of the most bestial and ferocious animals. He is not content merely with the consummation of his purpose, but takes that fiendish delight in the degradation of his victim which he always shows when he can reek his vengeance upon one whom he has hitherto been compelled to fear; and, here the white woman in his power is, for the time being, the representative of that race which has always over-awed him. (Williamson 88–89)

One hardly has the conceptual apparatus to describe this passage: a combination of demonizing and bestializing, a kind of male hysteria within a nightmare construct of history; and within the national arena views like this went virtually unchallenged at the end of the century.[2] At the same time as the "experts" raised their monitory voices about the degeneration of blacks, a number of moves were simultaneously taking place in other discursive arenas that would insure the relegation of African Americans to the far margins of the national imaginary. Booker T. Washington sealed the economic compact between North and South in his Atlanta Compromise speech (1895); *Plessy v Ferguson* (1896) confirmed the constitutionality of the idea of "separate but equal"; and the Dunning school of Reconstruction historiography was beginning to attribute the failure of the Reconstruction to what it called "Negro incapacity." This, then, is the context which I would like to bring to bear against these texts of Crane and Chesnutt, with their central black male characters, and I want to reread both texts in that context. Of course, I realize that I'm defining "context" here in a somewhat unusual way: I'm not attempting to read the complicated position(s) of African Americans in the late nineteenth century synoptically. Rather, I'm defining context as "other racist texts" (Gates xxv), like Bruce's, against which I will read *The Monster* and *The Conjure Woman*. In doing so, I also want to show how two stereotypes employed by Crane and Chesnutt, the Sambo and the plantation darky, exist in an uneasy relation with the stereotype of the black beast rapist.

Considering the end-of-the-century consensus about race, Crane's *The Monster* has been read, almost perversely, as abstracted from any historical context. As Michael Warner has written, the story has been most often interpreted as a critique of the "social hypocrisy of the townsfolk" (Warner 87): a universalized townsfolk who, in contrast to the local colorists, are curiously without a meaningful sense of place. Warner's analysis of this received interpretation of social hypocrisy, while interesting, fails to take into account how precisely Crane situates his black man, Henry Johnson, and how aware, on whatever level of intentionality, Crane seems to be of the intersection of the discourses of race and gender.[3] From the moment of his introduction, Johnson is less a character than a congeries of racist stereotypes. But these stereotypes are destabilized, I will argue, by what is unrepresented in the text: fear of black men as bestial rapists and, in particular, fear of post–Civil War black men. Williamson argues, for instance, that from the point of view of racial radicals, the decade of the 1880s was one of high cultural anxiety because by the "mid-eighties young Negroes were coming into manhood who had been born free and had never felt the civilizing effects of slavery. By 1889, the 'New Negro,' as white contemporaries labeled him, might be twenty-four years old. Indeed, he *was* a new man, and his potential *was* unknown" (Williamson 78–79).

Crane's "new Negro," Henry Johnson, when he first appears seems far from the figure of cultural anxiety that I have been evoking. Although a mature man, the narrator tells us that he is the equivalent of a child; he is like Jimmy, the son of Dr. Trescott, who is only four or five years old. Johnson "grinned fraternally when he saw Jimmy coming. These two were pals. In regard to almost everything in life they seemed to have minds precisely alike" (Crane, *Maggie*, 66). Although here he is represented as childlike, the second scene in which he appears alerts the reader to what is being suppressed in that characterization, or rather to what his childishness inevitably, in the national imaginary of late-nineteenth-century America, masks.

In the next scene, Johnson throws off the costume of the stable hand, and "like a priest arraying himself for some parade of the church" he dons "lavender trousers" and a "straw hat with its bright silk band" (68). The narrator comments significantly that the change he has undergone "was somewhere far in the interior of Henry. But there was no cakewalk hyperbole in it" (68–69). After indulging in stereotype throughout the tale, Crane tries here to stave off yet another stereotype by asserting that Johnson doesn't fall into it. In this slightly vertiginous moment in the text, it is as if Crane were ascribing a kind of dignity to this character that he everywhere else denies him. Johnson refuses to become a stereotype darky here, but as Eric Sundquist has shown, the cakewalk in its evolution is an ambiguous cultural form, because it encompasses the possibilities of double parody. "In plantation cakewalk . . . black slaves . . . donned exaggerated finery to parody their masters" (Sundquist 282), but then white minstrels adapted this cultural form and "put on grotesque makeup and outlandish clothing in order to caricature black life" (281–282). In Crane's characterization, Johnson clearly has all the disadvantages of having been born in the postbellum period. Having no experience of slavery, he seems innocent of the subversive and parodic impulses in the cakewalk. Johnson is incapable, in Crane's view, of parody of white folks (or, at this moment, of a parody of himself). Instead he has become a stereotype, one of the two enduring minstrel stereotypes. He is the parodic "city dandy" (Boskin 75), transplanted to this rural town. He inhabits the stereotype so fully that when one of the townsmen calls out to him to ask where he's "[g]oing to walk for a cake tonight" (Crane, *Maggie*, 69), Johnson experiences this stereotypical jibe as one of a series of "compliments" that give him "an underground complacency of superior metal" (70). Johnson, then, quickly becomes a black man in blackface who "was not at all oblivious of the wake of wondering ejaculation that streamed out behind him. On other occasions he had reaped this same joy, and he always had an eye of the demonstration" (71). It would seem that a precondition of racist ideology in this period is that blacks were monologic. In other words, popular representations, such as those published in the magazine *Puck*, derived their power from the assumption that blacks, in contrast to Du Bois's later assertion, do *not* possess a "double consciousness," and that they are serenely unaware of the effects of racism on them.

Johnson is not merely parading through the town in order to stroke his self-esteem, and he is normalized by the men in the barber shop as a regular sight: "'he always dressed like that when he wants to make a front! He's the biggest dude in town—anybody knows that'" (70). He is trying to make an impression because he is going courting, to see the "saffron Miss Bella Farragut," and her mother receives him.

> After a great deal of kowtow, they were planted in two chairs op-
> posite each other in the living-room. Here they exchanged the
> most tremendous civilities, until Miss Bella swept into the room,
> when there was more kowtow on all sides, a smiling show of teeth
> that was like an illumination. . . . They bowed and smiled and ig-
> nored and imitated until a late hour, and if they had been the oc-
> cupants of the most gorgeous salon in the world they could not
> have been more like three monkeys. (71)

Under the parody of civility is the jungle. The blacks are "monkeys," and in the eyes of the narrator, their hilarious civility serves only to mask their animality. Although that animality is rendered relatively harmless by calling them "monkeys," I would argue that "monkey" is a mask of a mask, a substitution for the mask of the brutal rapist. John-son's parodic civility is simply a mask for his essential animality.

Johnson, though, is transformed from dude to monster when he selflessly rescues little Jimmy from Dr. Trescott's burning house. His face is burned away, and he is left with no physiognomy and no mind. Most commentators on the story, at this point, shift the focus to the white doctor and his heroic effort to do the right thing in saving John-son's life and in continuing to care for him.[4] Most also stress the hypoc-risy of the community, but I want to focus for a moment on the meaning of this transformation of Johnson from a young and prepossessing "new Negro" to a monster who is certainly meant to evoke tales of horror. Crane never attempts to describe Johnson's face, but lets us infer what he must look like from the reactions of a white child and some of John-son's former neighbors. For the purposes of my analysis the reaction of this child is crucial. A group of young children are having a party; when one of them hears a noise, she turns to look out a window.

> Instantly she screamed and sprang away, covering her face with her hands. "What was it? What was it?" cried every one in a roar. Some slight movement of the eyes of the weeping and shuddering child informed the company that she had been frightened by an appearance at the window. . . . She was not coherent even to her mother. Was it a man? She didn't know. It was simply a thing, a dreadful thing. (99–100)

What Crane has done here is to literalize the image of the black brute that is epidemic in his culture, the terror of the black brute experienced by the white girl child. In terms of the national narrative of black men, the appearance at the window is not even a "man"; it is a "dreadful thing," the nameless, faceless terror evoked by a nation bent on denying black men their manhood in denying them their vote and moving as quickly as possible to try to impose clear and vivid lines of segregation in public facilities and private organizations.

The terror is repeated among Johnson's black friends when he unexpectedly appears among them, talking as he did before his disfiguration, as if he were unaware of the horror he inspires in those around him (just as, before he lost his mind, he seemed to be unaware of the racist reactions of the townspeople). Johnson has come again to court Miss Bella Farragut, but at sight of him, she "grovelled in a corner of the room. . . . In a last outbreak of despair, the girl, shuddering and wailing, threw herself face downward on the floor" (101). Although no one in the town can abide the sight of Johnson, the doctor perseveres in his heroic resolve to care for the man who saved his son's life. Indeed, it seems as if the doctor is going to let his career be ruined in the face of the town's disapproval of his actions, but he is finally broken by the pressure that the women of the town both indirectly and directly bring to bear. He is visited by an all-male ad hoc committee of leading citizens who try to convince him to give up his heroic resolve to care for Johnson:

> "You have changed from being the leading doctor in town to about the last one. It is mainly because there are always a large number of people who are very thoughtless fools, of course, but then that doesn't change the condition."
>
> A man who had not heretofore spoken said, solemnly, "It's the women." . . .
>
> "And there are a good many of us that admire you for it im-

mensely . . . but that isn't going to change the minds of all those
ninnies."

"It's the women," stated the advocate of this view again. (116)

Although the idea that the women are at fault seems at this point to be
only a minority point of view, the exchange does make out women, however provisionally, to be "very thoughtless fools" and "ninnies." The
binary I'm perceiving in the story is complicated, however, by the father of the girl who sees Johnson at the window, and who leads the campaign against Dr. Trescott. A later conversation among several women
casts doubt on the psychic trauma suffered by his daughter, and it
makes out not only the father, but also the whole town, to be "'silly
people'" (113). These silly people, both men and women, participate in
this civic hysteria, but the women, with their "finer" and "more sympathetic" natures, become the core of the campaign for Johnson's expulsion. This view is validated by the experience of Alek Williams, a black
man the doctor hires to care for Johnson, and finally by the experience
of the doctor's wife. Williams complains that "'my ol' 'ooman she cain't
'ceive no lady callahs, nohow. . . . Noner ma wife's frien's ner noner ma
frien's'll come near ma res'dence'" (90). The judge to whom Williams
goes to complain treats his complaint with contempt. Just as the narrator is allied with the townsfolk in seeing the ludicrousness of black
people trying in any way to imitate whites, the judge takes much the
same line as the second speaker in the exchange I just quoted. He says
the ladies who refuse to visit Williams's wife are "silly people" (90), and
he buys Williams off with (or Williams manipulates him into paying)
an extra dollar a week for caring for Johnson.

What we see developing in the story, then, is a kind of binary structure of parody/horror or parody/tragedy. When the wife of a black man
is unable to receive her friends, the narrator and townspeople see this as
parody, but when the doctor's wife is ostracized by the women of the
town on her day for receiving visitors, then his heroic resolve to do the
right thing crumbles. In the face of his wife's social isolation, he will,
the narrative implies, expel Johnson, purging Whilomville of a disturbing and disruptive presence and returning it to a suspect stability. And
although critics have argued that Crane's Whilomville stories portray a
kind of "middle-class utopia" (Crane, *Tales of Whilomville*, xiv), one
that "exists outside of time, exempt from progress"[5] (xiii), I would argue that in its depiction of a "new Negro" the tale is eerie in its reflection of and contribution to the national consensus on race. Black men
must, in all cases, be marginalized, and Crane takes Johnson through

the whole repertory of roles ascribed to black men in this period: an adult who is inoffensive and childlike; the comic, overdressed Sambo, a figure familiar in cartoons; and the black beast. The continued existence, the internal balance of this community is dependent on what it must expel—the bestial black man. Johnson becomes a kind of *pharmakos*, a ritual scapegoat in the Greek sense, an embodiment, as Donald Gibson has written, "of the deepest fears of the community. Henry *seems* to Whilomville to be what Bigger Thomas in Richard Wright's *Native Son* actually is: a monster created by his condition as a Negro in America" (Gibson 138).[6] Gibson's linking of these two texts makes explicit what's only latent in Crane: the fear that is unnameable in Whilomville in 1899, the fear of the black brute rapist, the very crime that the lawyer, Max, tells Bigger he's actually being tried for in *Native Son*. But this literalization of an unspoken and unspeakable fear is made all the more potent by its repression. Whilomville, Crane's critics would have us believe, unlike the turn-of-the-century South, is a kind of timeless utopia, but if it is one, it must repress its deepest fears, simultaneously denying them and participating in a communal expulsion of them. Possibly what the culture conceives to be the more "sympathetic" nature of women makes them, in Whilomville, prey to the horrors of appearance, prey to the fears of the black beast rapist. Although the doctor can insist, even in the face of economic ruin and male censure, on a kind of traditional morality, he is helpless in the face of women, in whose name he will enforce, in Showalter's terms, strict border controls. Although Johnson will be expelled rather than killed, the action here uncannily duplicates the structure of lynching in this period: men acting *for* women will summarily deal with the monster, and their rationale will be that they were, after all, only protecting their own women, while from our perspective they were, of course, acting on their own fears.

In Charles W. Chesnutt's *The Conjure Woman*, the necessity for border controls is both subverted and, I will argue, unintentionally affirmed. The situation in these stories is more complicated than in *The Monster*, and that complication is crucial to Chesnutt's rereading of racial radicalism through the genre of the plantation tale. Some time after the Civil War, a Northerner and his wife move south and buy a vineyard, and each of the stories is narrated by this Northern man (and crucially, the narrator's wife, Annie, is present during each telling of a tale). Her husband frames and then renarrates the stories of Uncle Julius McAdoo, a former slave, a character who, in this period, is going to be read inevitably as a plantation darky—simple, superstitious, and loyal. Because of the omnipresence of the discourse of racial radicalism, Chesnutt is very careful to domesticate Julius. As a former slave, he is immediately less suspect than Johnson, because McAdoo has been exposed to the "civilizing" effects of slavery. In addition, he's old and asexual. The narrator describes him this way:

> [H]e was a tall man, and, though slightly bowed by the weight of years, apparently quite vigorous. He was not entirely black, and this fact, together with the quality of his hair, which was about six inches long and very bushy, except on the top of his head, where he was quite bald, suggested a light strain of other than negro blood. There was a shrewdness in his eyes, too, which was not altogether African, and which, as we afterwards learned from experience, was indicative of a corresponding shrewdness in his character. (Chesnutt, *Conjure Woman*, 4)

Elsewhere, the white narrator talks about the "wildly extravagant . . . Oriental cast of the negro's imagination" (16), and we can easily see, from the beginning, the potential complications of these narratives. For the narrator, is McAdoo as a man of mixed racial heritage a confusingly liminal figure, who possesses white "shrewdness" and a black "Oriental imagination"? Is this a critique of American racial essentialism? Or is this Chesnutt buying into the essentialism of American constructions of race? Or are these tales Janus-faced and double-voiced from the ground up, so that different readers can read the tales as either affirmation or critique?

This doubleness is reflected in the structure of the stories, in which there are always two auditors, the male narrator and his wife. The narrator is instrumental and scientific in his assumptions, which he articulates most clearly in "Sis' Becky's Pickaninny": "'Julius,' I observed, half to him and half to my wife, 'your people will never rise in the world until they throw off these childish superstitions and learn to live by the light of reason and common sense'" (52). Note the double address. He is trying to educate both Julius and his wife, Annie, because the narrator (and the culture) sees that black men and white women, despite the threat one poses to the other, share certain "essential" characteristics: both tend to be less "rational" than white men, thus more prey to groundless fears. In these stories, then, Annie is a bridge between a white man and a black man; she "functions as an interpreter, broker, buffer, and guide, not only between the two men but between Julius' fictions and the reader" (Duncan 92). Although she occasionally expresses some doubt about Julius's tales of conjuration (particularly in

"The Conjurer's Revenge"), her relation to him is fundamentally different from her husband's. He recognizes that she shares with Julius "a very sympathetic turn of mind" (Chesnutt, *Conjure Woman,* 15), almost as if Chesnutt were signifying on Harriet Beecher Stowe's well-known conclusion to *Uncle Tom's Cabin:* "the man or woman who *feels* strongly, healthily, and justly, on the great interests of humanity is a constant benefactor to the human race. See, then, to your sympathies in this matter" (Stowe 385). This "turn" of sympathy allows Chesnutt to open some space between Annie and her husband in the second story of the volume, "Po' Sandy." In Julius's tale, a male slave, Sandy, is constantly being hired out, moved from plantation to plantation by his master. His "wife" has been sold away, and he has taken up with Tenie; everyone on the plantation "'mence ter talk about how lovin' dey wuz'" (Chesnutt, *Conjure Woman,* 16). Tired of being moved around, Sandy asks Tenie, a conjure woman, to turn him into a tree, which she unconjures at night so that they can spend time together. But the tree who is Sandy is cut down, and Tenie goes insane. After Julius finishes the story, husband and wife have this exchange:

> Annie had listened to this gruesome narrative with straitened attention.
> "What a system it was," she exclaimed, when Julius had finished, "under which such things were possible!"
> "What things?" I asked in amazement. "Are you seriously considering the possibility of a man's being turned into a tree?"
> "Oh, no," she replied quickly, "not that"; and then murmured absently, and with a dim look in her fine eyes, "Poor Tenie!" (23)

From early in the collection of stories, then, the reception of these tales by husband and wife is gendered in terms of instrumental rationality vs. sympathy. As a no-nonsense Northern capitalist, the narrator reads the tales in terms of the national consensus, as the superstitious, primitive narrative of a representative of a race that hasn't evolved very far. He dismisses Julius's tales as "wildly extravagant . . . [and] Oriental," while Annie, being sympathetic, responds to another aspect of Julius's narrative, the human cost of the slave system. Indeed, one might argue that Chesnutt, in these two modes of reception, is evoking two different literary traditions: a realistic "male" tradition and a devalued sentimental "female" tradition. By doing so, he is indicating to his white audience that not only are Julius's tales double-voiced, but the dominant culture is also double in these gendered traditions of writing and reading.

The terms which I am invoking to describe the interaction between

Julius and the white folks are fairly conventional ones, but Chesnutt, in what I think of as the linchpin of the collection, "Sis' Becky's Pickaninny," redeploys the characters' predispositions in quite unexpected ways. Here I am reading *The Conjure Woman* as an internally coherent sequence of stories,[7] as a proto-form that will be more fully realized by Sherwood Anderson in *Winesburg, Ohio*. In the first story of the collection, John says her "poor health" is the reason they moved from Ohio to a "warm and more equitable climate" (1). In "Sis' Becky's Pickaninny," however, the project of relocation seems to have failed; her health had improved at first, but "[t]oward the end of our second year . . . her ailment took an unexpected turn for the worse. She became the victim of a settled melancholy, attended with vague foreboding of impending misfortune. . . . [N]othing seemed to rouse her from the depression into which she had fallen" (51). Although Richard Brodhead has written that the depression Annie suffers from is a result of "boredom—a boredom induced by her way of life" (11), I want to argue that the sources of her depression, while partly located in the social, are also more intimate and private.

At the opening of "Sis' Becky's Pickaninny" Annie's depression is so deep that she "was apparently without energy enough to speak for herself" (51); she was unable to respond to a question of Julius's. His response is to tell her a tale of a slave woman whose master sells her away from her newly born child. Her friend, Aunt Nancy, uses a conjure woman to aid both child and mother, and the tale involves magical transformations and a happy ending. Again the interchange at the end of Julius's narrative between husband and wife is crucial:

My wife had listened to this story with greater interest than she had manifested in any subject for several days. I had watched her furtively from time to time during the recital, and had observed the play of her countenance. It had expressed in turn sympathy, indignation, pity, and at the end, lively satisfaction.

"That is a very ingenious fairy tale, Julius," I said, "and we are very much obliged to you."

"Why, John!" said my wife severely, "the story bears the stamp of truth, if ever a story did."

"Yes," I replied, "especially the humming-bird episode, and the mocking-bird digression, to say nothing of the doings of the hornet and the sparrow."

"Oh, well, I don't care," she rejoined, with delightful animation; "those are mere ornamental details and not at all essential. The story is true to nature, and might have happened half a hundred times, and no doubt did happen, in those horrid days before the war." (61)

Something magical has happened here in the conjuration of the tale. In fact, one might argue that Julius's narrative *is* conjure, and his cure of Annie begins by his evocation of sympathy in her. The subtle and complicated interaction between an old black man and a young white woman results in her being cured of depression. If the white women in *The Monster* insist on the expulsion of the *pharmakos*, the black beast, the white woman here forges a solidarity of sympathy with an old black man and with the experience of black people, a solidarity between white female and black male that is only possible in *Uncle Tom's Cabin* between the saintlike Tom and the angelic Eva. This sympathy is signaled by an asymmetrical exchange in "Sis' Becky's Pickaninny." The story begins with the narrator seeing Julius's rabbit's foot and casting scorn on it as foolishness and superstition. Despite the narrator's genial contempt, Julius insists on the utility of the charm: "'dey ain' no 'moun er money could buy mine, suh. I mought len' it ter anybody I sot sto' by, but I would n' sell it, no indeed, suh'" (52). At the end of the story, the narrator records, without comment, having found the rabbit's foot in his wife's possession. Her possession of the good-luck charm, then, signals an exchange of mutual sympathy because Julius is a kind of seer, like the figure of Lebert Joseph in Paule Marshall's *Praisesong for the Widow*, one who was "marked . . . as someone who possessed ways of seeing that went beyond mere sight and ways of knowing that outstripped ordinary intelligence (*Li gain connaissance*)" (Marshall 172). Uncle Julius, unlike Annie's husband, can see not only her depression, but the sources of her pain in her childlessness, her boredom, and her isolation.

"Sis' Becky's Pickaninny," moreover, is the only story in *The Conjure Woman* in which Julius's story seems entirely selfless. In the other stories, his narratives are, in their own sly way, instrumental; he is trying to get his white "boss" to do (or not to do) something to benefit Julius. Although he fails to prevent the narrator from buying the plantation in "The Goophered Grapevine," most often Julius manages, as William L. Andrews has observed, to conjure the narrator (Chesnutt, *Collected Stories*, xii) and to gain some tangible benefit from the telling of the tale. In "Sis' Becky's Pickaninny," in contrast, Chesnutt leaves the reader in some doubt about whether Julius does benefit. Chesnutt chooses not to say whether Julius's assertion that "'dey ain' no 'moun er money could buy'" his rabbit's foot is merely a beginning gambit in a complicated negotiation. Chesnutt wants to leave open the possibility that Julius *gives* Annie his rabbit's foot and gets in return nothing but her sympathy. From Harriet Beecher Stowe's perspective, this exchange of sympathy would signify the deepest of understandings, but if one posits a different tradition of female readership and reception,[8] then Chesnutt here enacts how the discourse of sympathy can override, at least momentarily, the ideology of racism, no matter how genteel that racism. In the end, though, I continue to be disturbed by the exchange because of the asymmetry of power relations, and because the exchange is predicated on Julius's asexuality, on his symbolic castration.

If Julius is symbolically castrated, he is not silent, the status to which, Henry Louis Gates has reminded us, blacks in this period had been increasingly relegated. From 1876 to 1915, Gates says, "the literary presence of the speaking black subject was replaced by the deafening silence of his absence; essentially as an object, a figure in the fictions of nonblacks, did the black then 'exist' in mainstream literature" (Gates xviii). What we see, then, in Crane's *The Monster* is black man as object, deprived of the ability to articulate his own experience, an object first of ridicule and then of fear. In Chesnutt's *The Conjure Woman*, the black man speaks, but not directly of his own experience in postbellum America (and *The Conjure Woman* is similar to Twain's *Pudd'nhead Wilson* in that respect). His plantation stories only indirectly speak to his own postwar experience, almost as if Chesnutt knew that the only way he, as a writer, could get a hearing was by using the mask of the plantation darky and by omitting one whole generation from his tales, the generation of Henry Johnson. The only other black male in these stories is Julius's grandson, Tom, in "Mars Jeem's Nightmare." Despite the absence of this whole generation, Chesnutt, in the period of racial radicalism, creates a solidarity of sympathy and knowingness between black man and white woman, a solidarity that marginalizes the rational and instrumental white man. I find this an astonishing achievement, but one which is accomplished at a certain cost because young black men, the "new Negroes," must be excluded from this interaction, even by—especially by—an African-American writer, who, ironically, becomes himself part of an artistic lost generation for Americans. Within the cultural constraints of the late nineteenth century, Chesnutt cannot imagine (or cannot afford to imagine) a solidarity between a young black man and a white woman which would not inevitably marshal all of the vicious stereotypes of racial radicalism. Indeed, one could argue the futility of his effort in these stories because (as I said earlier) they could just as easily be read as confirming the marginality of blacks and women. For me, then, Chesnutt's accomplishment in *The Conjure Woman* is to have created a double-voiced narrative that attempts to undermine the presupposition of racial radicalism, but

clearly, and sadly for us and for our culture, Crane's vision of the necessary expulsion of the black beast has had much more staying power.

Notes

This essay was written with the support of an NEH Summer Seminar for college teachers, "Slavery, Reconstruction, and the U.S. Civil Imagination," under
the direction of Donald Pease. I would like to thank Marjan van Schaik and my
colleague John Patterson for helpful reading of drafts of this essay.

1. *The Red Badge of Courage* quickly became part of the high school curriculum, which also tended to perpetuate Crane's "centrality."

2. Of course, male African-American writers such as Chesnutt and Du Bois,
   and woman writers such as Anna Julia Cooper, Ida B. Wells, and Pauline
   Hopkins, were publishing in this period, but even the most visible of their
   works had a negligible effect on the turn-of-the-century racial consensus.

3. Crane, with his ear attuned to popular culture (for example, the scenes of
   popular entertainment in *Maggie* [1893]), will have been aware of the
   vogue for coon songs and the number of large-scale revues throughout the
   1890s in which coon songs and the cakewalk were performed.

4. Thus Johnson becomes an occasion for the white man to struggle with self-
   definition, a dynamic pointed out in Toni Morrison's *Playing in the Dark*.

5. When I taught these two texts in the graduate American Studies class of
   my colleague John Patterson, one of his students, Beth Bisbano, pointed
   out how careful Crane is to situate Whilomville on the cusp of modernity.
   For instance, there are both electric and gas lights in the town, and while
   there are electric street cars, fire engines are still dragged to fires by crowds
   of men. She argued that the expulsion of Johnson was an implicitly anti-
   modern move, but my sense is that his expulsion can be read as Crane's
   participation in the national consensus forged at this time. In order for
   America to "progress" and to "develop," particularly in the South, the
   problem that African Americans represented had to be made to disappear.
   And so the monster, and the unnameable threat that he represents, must be
   expelled.

6. Although Gibson is acute on this point, he also retreats into a rather standard reading of the text that focuses on the moral dilemma of the central
   white character: "despite the racial theme . . . *The Monster* is finally a story
   about human responsibility" (138).

7. Given the number of Uncle Julius stories *not* reprinted in *The Conjure
   Woman*, including a masterpiece like "Dave's Neckliss," I think that one
   must attribute this kind of coherence to the volume. In addition, as Richard
   Brodhead has made clear, the intervention of Chesnutt's editor, Walter
   Hines Page, was crucial: he identified the best of Chesnutt's corpus of sto-
   ries, and "it would be easy to argue that Page's letter helped Chesnutt en-

vision the whole, coherent work. . . . He shows no signs of having envisioned it on his own" (Chesnutt, *Conjure Woman*, 17).

8. It is beyond the scope of this article, but one could argue that Julius's intervention in the last story of the volume, "Hot-Foot Hannibal," also points to the sympathetic solidarity between Julius and Annie. In the story, Julius is instrumental in reconciling the sister-in-law of the narrator with a local man, and thus ironically he helps to conclude the volume on the note of a North-South marriage, symbolic in this period of national reconciliation, a reconciliation that is only made possible in the national arena by the willingness of the North to collude with the South on the question of race.

Works Cited

Boskin, Joseph. *Sambo: The Rise and Demise of an American Jester.* New York: Oxford University Press, 1986.

Chesnutt, Charles W. *The Conjure Woman and Other Conjure Tales.* Edited and with an introduction by Richard Brodhead. Durham: Duke University Press, 1993.

———. *Collected Stories of Charles W. Chesnutt.* Edited and with an introduction by William L. Andrews. New York: Mentor, 1992.

Crane, Stephen. *"Maggie: A Girl of the Streets" and Other Short Fiction.* New York: Bantam, 1986.

———. *Tales of Whilomville.* Vol. 7 of *The University of Virginia Edition of the Works of Stephen Crane.* Edited by Fredson Bowers. Charlottesville: University of Virginia Press, 1969.

Duncan, Charles. *The Absent Man: The Narrative Craft of Charles W. Chesnutt.* Athens: Ohio University Press, 1998.

Gates, Henry Louis, Jr., and Charles T. Davis. Introduction to *The Slave's Narrative*, edited by Charles T. Davis and Henry Louis Gates, Jr. New York: Oxford University Press, 1985.

Gibson, Donald B. *The Fiction of Stephen Crane.* Carbondale: Southern Illinois University Press, 1968.

Marshall, Paule. *Praisesong for the Widow.* New York: Dutton, 1984.

Showalter, Elaine. *Sexual Anarchy: Gender and Culture at the Fin de Siècle.* New York: Viking, 1990.

Stowe, Harriet Beecher. *Uncle Tom's Cabin.* Edited by Elizabeth Ammons. New York: Norton, 1994.

Sundquist, Eric. *To Wake the Nations: Race and the Making of American Literature.* Cambridge: Harvard University Press, 1993.

Warner, Michael. "Value, Agency, and Stephen Crane's *The Monster.*" *Nineteenth-Century Literature* 40, no. 1 (1985): 76–93.

Williamson, Joel. *A Rage for Order: Black/White Relations in the American South since Emancipation.* New York: Oxford University Press, 1986.

Fourteen

"Moral Authority," History, and the Case of Canonization
William Wells Brown's Clotel and Clotelle

Gillian Johns

I

Since the American civil rights movement of the 1960s, literary critics and others have invested much energy in the recuperation, republication, and reinterpretation of many lost or undervalued texts originally produced by African Americans. Such nineteenth-century works as Harriet E. Wilson's *Our Nig* (1859) and Harriet A. Jacobs's *Incidents in the Life of a Slave Girl* (1861) have been republished in trade formats that make them newly accessible to twentieth-century readers, and later authors such as Charles W. Chesnutt and Zora Neale Hurston have been complimented not only with republication but also with a renaissance of interpretive attention. The ex-slave William Wells Brown—long recognized as the first African American to write a novel—is among the authors receiving increased levels of attention. J. Noel Heermance's 1969 massive critical biography of Brown, which included a reissue of Brown's 1864 novel of slavery, *Clotelle: A Tale of the Southern States*, claimed for the author "significant and deeply impressive" (Heermance 23) pioneering efforts in expressive genres restricted by the ideology of abolition. By 1978, in their reference guide to both Brown and Martin R. Delany, Curtis W. Ellison and W. E. Metcalf, Jr., observed, "Interest in [Brown's] life and work continues; between 1969 and 1975, at least ten reprints of his books, as well as a number of articles about him and a major biography, were issued" (Ellison and Metcalf 3). And Henry Louis Gates, Jr., and William L. Andrews republished the 1853 *Clotel;*

or, the President's Daughter in their identically entitled 1990 anthologies *Three Classic African-American Novels.*

William L. Andrews describes the general canonical shift thus:

> As the study of Afro-American history, literature, and culture boomed in the 1960s and 1970s, the significance of the black writer in the literature of the South underwent considerable re-evaluation. Not surprisingly, the desegregation of southern literary history and criticism received its impetus from black researchers and commentators. It was they who began to argue that the autobiographical writing of ex-slaves like Frederick Douglass and William Wells Brown served as a critique of the plantation tradition and ante-bellum southern literature. In their analyses, the fiction of Chesnutt had to be read as a corrective to the excesses of Harris and Thomas Nelson Page. James Weldon Johnson, Jean Toomer, and Zora Neale Hurston offered insights into the folk traditions of the South that could not be found in DuBose Heyward, Paul Green, or Erskine Caldwell. (Andrews, "Authority," 1–2)

What is significant about this account of the current status and function of African-American literature is that it presumes and contextualizes a broader range of value and influence for the tradition than American critics and readers have historically offered it. If, as Andrews asserts, landmark Southern white writers must be read against their black contemporaries, these African-American writers are now read not merely for what they reveal about the lives of their own oppressed people, or the "Negro Problem"—the way many of us learned initially to view them—but also for what they say, or "correct," about the mythologizing of a larger American public. Indeed, Andrews asserts that currently "the margin and the center have been reversed" to a degree that "testifies to the moral authority that black southern literature has been gaining in competition with much white southern literature for this era's interpretation of the racial past" (Andrews, "Authority," 2). For him, then, early black authors currently have the clout—or "moral authority," to use his term—to write our nation's whole crucial political history.

Yet notwithstanding the "moral authority" Andrews discovers for African-American authors in the present literary climate, it is interesting to find him wondering on the same page of the same essay, "Is it advisable . . . simply to slip the yoke of marginality from one group of writers to another without changing the joke that southern literary historians and critics have been playing on themselves and their readers, namely, that a single race or sex or mode of southern writing can be awarded plenary or representative status?" And this provocative query raises a red flag for us; Andrews is warning scholars here to beware the frugality they often cultivate when organizing literary traditions. More importantly, even, his question points to general concern about whether our old, perhaps comfortable, literary practices—discovering the major works for any given period or people and then clustering minor works around them—are still appropriate given our new "literary" interest in cultural history for its own sake. That is, implicit in the new canonical problem is a debilitating confusion or mystification of intention in the field about what we are reading and writing for and how to achieve those objectives. We sometimes don't know, of course, and other times don't say. Nevertheless, what I have called a confusion of scholarly intention results, at least in the case of William Wells Brown, in canonization practices assuming an unnecessary degree of scarcity of "plenary" space or "moral authority" for one author of multiple "versions" of what has come to be known as "the first African-American novel." For while it is true that Brown's work has received a great deal of critical attention —indeed, surely enough to preserve his name during this important era—accompanying the explication of his literary efforts is a tendency to privilege only one or the other of his very distinct 1853 and 1864 novels as *the* exemplary text, as if only one of the works can contain authentic historical matter. Following Andrews's lead, however, I want to explore how our scholarly tendency to read only one text at a time affects our critical understanding of Brown's work, and to suggest that both of these novels are interesting for different reasons and both consequently warrant preservation and widespread reading, preferably as a pair.[1]

II

In the introduction to his *Three Classic African-American Novels*, Gates provides the general reader with the following explanation of Brown's career and *Clotel*'s publication history:

> Brown enjoys the distinction of being the first American of African descent who earned a living as a writer. . . . Overshadowed by the awesome presence of Frederick Douglass, however, Brown's career and significance to the tradition have not fully or adequately been assessed.
> Brown wrote four distinct versions of *Clotel*, the first of which,

curiously enough, was not published in America until 1969, perhaps because of its claim that Thomas Jefferson had kept a mistress who was a slave, Sally Hemmings, that she had borne his
children, and that Jefferson had sold them. References to Jefferson's paternity disappear completely in the other American editions of *Clotel*. (Gates x)

Gates is certainly right to observe *Clotel*'s "curiously" long absence for
American readers. And his implicit point that Brown's first anti-slavery
novel (which does indeed assert the inconstancy and moral negligence,
at best, of a venerated American father) was too impolite for general
readers for over a hundred years is surely convincing to many students
of American history. I find it more curious still, however, that while
Gates acknowledges that the scholarly community has long been aware
of multiple "versions" of Brown's pioneering anti-slavery novel and that
the author's "significance to the tradition" warrants further critical assessment, he himself takes the opportunity to anthologize only one—
or, in effect, to replace one neglected, rarely available "version" with
another—rather than, say, to argue explicitly for the value of all of the
texts. Although no one editor could endorse all of the tradition at one
publication moment, Gates's language and choice seem to promise his
reader the special titillation of access to a censored text that must, by
virtue of its proscription, be the better read. Also consider the fact that
Andrews (whom we recall as the scholar who, in his essay "Mark Twain,
William Wells Brown, and the Problem of Authority in New South
Writing," advocates a confrontation of the "mystification of authority"
in our literature and invites recognition that writers such as Twain and
Brown indicate that "authority is transactional" and should thus "acknowledge its own provisionality" [Andrews, "Authority," 8, 11–12])
also reissues Brown's first novel as part of an anthology of classics in
1990. Yet he likewise does not direct his reader to the author's other
"correctives" of the American "racial past"; he refers to them simply as
"three more versions of *Clotel*" (Andrews, *Three Classics*, 15). While it
is a privilege to witness nineteenth-century anti-slavery literature becoming available to general American readers, it seems to me that by
recognizing Brown's multiple fictional accounts of slavery as "versions"
of a singular American tale and opting to publish one, both of these
premier scholars of African-American literature suggest that, for all
practical purposes, a student of American literature need be familiar
with only one, the one they have made the extra effort to republish in
trade format.[2] Indeed, presented with the authoritative introduction

that normally accompanies paperback editions such as both *Three Classic African-American Novels*, a general reader is led to take on faith the
word of the expert.

Heermance, however, held a very different view of Brown's fiction. In
1969, he argued that the 1864 *Clotelle* represented the intended final
work of the artist. Describing Brown as a writer developing an "awareness of effect, both psychological and literary, and an understanding of
how certain perspectives and techniques work on an audience" (Heermance 135) over the course of his expressive career, this scholar opted
to reissue *Clotelle* along with two hundred pages of critical and biographical background explicating how the author's work culminated in
the 1864 novel. Indeed, Heermance asserted that the 1864 novel represents "artistry enough" to warrant study since, "though Brown's 'firstness' as a novelist lies in the 1853 date of his first *Clotel; or, The President's Daughter*, published in London, it is the 1864 edition which gives
us our understanding of the artist who is finally pleased enough with
his work so that he does not revise it again, and does, in fact, copyright
and publish it himself three years later" (Heermance 133). According to
Heermance, moreover, Brown became increasingly committed—before
and during the Civil War, *after* the initial 1853 publication of *Clotel*—to
black life and nationalism, and this shift was accompanied by later non-
fictional efforts to rewrite American images of blacks (in, for example,
his histories *St. Domingo: Its Revolutions and Its Patriots* [1855] and *The
Black Man: His Antecedents, His Genius, and His Achievements* [1863]),
given what the author saw as "the need for the country to change its
attitudes and preconceptions about Negroes" (Heermance 20). With
this argument, of course, the implication is that *Clotelle* is not only the
better "artistic" work but also the more historically interesting artifact.
In 1969, then, Heermance argued the other side of Gates's coin; yet
notwithstanding his archival and interpretive efforts and perhaps those
of others of his critical generation, his position has disappeared from
view for the current would-be general reader of Brown's fiction.[4]

My point in observing the resituation of *Clotel/Clotelle* by these
scholars is neither to advocate one editor's position over another's nor to
make a new case for *Clotelle*'s being the sole text of Brown's worthy of
preservation. Rather, I want to suggest that we re-examine the basic
assumption that any editor or scholar aiming to preserve early African-
American literature must choose one of Brown's texts and promote it as
the truest or most important. Stated simply, if Heermance, Gates, and
Andrews—all of whom possess authority as critics—must keep making the same kinds of arguments for the worth of just one of Brown's

"versions" to prevent the wholesale disappearance of this black author's name and "firstness," then none of them can present complex readings that would detail the richness of this early author's multiple texts and his relationships to his contemporary readers, let alone explicate why more of his works might be particularly interesting to readers today. Moreover, their predicament seems to mark more than a mere shortage of physical publication space, for other critics as well, while commenting analytically on several early African-American works simultaneously, have made similar arguments for the "moral" precedence of one text over another. In his 1990 essay "Race, Violence, and Manhood: The Masculine Ideal in Frederick Douglass's 'The Heroic Slave,'" for example, Richard Yarborough posits that Brown's *Clotelle*—in which the term "Negro" is replaced by the more nationalistic term "African" for character description—depicts an ideological development in the author's textual struggle with African-American manhood. Yarborough writes that this "change, although apparently minor, in fact manifests Brown's rejection of some of the racist ideological assumptions that supported popular white conceptions of blacks" (Yarborough 170); thus he characterizes Jerome, Brown's final and actually *black* (rather than the earlier mulatto) "male lead" of *Clotelle,* as an important legacy to later African-American writers. Yet while Jean Fagan Yellin has also identified a trajectory in Brown's fiction, for her it is an unfortunate ideological regression—or decrease in authenticity—in the author's accounts of slavery. Yellin discovers the literary importance of the first *Clotel* to lie in its "powerful realistic scenes of slave life" (Yellin 174) but writes that "[i]n revision the realistic passages have been weakened. . . . The tone is now smooth. The rough humour, stark brutality, and pointed debate which gave the novel vitality are trimmed, toned down, almost obliterated. If the skin of its hero were not colored black, the book would be a conventional sentimental anti-slavery novel" (Yellin 175–176). For Yellin, by the time *Clotelle* appears, whatever was "realistic" in Brown is gone.

It is further telling that in "Her Side of His Story: A Feminist Analysis of Two Nineteenth-Century Antebellum Novels—William Wells Brown's *Clotel* and Harriet E. Wilson's *Our Nig*," Angelyn Mitchell goes so far as to argue that Wilson's more "personal" tale of slavery is more authentic than, and therefore altogether superior to, Brown's "discursive" account, effectively assigning the first fictional black utterance on African-American women to Wilson rather than Brown. Remarking on what she terms the "flatness" of Brown's characterization, Mitchell writes:

Wilson's novel springs, it seems to me, from what might be called a "secret well of immanent femininity." . . . Wilson portrays her female characters' quest for freedom through hyperbolic renderings of interpersonal, familial, and social interactions. Brown is also concerned with women and their quest for freedom; however, his female characters seek freedom through heroic deeds such as daring escapes and other adventures. . . .

. . . But when women are allowed to speak for themselves, as Mary Helen Washington says of black female writers, their literature takes the trouble to record the genuine "thoughts, words, feelings, and deeds of black women, experiences that make the realities of being black in America look very different from what men have written." And as recent discourse theory has made clear, the ability to talk, to give utterance, about one's life and to interpret it, is integral to leading that life rather than being led through it. (Mitchell 8)

In the case of these two authors, it would seem, twentieth-century readers are asked to decide which gender should be awarded Andrews's "moral authority" to *record the genuine* regarding historical black women. In fact, however, given that *Our Nig* (1859) was published only six years after *Clotel* (which was published in 1853—and only in Britain), if *Our Nig* is deemed the better, more authentic novel in general, it might obtain the coveted literary position of "the first African-American novel," gender questions aside.

I believe that the critics are right. *Clotel* and *Clotelle* really *are* different tales; and *Our Nig* is still another. We have many early African-American novels to read and explicate, even of a single author, for, as Richard O. Lewis writes, "Brown's *four novels* include *Clotel* . . . and *Clotelle*" (Lewis 130; emphasis added). But what is at stake in the way that critics currently choose to advocate the value of a particular text is nothing less than that text's authority to speak for ideological history; with Andrews's critical "joke/yoke" very much alive, we take on faith not only that there can be only one "plenary" or "first" African-American novel but also that only one "version" of that novel can deserve our attention. What this means is that how we select and organize our exemplary texts hinges more on our particular ideological aims, interests, and limitations as both readers and critics than on any static or inherent historical value possessed by the texts. When writing and reading in the service of recuperating nineteenth-century representations of black manhood, we locate one "plenary" text; when after "authentic" slave life, we shift our orientation to another; and when in search of complex renderings of black women, we move to yet another. However, if Andrews is right that we can stop playing the critical "joke" on both ourselves and our readers that only one text can speak at once, and it can make only one argument—that we might dare to no longer obediently observe a monolithic, hierarchical notion of history and canonization—then we might begin to be more forthright about our readings. We might, when we know, tell our readers what particular "literary" values and ideological "histories" we, ourselves, are reading and writing in the service of at any given moment and let them choose these or others. We might, when we can, place in check our own stinginess regarding writers who offer multiple, often conflicting, interpretations of America's "racial past." We might, that is, imagine offering our books and authors more than one textual space at a time, if we already agree, as Andrews suggests we do, that the voices of African Americans count centrally and diversely in descriptions of our general American past. And with that said, I want now to take a brief look at the 1853 *Clotel* before focusing more closely on the particular publishing moment and on the characterization and plot changes made for the 1864 novel, both because the later novel, *Clotelle,* is currently the less available of the two (and thus, by critical suggestion, less valuable to readers) and because Brown's revisions to it make for a reader/text alliance revealing a particularly Civil War–time fictional dream of post-emancipation American racial unity.

III

The 1853 *Clotel* is by far the longer of the two novels and includes within its pages much matter beyond the narrative: several simultaneously enacted plots; newspaper advertisements, editorials and news accounts, and speeches; and anecdotes, discussions, songs, and poetry about antebellum Southern life for both blacks and whites. Brown begins the novel, for example, not with an introduction to particular fictional characters but rather with a five-page commentary—quoting both Southern state laws and the voices of public officials—on the legal and actual restrictions on the marriages of "half-whites" during slavery's late stage in America. After this "documentation,"[3] the author addresses his British reader directly, writing,

> Reader, when you take into consideration the fact, that amongst the slave population no safeguard is thrown around virtue, and no inducement held out to slave women to be chaste, you will not be surprised when we tell you that immorality and vice pervade the cities of the Southern states in a manner unknown in the cities

and towns of the Northern states. Indeed most of the slave women have no higher aspiration than that of becoming the finely-dressed mistress of some white man. (*Clotel* 63)

Already, in his preface, Brown has placed the burden of correcting slavery's general social and moral disorder squarely on that same intended reader, writing, "If the incidents set forth in the following pages should add anything new to the information already given to the Public through similar publications, and should thereby aid in bringing British influence to bear upon American slavery, the main object for which this work was written will have been accomplished" (16). With this combination of introductory "argument" and extra-narrative frame, then, Brown anticipates both his readers' discomfort and their lack of information about the institution of slavery and charges them not only with suspending moral judgment of American slaves, but also with the perhaps more difficult task of taking a sweeping view of the lifestyle accompanying slavery.

When Brown introduces the novel's primary characters, Currer and her two daughters Clotel and Althesa (who is also Thomas Jefferson's daughter), then, and announces their impending sale, his readers are already primed to view them as textual guides to America's Southern chaos. And through the narrative portrayal of the breakup of Currer's family and the particular dangers the three mulatto women (and, later, Clotel's daughter Mary) subsequently confront alone, Brown is able to record his vision of what Yellin has aptly termed "slave life" in various Southern environments. For example, he details the texture of the daily lives of Natchez slaves and slaveholders while tracing Currer's fate in the hands of a Southern white Methodist parson, including individual chapters exploring contradictions in slaveholder-sanctioned sermons that advocate a docile form of Christianity only for their slaves, self-deluding ideas that poor Southern whites have about their superiority over blacks, and ways in which black slaves manipulate their white masters with overtly officious behavior while they undermine their authority in private song. As Yellin has noted, all of this cultural-historical material is deleted from the more focused narrative action presented in *Clotelle*, which means that we can preserve it only by preserving Brown's first novel.

Regarding the value of *Clotelle*, Brown's later novel—published at the height of the war—however, it is worth recalling that the American Civil War was at no point an easy win for abolitionists. James M. McPherson notes in his landmark history *The Struggle for Equality:*

Abolitionists and the Negro in the Civil War and Reconstruction that President Lincoln signed the Emancipation Proclamation in January of 1863 —three years into the war—primarily because of increasing public belief that it was a military necessity: the North had to destroy the advantage white Southerners were enjoying in the dragging conflict in being able both to leave their property in the hands of black male slaves while fighting and to exploit slave labor to maintain their army. The moral question of whether American slaves had the right to freedom remained open throughout the war, and committed abolitionists remained fearful of and disillusioned by the climate. McPherson writes,

> A young abolitionist in the army reported to Garrison that many of his fellow soldiers had become "emancipationists" only because they wanted to end the war and go home. They still disliked the Negro as much as ever: "Though these men wish to abolish slavery, it is not from any motive outside of their own selfishness; and is there not a possibility that at some not very distant day, these old rank prejudices, that are now lulled to sleep by selfish motives, may again possess these men and work evil?" Frederick Douglass felt the same fear and expressed it in a speech at the Cooper Union: "Much as I value the present apparent hostility to Slavery at the North, I plainly see that it is less the outgrowth of high and intelligent moral conviction against Slavery, as such, than because of the trouble its friends have brought upon the country." (McPherson 92–93)

James Redpath, the publisher of Brown's *Clotelle*, was one of those abolitionists doubtful of the capacity and willingness of Northerners to reimagine black slaves as American citizens. McPherson quotes him as remarking, six weeks into the war, "'[T]he drift of public sentiment appears, day by day, to be steadily setting against even the recognition of the slave in this contest'" (McPherson 58). It is surely this frame of mind that led Redpath to publish Brown's *Clotelle* as part of his "Books for the Camp Fires" series, which included Balzac's *The Vendetta*, Swift's *Gulliver's Travels*, and Hugo's *The Battle of Waterloo*. And, indeed, one could say that the authorizing documentation of the 1853 novel is replaced by the blatantly propagandistic packaging of the November 1864 novel, for Redpath directly targeted the book's cover to Union soldiers with the "camp fire" inscription in bold type above a drawing of soldiers around a fire, and the novel bore the following message on its last page: "NOTE—The author of the foregoing tale was formerly a Kentucky Slave. If it serves to relieve the monotony of camp-life to the soldiers of the Union, and therefore of liberty, and at the same time kindles their zeal in the cause of universal emancipation, the object both of its author and publisher will be gained" (*Clotelle* 104).

According to McPherson, Brown revised and circulated *Clotelle* for the first time in America "for the express purpose of dispelling popular notions about the Negro in order to help mobilize popular support for Lincoln's newly adopted emancipation policy" (McPherson 139). In 1955, reissuing *Clotelle* in "the first American edition reproduced in facsimile from the copy of The Library Company of Philadelphia," editor Maxwell Whiteman likewise calls attention to the importance the novel's packaging and historical moment had for its publisher. He writes in his introduction,

> Eleven years were to pass before an American public in the midst of a bitter war was to read it. The second edition was rewritten, the name respelled to *Clotelle*, and the president was substituted by the senator. James Redpath, the publisher of the first American edition in 1864 directed its sale "to the Soldiers of the Union" not only to relieve the monotony of camp life but with hopes that "at the same time [it] kindles their zeal in the cause of universal emancipation." (*Clotelle* vii)

For both scholars, Brown produced his "art" for social reasons; he used "art," we might say, to change minds. And given this explicitly propagandistic nature of Brown's work, scholars might be tempted to deem it to have little relevance to late-twentieth-century readers: we might find it to be less authentically representative of nineteenth-century black expression and audience than we would have our early African-American literature; or we might think it unreliable to read historically a book published "expressly" to influence Union solders in camp. Yet, by definition, all of what we consider to be the "literature of slavery"—from *Uncle Tom's Cabin* to *Narrative of the Life of Frederick Douglass*—possesses propagandistic intent. As Lewis contends,

> Since "truth is stranger than fiction," such melodrama as pervades much of Brown's fiction draws charges that his works are propagandistic, which is accurate but which nonetheless fails to recognize the informative value of such social-protest literature. Are not the works of Dickens, Hugo, Tolstoy, and Stowe "propagandistic" fiction? The verisimilitude of the "propaganda" is the test of its social value. And Brown, in the tradition of Washington Irving, manipulates his material to bolster a sense of historical credibility. (Lewis 149)

Propaganda is often a feature of literature situated firmly in its own historical moment, not a reason to discard texts. And I would contend further that one key source of the particular value of Brown's 1864 *Clotelle* lies within the very explicit packaging that might offend us as "literary" readers. That is, when reading for the cultural history represented in expressive work, we often would like to know who any given author is talking to, or what the text might say about the dreams and fears of its readers in addition to its author. And while audience is a factor we tend to have trouble pinning down for much of our literary tradition (perhaps especially of the nineteenth century), with *Clotelle* scholars are fortunate enough to find themselves in a position to speculate on the historical relationship between text and specific intended reader. We can, that is, see what an American ex-slave thinks he needs to tell those fighting reluctantly and indirectly—yet *at that very moment* —for his freedom. In this light, surely we can imagine the unique historical value—for a reader interested in American sentiments about slavery—of a novel circulated to inspire white Union soldiers with "the cause of universal emancipation" during the height of the American Civil War.

IV

It is often observed that Thomas Jefferson is no longer a feature of Brown's *Clotelle* and suggested that his deletion marks an ideological retreat on the author's part in order to gain the sympathies of an American readership. Yet there has been little consideration of the possibility that Brown's thoroughgoing revisions of names and emplotment, including the erasure of Jefferson, might not generally mitigate for American readers the implications of slavery on their soil.

I want to argue that, read in contrast to the structural and narrative choices the author makes in *Clotel*, his 1864 novel transfers personal responsibility for the familial chaos and hence moral resolution necessary in the South to all Americans at the same time that it leads soldiers, in particular, to watch their race-based expectations and comfort collapse. Several character and plot changes reveal the important ideological shift, and Brown's opening sets the stage, for here he replaces his earlier caveat about judging the morality of "half-whites" with a terse but telling two-paragraph description of the number and plight of American mulattoes. Indeed, Brown cuts right to the chase, in the second paragraph, with the same statement he had used in his first novel to absolve black slaves of moral responsibility; but it is now addressed to "we" northern Americans rather than "you" British. He writes,

"When we take into consideration the fact that no safeguard is thrown around virtue . . . we will not be surprised when told that immorality and vice pervade the cities and towns of the South to an extent unknown in the Northern states" (*Clotelle* 5–6). Brown does not promise to neatly dress up, for his American readers, the moral degradation they will witness. Nor does he offer "authoritative" documentation for the accuracy of his vision to follow; no structuring justification for this account is presented here via the testimony of other speakers or state law. Instead, readers are simply directed to "not be surprised" when his previously enslaved black voice utters the last word on how the Southern world looks.

Brown's audacious reach for authority is accompanied in *Clotelle* by a new hierarchy of moral order and action that does not always reinforce earlier literary conventions allied to the ideology of abolitionism. For example, in a revision perhaps more complicated to describe than to read, Clotelle, Brown's mulatto heroine in this novel (the counterpart to Mary in *Clotel*), who is marked as a heroine by her highlighted presence throughout the narrative action as well as by her eponymous name, does not die the "tragic" death that her name double of the earlier novel does. In *Clotel*, Clotel "ran for her life" (217) into the Potomac River; in *Clotelle*, she is privileged to end the tale living free in France, married, as Yellin has observed, "no longer [to] the rebellious mulatto George, but [to] the black slave rebel, Jerome" (Yellin 174). And while Yellin argues that the changes to Brown's heroine have an effect—if any—only at the level of the language of race (that is, Brown's move to include a fully *black* character), the circumstances surrounding Clotelle's fate and family in fact mark a grander realm of possibilities for the American mulatto heroine than is conventional in American fiction: she is reunited with her deliriously repentant white slaveholding father in Europe, and she, he, and her chosen husband Jerome resolve to live together as black, mulatto, and white members of one expatriate American family. While Mary, Brown's earlier heroine (the only mulatto female to live through the American drama of slavery), is likewise reunited with her first love at the end of *Clotel*'s narrative (after enduring multiple forms of mistreatment and being rescued by a lucky marriage and removal to Europe), she never merges with the white line of her biological roots.

In the revised characterization of George-Jerome—aptly described by Yarborough as Brown's "male lead" (Yarborough 171)—we can see more of the author's expanding realm of possibilities. While Mary's husband George in *Clotel*, "too, could boast that his father was an American statesman," and Brown asserts the character's heroism editorially, as critics have noted, George's physical strength is never actually depicted. By the time Brown writes his Civil War novel, however, he imagines a male hero who both is black and resembles the young Douglass of *Narrative of the Life of Frederick Douglass* in his sense of his own manhood. In language similar to that of the slave narrative—in which Douglass writes that "the white man who expected to succeed in whipping, must also succeed in killing me" (Douglass 79)—Brown writes, "Jerome felt his superiority, and always declared that no master should ever flog him." Threatened with a whipping, the slave responds, "'I will serve you, Master Wilson, I will labor for you day and night, if you demand it, but I will not be whipped'" (*Clotelle* 58). Jerome in fact subsequently strikes his master and escapes; yet after being caught and imprisoned, he still remarks remorselessly,

> My liberty is of much consequence to me as Mr. Wilson's is to him. I am as sensitive to feeling as he. If I mistake not, the day will come when the negro will learn that he can get his freedom by fighting for it; and should that time arrive, the whites will be sorry that they have hated us so shamefully. I am free to say that, could I live my life over again, I would use all the energies which God has given me to get up an insurrection. (65)

Moreover, after Clotelle has assisted him in escaping hanging, on his way north Jerome risks his own life to rescue a white child from a burning house, and later, while on a ship headed for Europe, he muses to himself, "'Though forced from my native land by the tyrants of the South, I hope I shall some day be able to return. With all her faults, I love my country still'" (88). Brown's readers witness here a black male who dares to refer to America as his "native land," his country that he loves, as if the bond is too deep to be broken by one race's misguided perceptions. Indeed, when Jerome arrives in Europe, Brown depicts him, in truly loyal American sarcasm, as made notably uncomfortable by the British caste system. Jerome, then, is smart, strong, and ethical; and he would fight for his country. Given Brown's targeted readership, we might conjecture that his strategy is to portray in this male character a potential black American citizen; the Civil War moment has stretched his limits for black male characterization.

Notwithstanding the importance of how Brown expands the range of action of his leading black characters (Clotelle and Jerome) for Civil War–time readers, it is also striking to note how he conspicuously lowers the status of other blacks and some whites in *Clotelle*, for what emerges from a close reading is an ideological pattern that equates (at least Brown's sense of) ethical behavior with narrative success and immoral choices with failure. For instance, early in the novel readers learn that, in contrast to Currer of *Clotel*, Agnes—the slave mother here—is an older black woman whom Brown describes as tasteless enough to "be heard boasting that she was the daughter of an American Senator" (*Clotelle* 5–6), and she dies in an unsympathetic footnote (unlike Currer, who lived for many narrative pages after her initial sale south). In this novel, then, a character's race does not dictate sympathetic narrative portrayal, for to his newly unbecoming black American Agnes, Brown adds revised language and action to describe the alliance between a black woman and a white man. In chapter 11, Brown refers to Clotelle's mother Isabella (one of Agnes's daughters), who lives alone in a cottage her master and lover Henry Linwood (Horatio Green in *Clotel*) has obtained for her, pejoratively as a "mistress," in sharp contrast to his romantic treatment of the same situation in *Clotel*. And while Green had been unabashedly in love with his slave Clotel and had remained committed and single throughout the couple's relationship, Brown's Linwood has been married for two years while enjoying his involvement with the unaware Isabella. When Isabella asks him about the woman she has seen him riding with in a carriage (having already sensed something amiss between them, since he no longer spends nights at the cottage), Linwood lies, saying that he has no one else, even though she has offered him the moral out of sending her and their daughter Clotelle out of his way to the free Northern states; Linwood then goes home to likewise lie to his brooding wife Gertrude about where he has been and who the slave child was who called him "papa" when they passed by in the carriage.

Brown goes on for several chapters with his depiction of the sordid betrayals wrought by Henry and Isabella's unholy union, and via this part of his story he introduces a white double to the tasteless Agnes. The character of Linwood's mother-in-law, Mrs. Miller, is unique to *Clotelle;* she is a "caged lioness" (36), according to Brown, and as duplicitous as Linwood yet far more powerful. She is a strong contrast to her sweet young white daughter, who has a "secret grief gnawing at her heart" and is in no way contentious but, rather, "sad," with "pale cheeks and eyes that showed too well that agony, far deeper than her speech portrayed, filled her heart" (*Clotelle* 35). Mrs. Miller is a harsh older Southern woman who believes in "asserting her rights." When she learns from her distraught daughter that, in his sleep, Linwood has repeated Isabella's name and professed he will never marry, she follows him to Isabella's house, triumphantly confronts the slave with Linwood's marriage, and later demands that her son-in-law give her power to do "as she should think best" with the two slaves Isabella and Clotelle. Linwood, although the man of the family, is no match for Mrs.

Miller: "Gertrude was Mrs. Miller's only child, and Henry felt little like displeasing a family upon whose friendship he so much depended, and no doubt, long wishing to free himself from Isabella, he at once yielded to the demands of his mother-in-law" (*Clotelle* 37–38). Isabella is hence sold south and her daughter Clotelle raised and tormented by Mrs. Miller as a working slave. Yet in his Civil War novel, Brown has created in Mrs. Miller more than another white literary figure responsible for chaos in the lives of slaves, for she also emerges ideologically as the greatest threat to Southern *white* tranquility, including her own: she takes to drinking, becomes, according to Brown, "the most brutal creature that ever lived," and then dies alone, "unlamented by a single person." Linwood, who could not stand to watch his daughter be abused yet was unable to change the situation, remorsefully learns too late—after Gertrude has already died of "melancholy"—that he had "blamed" his wife "wrongfully" for his mother-in-law's cruelty toward his daughter (102).

Another notable aspect of the hierarchy of ethics as represented in *Clotelle* is that Linwood's position changes in Brown's revised novel, for while he is both ethically and materially weak in the early part of the narrative, his sense of ethics has evolved by the end. Brown adds two new chapters here, "Clotelle Meets Her Father" and "The Father's Resolve," in which the reunited Clotelle and Jerome accidentally come upon Linwood in France while the slaveholder is in a sad state:

> Stretched upon a mattress, with both hands tightly bound to the bedstead, the friendless stranger was indeed a pitiful sight. His dark, dishevelled hair prematurely gray, his long, unshaven beard, and the wildness of the eyes which glanced upon them as they opened the door and entered, caused the faint hope which had so suddenly risen in Clotelle's heart, to sink, and she felt that this man could claim no kindred with her. (*Clotelle* 101)

Beaten and wracked with guilt, the delirious Linwood is tied up as a slave might be; and with his material condition lessened, Clotelle is in the comparative position of power—he is the one who can make no claim of being kin to her. Clotelle spends two days nursing her father before he can speak, during which time he comes to accept her black husband. The trio then tour Europe together as a family for a time, and during the trip Linwood—due to both the young couple's influence and the non-racist example of the Europeans—resolves to set his slaves free, settle them in a Northern state, and return to live with his daughter and her husband in France. Thus Brown's Civil War novel—directed to Union soldiers who need inspiration to finish "the cause of universal emancipation"—ends, appropriately, on the note of this American slave-holder's new "resolve" rather than with the realization of his slave's actual freedom.

It is safe to say that Brown refashions the characters and plot of his earlier *Clotel* into his first *American* African-American novel, *Clotelle*, in a manner that will meet at least his own need for an American dream of post–Civil War national unity. He has written into his novel an entirely new order which shifts the burden of moral responsibility to the young and kind and presents the possibility of the happy American ending of a harmonious multiracial "family." Clotelle—a mulatto woman—earns status as the only female survivor of her family and, indeed, the family's strongest member, taking over the earlier role of the mature white woman as director of her family's male head. And perhaps even more significant than the introduction of this triumphant mulatto to American fiction is the concurrent erasure of villainous traits in Gertrude, her ideological young white double. In fact, Brown's dream dictates a wholesale transfer of power from his central white patriarch and matriarch to young people who possess the moral virtue necessary for racial reconciliation and peace. I contend that in this, *Clotelle* has significance today as a historical record of the American expressive-political imagination. Overall, the storylines I have summarized here suggest that the "propaganda" in Brown's novel presents—at its very timely moment—the ideological promise of a post-emancipation future for Americans as members of families who live through an internal experience of slavery. Reading this story, one might find oneself imagining its intended readers, Union soldiers, and hypothesizing that the narrative might tend to inflate their sympathy for the young, vulnerable Southern women they would likely meet during the chaos of war; similarly, it might deflate their sense of the manhood of Southern men—here shown as duplicitous, adulterous, and ineffectual as leaders of their families—whom they must be prepared to fight. In short, the novel makes much historical sense as an expressive document bound to the American Civil War, or, in other words, as a fictional effort to imagine a peaceful American future should the Union win. Combining it with Brown's first *Clotel*, we have a rich combination of cultural materials through which to read American antebellum struggle and hope.

Notes

1. A longer project needs to be pursued, of course, that would consider the relationships among all of Brown's four anti-slavery novels offered as

Clotel[le] and their relevance to past and present readers, but the general problem of the scholarly tendency to privilege one "authentic" example of the author's "novel" is visible in the canonization history and critical discussion surrounding the author's 1853 and 1864 works.

2. By using the term "trade," I mean to suggest the readers and accessibility of a text, not a judgment of taste. Compared to the publications of university presses, the two collections edited by Gates (published by Vintage and selling for $16) and Andrews (published by the New American Library and selling for $6.99) are widely available in bookstores with sections of African-American literature and, because of their prices, are attractive to teachers and students in survey courses in American literature.

3. This technique is of course not unique to Brown; rather, he borrows from the slave narrative form here, which typically includes authenticating documentation along with the narrative of the life of the speaker. What is notable to those with an interest in cultural history is that this strategy for achieving textual authority makes its way into the African-American novel with Brown.

4. It might come as no surprise, moreover, that a cursory glance at recent critical analyses of Brown's novels finds the majority of them to center on *Clotel* (1853) rather than *Clotelle* (1864). See, for example, Peter A. Dorsey, "De-authorizing Slavery: Realism in Stowe's *Uncle Tom's Cabin* and Brown's *Clotel*" (*ESQ* 41, no. 4 [1995]: 256–288); Robert S. Levine, "'Whiskey, Blacking, and All': Temperance and Race in William Wells Brown's *Clotel*," in *The Serpent in the Cup: Temperance in American Literature*, ed. David S. Reynolds and Debra J. Rosenthal (Amherst: University of Massachusetts Press, 1997), 93–114; Ashis Sengupta, "William Wells Brown's *Clotel:* A Critique of Slave Life in America," in *Indian Views on American Literature*, ed. A. A. Mutalik-Desai (New Delhi: Prestige, 1998), 117–125; Adeleke Adeeko, "Signatures of Blood in William Wells Brown's *Clotel*," *Nineteenth-Century Contexts* 21, no. 1 (1999): 115–134; R. J. Ellis, "Body Politics and the Body Politic in William Wells Brown's *Clotel* and Harriet Wilson's *Our Nig*," in *Soft Canons: American Women Writers and Masculine Tradition*, ed. Karen L. Kilcup (Iowa City: University of Iowa Press, 1999), 99–122; Lee Schweninger, "Brown's *Clotel* and the Historicity of the Anecdote," *MELUS* 24, no. 1 (1999): 21–36; and Ryan Simmons, "Naming Names: *Clotel* and Behind the Scenes," *CLA Journal* 43, no. 1 (1999): 19–37.

Works Cited

Adeeko, Adeleke. "Signatures of Blood in William Wells Brown's *Clotel*." *Nineteenth-Century Contexts* 21, no. 1 (1999): 115–134.
Andrews, William H. "Mark Twain, William Wells Brown, and the Problem of

Authority in New South Writing." In *Southern Literature and Literary Theory*, edited by Jefferson Humphries, 1–21. Athens: University of Georgia Press, 1990.

———, ed. *Three Classic African-American Novels*. New York: Mentor, 1990.

Brown, William Wells. *Clotel; or, The President's Daughter*. 1853. Reprint, New York: Carol Publishing Group, 1989.

———. *Clotelle: A Tale of the Southern States*. 1864. Reprint, edited by Maxwell Whiteman. Philadelphia: Albert Saifer, 1955.

Dorsey, Peter A. "De-authorizing Slavery: Realism in Stowe's *Uncle Tom's Cabin* and Brown's *Clotel*." *ESQ* 41, no. 4 (1995): 256–288.

Douglass, Frederick. *Narrative of the Life of Frederick Douglass, an American Slave, Written by Himself*. Edited by David W. Blight. Boston: Bedford, 1993.

Ellis, R. J. "Body Politics and the Body Politic in William Wells Brown's *Clotel* and Harriet Wilson's *Our Nig*." In *Soft Canons: American Women Writers and Masculine Tradition*, ed. Karen L. Kilcup, 99–122. Iowa City: University of Iowa Press, 1999.

Ellison, Curtis W., and E. W. Metcalf, Jr. *William Wells Brown and Martin R. Delany: A Reference Guide*. Boston: G. K. Hall, 1978.

Gates, Henry Louis, Jr., ed. *Three Classic African-American Novels*. New York: Vintage, 1990.

Heermance, J. Noel. *William Wells Brown and Clotelle: A Portrait of the Artist in the First Negro Novel*. [Hamden, Conn.]: Archon, 1969.

Levine, Robert S. "'Whiskey, Blacking, and All': Temperance and Race in William Wells Brown's *Clotel*." In *The Serpent in the Cup: Temperance in American Literature*, ed. David S. Reynolds and Debra J. Rosenthal, 93–114. Amherst: University of Massachusetts Press, 1997.

Lewis, Richard O. "Literary Conventions in the Novels of William Wells Brown." *CLA Journal* 29 (1985): 129–156.

McPherson, James M. *The Struggle for Equality: Abolitionists and the Negro in the Civil War and Reconstruction*. Princeton: Princeton University Press, 1964.

Mitchell, Angelyn. "Her Side of His Story: A Feminist Analysis of Two Nineteenth-Century Antebellum Novels—William Wells Brown's *Clotel* and Harriet E. Wilson's *Our Nig*." *American Literary Realism, 1870–1910* 24, no. 3 (1992): 7–21.

Schweninger, Lee. "Brown's *Clotel* and the Historicity of the Anecdote." *MELUS* 24, no. 1 (1999): 21–36.

Sengupta, Ashis. "William Wells Brown's *Clotel*: A Critique of Slave Life in America." In *Indian Views on American Literature*, ed. A. A. Mutalik-Desai, 117–125. New Delhi: Prestige, 1998.

Simmons, Ryan. "Naming Names: *Clotel* and Behind the Scenes." *CLA Journal* 43, no. 1 (1999): 19–37.

Yarborough, Richard. "Race, Violence, and Manhood: The Masculine Ideal in Frederick Douglass's 'The Heroic Slave.'" In *Frederick Douglass: New Liter-*

ary and Historical Essays, edited by Eric J. Sundquist, 166–188. Cambridge: Cambridge University Press, 1990.

Yellin, Jean Fagan. "William Wells Brown." In *The Intricate Knot: Black Figures in American Literature, 1776–1863*, 154–182. New York: New York University Press, 1972.

Fifteen

Mark Twain and the Multicultural Imagination

Joe B. Fulton

In the September 1882 issue of *The Century*, William Dean Howells identified the "ethical intelligence" of Mark Twain's writing in his review of "The Facts Concerning the Recent Carnival of Crime in Connecticut" (Howells 782). Since that time, critics have generally, if tacitly, accepted the idea that questions of ethics are integral to Twain's practice of realism. Despite what Wayne Booth characterizes as "floods of moral criticism" on Twain (Booth 459), however, a few critics, including Gladys Bellamy, have suggested the intimate connections between "the aesthetic inclination which leads him to create and the ethical inclination which leads him to teach" (Bellamy 155). For the most part, contemporary critics have been reluctant to discuss the specific ethical elements that contribute to Twain's importance as a writer.

Recently, Michael Davitt Bell, in *The Problem of American Realism*, has even suggested that Twain, because he failed to meet the moralistic standards of his friend Howells, was no realist at all. I think, however, that the critical problem with American realism generally and with Twain in particular is one of approach. The classic definitions of realism offered by Howells, Auerbach, and Wellek all include some variation of the belief that realism engages primarily external components of the world. Wellek, for example, defines realism as the "objective representation of contemporary social reality" (Wellek 240–241).

Reprinted from *Mark Twain's Ethical Realism: The Aesthetics of Race, Class, and Gender*, by Joe B. Fulton, by permission of the University of Missouri Press. Copyright 1997 by the Curators of the University of Missouri.

Twain, however, offered a divergent definition. He sensed that realistic writing was implicated not just in the aesthetic surface, but in a normally inaccessible inner life. Consider his estimation of his friend and fellow realist Howells, as outlined in a letter dated January 21, 1879:

> And only you see people & their ways & their insides & outsides as they are, & make them talk as they do talk. I think you are the very greatest artist in these tremendous mysteries that ever lived. There doesn't seem to be anything that can be concealed from your awful all-seeing eye. It must be a cheerful thing for one to live with you & be aware that you are going up & down in him like another conscience all the time. (Twain, *Twain-Howells Letters*, 1:245)

Twain portrays the author as one engaged in ascertaining the way a person sounds and appears from the outside, but also as one who breaks through this exterior to experience the interior. Thus, one sees people "as they are" only in the unity of their inner and outer lives. Moreover, the inside is implicated in the outside, and Twain marries the two aspects into an aesthetic unity of accurate portrayal. For the realist agenda, this means that the "outsideness" or otherness of the hero or heroine—typically reflected in the use of dialect, whereby characters achieve authentic voices—is the result of an "insideness" by which the author comprehends that otherness.

This recalls Twain's attitude in his review "What Paul Bourget Thinks of Us," where he argues that "A foreigner can photograph the exteriors of a nation, but I think that that is as far as he can get. I think that no foreigner can report its interior—its soul, its life, its speech, its thought" (Twain, "What Paul Bourget," 152). Once again, Twain defines realism as concerning more than the outside, which one might photograph, and asserts that it involves the inside as well. Twain then declares that one apprehends the interior by "absorption; years and years of intercourse with the life concerned; of living it" (152). Twain's desire to "be authentic" reflects the attempt to gain a privileged intrusion into the other's life, to live that life from the inside. That the author, in Twain's letter to Howells, becomes "like another conscience" explicitly links the aesthetic completion of the work of art with the ethical interaction of author and character.

For Mark Twain, then, the composing process is guided by what I would call a "multicultural imagination." Twain experienced the act of writing as an act of what the Russian philosopher Mikhail Bakhtin terms *vzhivanie* or "living into" the other person. Bakhtin conceives of authorship as an imaginative switching of places with another person, a heightened empathy: "I must empathize or project myself into this other human being, see his world axiologically from within him as he sees this world; I must put myself in his place" (Bakhtin, "Author and Hero," 25). "Insideness," akin to "walking a mile in the other's shoes," leads to a greater understanding of the other person that is reflected in realistic characters.

In Twain's case, his usual subjects were those on the other side of the race or class line, those separated by convention and ideology. Reflecting in his autobiography on his early boyhood, Twain noted that the local black children were "comrades and yet not comrades; color and condition interposed a subtle line which both parties were conscious of and which rendered complete fusion impossible" (Twain, *Autobiography,* 6). Class lines produced similar restrictions, as they "were quite clearly drawn" (28). Twain fought these restrictions, and the desire for "complete fusion" where lines of difference are "clearly drawn" is a defining characteristic of his fiction. Fusion and difference engage in a tug of war that at times unifies Twain's writing, and at times threatens to pull it apart. But always his fiction builds on this background to posit an ethics of the other, where the other's "otherness" is essential to the identity of the "I." Daniel Borus describes the realists' attempting "the construction of a common culture in which all classes could participate" (Borus 4). Twain imagines such a society by working toward the construction—for himself, and through him for his readers—of an individual "multicultural imagination" in which all races and classes play a role. As the subsequent discussion will reveal, this does not mean that, as Amy Kaplan argues in her analysis of American realism, "social difference can be ultimately effaced by a vision of a common humanity" (Kaplan 21). Rather, common humanity is revealed by a need for what is different about the other.

Twain models within his fiction the process whereby the multicultural imagination is created. Critics usually ascribe the presence of doubled and switched characters in his writing to psychological fractures, and ultimately to what James Cox has called "the primal creative act of inventing Mark Twain" (Cox 21). Perhaps, though, in his use of doubles, Twain looks outward (and backward) as well as inward. For in each use of doubles, the switch of characters inscribes in the text society's fear of becoming the other, a fear Twain experienced in his childhood: one senses the dread of the lower class in *The Prince and the Pauper,* and the even greater dread of blacks and miscegenation in *Pudd'nhead Wilson.* Doubles often signify the expunging of the other from consciousness, individually and socially. In Stevenson's *Dr. Jekyll and Mr. Hyde,* for example, Hyde represents on some level the Victo-

rian era's attempted repression of man's more animalistic qualities.
Twain similarly uses doubles to confront consciousness (and conscience)
with the elements it has rejected. The use of doubles reflects Twain's
imaginative reach to embrace those whom genteel society has shunted
off to the "other" side of race and class lines. Susan Gillman's belief
that "Mark Twain presses his investigations of twinness to the point
where coherent individual identity collapses" speaks directly to this issue (Gillman 1). For the doubles look inward to the creation of identity,
but are also implicated in Twain's youth, and look outward to society at
large. Bakhtin maintains that a unitary identity does not exist, and that
one constructs identity throughout life by the constant accretion of elements "transgredient" to consciousness. "Transgredient," as Todorov
explains, refers to "ingredients" of consciousness "that are external to
it, but nonetheless absolutely necessary for its completion" (Todorov
95). The doubles in Twain's fiction illustrate Bakhtin's claim that a
"person has no internal sovereign territory. . . . looking inside himself,
he looks into the eyes of another" (Bakhtin, *Problems*, 287).

Twain uses doubles to forge individual and social multicultural identities in a society where "color and condition" work against "complete
fusion." While Bakhtin conceives of *vzhivanie* as an imaginative switch,
Twain employs actual switches to throw characters into the unique,
particularized zone of the other. The ethical intelligence Twain displays
in this case adumbrates the changes that each undergoes as he lives
out the life of the other. In *The American Claimant* (1892), Lord Berkeley adopts the disguise of the cowboy desperado "one-armed Pete" in
America but later returns to his post in England only after the "condition of his mind" is "reorganized" through interaction with all sorts of
people (Twain, *American Claimant*, 124).

One can see in this central, recurring pattern evidence of William
Lecky's *History of European Morals*, a book Twain adopted into his phi-
losophy after first reading it in 1874 (Paine 1:510–511). From Lecky,
Twain gleans his central idea that environment determines character. In
What Is Man? for example, Twain illustrates his view:

I mean all the outside influences. There are a million of them.
From the cradle to the grave, during all his waking hours, the human being is under training. In the very first rank of his trainers
stands association. It is his human environment which influences
his mind and his feelings, furnishes him his ideals, and sets him
on his road and keeps him in it. . . . He is a chameleon; by a law of
his nature he takes the color of his place of resort. (Twain, *What
Is Man?* 161)

This "human environment" Twain speaks of consists of the others with whom one interacts, the myriad voices with which one connects. If ethical or unethical behavior is a function of one's environment, it follows that by changing this linguistic milieu one changes one's outlook, even one's imagination, that is, the ways in which one habitually conceives of things. Twain tests his hypothesis most obviously in *Pudd'nhead Wilson*. In this book, Twain switches black and white infants to see if man truly is a "chameleon" who "takes the color of his place of resort."

In *Pudd'nhead Wilson*, Twain's switched characters become "like another conscience" for each other, and they each gain a privileged intrusion into the other's life that reveals itself in altered language and altered ethics. Roxy, mother of the legally black but outwardly white Valet de Chambre, fears he will be sold "down river" and switches him with the master's child, Thomas á Beckett Driscoll. The two appear so similar that no one, not even Tom's father, can tell the difference between them. More importantly, the two boys cannot tell the difference, and so as they grow up each becomes the "racial other" he thinks himself to be, thus destroying the theoretical foundation for a racism that espouses a blood-based origin of cultural condition. Twain compounds the irony of the fable by having the real Tom, hereafter called Chambers, develop a sound heart while the false Tom develops a deformed conscience and habitually steals from the townspeople. Although Roxy blames Tom's duplicity on the one-thirty-second part "nigger" in his blood, his bad behavior seems due to his "training" as the scion of a proud First Family of Virginia (FFV).

The primary act of the book, Roxy's switch of the two infants, comes about largely because of a sermon she heard on free grace. Roxy's sermon is given voice by a woman willing and able to usurp, as F. R. Leavis phrases it, "the prerogative of the predestinating Deity" (Leavis 28).

> Now I's got it; now I 'member. It was dat ole nigger preacher dat tole it, de time he come over here fum Illinois en preached in de nigger church. He said dey ain't nobody kin save his own self— can't do it by faith, can't do it by works, can't do it no way at all. Free grace is de on'y way, en dat don't come fum nobody but jis de Lord; en He kin give it to anybody He please, saint or sinner—He do't k'yer. He do jis' as He's a mineter. He s'lect out anybody dat suit Him, en put another one in his place, en make de fust one happy forever en leave t'other one to burn wid Satan. (*Pudd'nhead Wilson* 15)

Critics have generally looked at how Roxy justifies the switch by arguing, as the passage continues, that white folks have done the same, not just historically in England by switching children, but also by usurping God's power alternately to confer grace or to damn. Roxy, as Robert Rowlette observes, responds directly to Percy Driscoll's threat to sell his slaves down South, and imitates his God-like power (Rowlette 92–93). Her language and her act thus subvert the Southern apologists' use of religion to justify slavery; or, if one views the book as Eric Sundquist does, Roxy's sermon critiques the Reconstruction era's increasing subjection of blacks.

Ironically, Roxy's use of the doctrine of free grace to justify the switch is literally a grace that sets one man free, even while enslaving another; but I believe Twain substitutes "love thy neighbor" for the doctrine of predestination. Although Roxy really does nothing to subvert the institution of slavery or the doctrine of predestination, as even her rewording of the argument that justified the initial theft merely elevates her own son to the status of master, the central lesson of the sermon is that "dey ain't nobody kin save his own self—can't do it by faith, can't do it by works, can't do it no way at all." In other words, Tom and Chambers cannot do anything to save themselves and, as children, depend upon Roxy for their very lives. Roxy later offers her own freedom to pay her son's debts, implicitly presenting a variation on her idea of free grace.

> Ain't you my chile? En does you know anything dat a mother won't do for her chile? Dey ain't nothin' a white mother won't do for her chile. Who made 'em so? De Lord done it. En who made de niggers? De Lord made 'em. In de inside, mothers is all de same. De good Lord he made 'em so. I's gwyne to be sole into slavery, en in a year you's gwyne to buy yo' ole mammy free again. (*Pudd'nhead Wilson* 80)

Here, Roxy becomes a kind of black female Christ who redeems and ransoms her child with her own life, again saving him by switching him, this time with herself as object as well as instigator of the exchange. In both speeches, Twain poses the helpless situation of the children as the situation of humanity, and he offers in this satire of miscegenation and American racial attitudes the very real message that each person, whether black or white, depends upon the other person for life, liberty, and even spiritual salvation.

And each person depends upon the other for identity. Mark Coburn discusses the issue of training in the novel and how training relates to the tyranny of communal opinion. Coburn observes that Twain "frequently presents 'the town' as if it were a single persona" (Coburn 21). More to the point, the inhabitants themselves conceive of identity as a univocal creation flowing from this "single persona." After Wilson tells his "half-a-dog" joke, for example, society brands him "Pudd'nhead" and he can do nothing to change his identity. Wilson's "half-a-dog joke" provokes a serious question: who owns identity? Twain similarly associates identity with ownership when discussing the "well fed, well petted, and properly revered cat" as necessary to "prove title" (*Pudd'nhead Wilson* 3). Proving title means, on its most basic level, proving one's identity, and even the legalistic flavor of the phrase highlights the way identity in this book involves the ownership of something or someone outside of the self. Such ownership relates, ultimately, to the holding of slaves. But if social identity in *Pudd'nhead Wilson* is a function of ownership—one either owns or is owned—doesn't this fact undermine the notion of a discrete selfhood? While the ultimate other in this story is society itself, which has the power to name people, there are many "others" whose voices are seldom heard, but who figure into the creation of identity just the same. While society defines blacks as slaves, and refuses to recognize their family names, the attempt to so define blacks acknowledges their voice even as that voice is suppressed. Slavery represents the extreme case of society bestowing selfhood, and so Roxy's subversion of racist ideology also subverts society's thinking about identity. If identity, perhaps even consciousness, reflects monologic society, what happens when a discordant voice intervenes? Although a slave and therefore legally a non-person, Roxy manipulates the language of the sermon into a subversion of the racist text that has been used to confer identity on both white and black in Dawson's Landing.

Roxy's sermon, then, is more subversive in theory than in actuality, yet it does provide an object lesson in the dialogic way identity is created, a creation at variance with the monologic identity society at large insists on. Roxy's version of the Illinois preacher's sermon depends on others in the sense that she responds to the already spoken words of both whites and blacks. Her sermon is, in Bakhtin's terms, "double-voiced," as she adopts the original sermon of the black preacher but expands the text to include her own situation (Bakhtin, *Problems*, 195). In effect, she imagines delivering her version of the sermon to a white audience just as, in a sense, Southern justifications of slavery were delivered not only to a white Northern audience, but also to a black audience that was the real, if unspoken, target of Southerners' guilt. Roxy, too, feels the need to justify the switch, not to her black brethren, but to the whites at the receiving end of her sermon. She anticipates the arguments of a white inhabitant of Dawson's Landing, arguing, in effect, "because you white folks done it, I can do it, too."

Roxy's sermon lifts off the page as much of *Pudd'nhead Wilson* does not, and bridges the ethical concerns of the novel and its often inadequate characterization. Although A. L. Nielsen has criticized, as have some others, the "white man's blackface speech" in the book (Nielsen 23), it seems to me he undervalues Twain's achievement of a voice that is both black and white. Twain took care to distinguish Roxy's dialect from the language of whites and blacks, and he situates her in liminal regions, socially and dialectally. For example, Twain edited the manuscript so that Roxy uses "myself" instead of "myseff" or "sef" (see Sidney Berger's discussion of the text in *Pudd'nhead Wilson*, 180). Twain's other major black dialectal creations are Jim in *Adventures of Huckleberry Finn* and Aunt Rachel in "A True Story." Both use "sef," as in Jim's powerful statement "Yes—en I's rich now, come to look at it. I owns mysef, en I's wuth eight hund'd dollars" (*Huckleberry Finn* 57). As in his previous works, Twain's realistic fiction here depends upon both an "outsideness" and an "insideness"; to record dialect he needs to be aware of the difference between his own and others' speech, but he also needs to get inside the other character to accurately reproduce that person's speech. If anything, Roxy's speech is really a white man's black woman's whiteface speech, as Roxy colors her sermon to justify her actions to a white audience. Perhaps, as Shelley Fishkin says of Jim, Roxy is "an eclectic amalgam of authentic black voices, and white caricatures of them" (Fishkin 92), while at the same time she is composed of authentic white voices and black caricatures of them. In short, Roxy's words illustrate the type of grace her sermon advocates; her dialogic response to the other's word depends upon an imaginative switch with the other person, an "insideness" that offers the newly dialogized word to the other as a recognition of the role the other plays in the formation of identity, an act akin to the bestowal of grace. Even Roxy's authentic language evidences a shared otherness that affirms, "ain't nobody kin save his own self."

Roxy, in her belief that people are mutually interdependent, proffers an ethics aptly suited to a multicultural society and so explains the conundrum of sameness and otherness. Even in their curious repletion, each of the inhabitants of Dawson's Landing is demonstrably incomplete, and Twain pairs characters in ways that suggest possibilities for consummation: Judge Driscoll is childless, for example, while his nephew Tom Driscoll has no father (in several respects), and the Italian twins are so interdependent they still bear the traces of their original identity as Siamese twins. Roxy and Tom, too, provide in their mixed white and black blood a metaphor for the complementarity of otherness in multicultural society; the white and black blood cannot be separated and leave a complete individual any more than Pudd'nhead Wilson could kill half a dog without killing the whole dog.

Twain structures this story of changelings and miscegenation, then, around the positive message of Roxy's secondhand sermon and the negative example of the switch itself. The effect on Chambers is perhaps the most obvious, as he acquires black dialect and manners. But just as pronounced is the effect on Tom, who acquires speech typical of the FFV. Roxy slaps and addresses Chambers "with severity" while she gives Tom only a "light pat" and speaks to him "humbly" (*Pudd'nhead Wilson* 15–16). David Sewell observes that Roxy's language and behavior create the "forms of speech they employ: the false Tom, addressed with submission, learns to be peremptory, while the new Valet de Chambre is broken and harnessed to the language of reverence" (Sewell 121). Like the prince and the pauper, these characters enter the unique linguistic arena of the other. Tom finds himself in a situation very like Tom Canty's as he is shuffled into a position of authority and almost absolute power. Like Tom Canty, Tom Driscoll acquires the absolute language task, and, if anything, he becomes too fluent in its use:

> When he got to be old enough to begin to toddle about, and say broken words and get an idea of what his hands were for, he was a more consummate pest than ever. Roxy got no rest while he was awake. He would call for anything and everything he saw, simply saying "Awnt it!" (want it), which was a command. When it was brought he said, in a frenzy, and motioning it away with his hands, "Don't awnt it! don't awnt it! . . ." (*Pudd'nhead Wilson* 18)

One clearly sees the influence of Lecky in this passage, as in the book as a whole. Wilson's calendar entry, "Training is everything. The peach was once a bitter almond; cauliflower is nothing but cabbage with a college education" (23), even mimics some of Hank Morgan's Lecky-influenced comments from *Connecticut Yankee*. By the light pats and the humble language directed toward him, Tom is trained to become white, and he bears out, in nearly literal terms, Twain's assertion in *What is Man?* that man "is a chameleon" and "takes the color of his place of resort" (161). The result is an "imitation white" whose will to own extends well beyond simple objects to the owning of other humans. This scene illustrates in specific detail the debt identity owes to the words spoken by others, as Tom and Chambers serve as targets for the self-forming language of others. In addition to illustrating that blackness and whiteness—apart from and sometimes including visually discernible color differences—are *socially* determined, the training that occurs

in these formative stages illustrates, in Althusserian terms, the way society reproduces its ideology.

A. L. Nielsen holds that, since Tom's training "comes entirely from
Roxy," he should not speak with the "'standard' Southern mode," but
with his mother's dialect (Nielsen 23). The "training" they receive is
more complex than that, however. In fact, Tom and Chambers both
speak languages that, like the racist attitudes they internalize and ultimately direct against themselves, result from many words and many
people. As I have argued, Roxy does alter her language as she addresses
the two children, and in this, she is herself a microcosm of society, with
her words forming the very words the children inevitably speak; even
linguistically they adhere to the expectations that society directs toward
them. It is no surprise when Twain tells the reader that Tom preferred
the tongs "above all other things," as they are a fitting symbol for the
acquisitive young man whose will to own and control exceeds his reach
(*Pudd'nhead Wilson* 18). In this same paragraph, Twain provides a litany
of Tom's expressive language, which one might call his "tong-tongue":
"Like it!", "Awnt it!", "Hab it!", "Take it!" Even as it is refined, Tom's
habitual language continues to express these selfsame attitudes.

While Chambers acquires the language of humility in much the same
way Edward does in his cross-country peregrinations with Miles Hen-
don, here the switch has no positive effect, just as Tom's acquisition of
absolute language has no positive effect: The characters remain mono-
lingual instead of becoming bilingual, psychologically monocultural instead of multicultural. Once Roxy informs Tom of the initial switch,
and he learns that he is not "marse Tom" but "Chambers," one might
expect him to awaken to a sense of responsibility toward the other, the
slaves for whom he is master. And dialogue does begin to take place as
Tom considers the implications of blackness and whiteness.

> Why were niggers and whites made? What crime did the uncreated
> first nigger commit that the curse of birth was decreed for him?
> And why is this awful difference made between white and black? . . .
> How hard the nigger's fate seems, this morning!—yet until last
> night such a thought never entered my head. (44)

Although Tom still looks at blackness from the outside, i.e., as a
"curse," his epiphany is stunning and one certainly expects that the
switch might produce for Tom an ethical relation with the racial other.
At this point, Tom realizes the "awful difference" between black and
white, the same "abyss" Roxy had observed earlier. In much the same
way that Edward in *The Prince and the Pauper* awakens to principles of
ethics, one expects Tom to begin behaving ethically. Instead, Tom con-

tinues to thieve and issue orders, with the additional irony that Roxy attributes his actions to his black blood. On the contrary, Tom's behavior radiates from his training, and he was trained as a white person. In one sense, his stealing from the town's citizens is a vengeful retribution on a smaller scale for the body-snatching perpetrated by the white citizens who hold slaves. In another sense, Tom's stealing illustrates the FFV principle of identity-through-ownership.

Roxy, ironically, forces Tom to acknowledge the "nigger" in him and change his outlook by changing his language:

> "Dah's one thing you's got to stop, Vallet de Chambers. You can't call me Roxy, same as if you was my equal. Chillen don't speak to dey mamies like dat. You'll call me Ma or mammy, dat's what you'll call me—leastways when dey ain't nobody aroun'. Say it!" (42)

Evan Carton has observed that "naming is the method by which [society] protects and preserves itself" (Carton 83), and here Roxy's attempt to name herself parallels society's naming of white and black. For these particular words, "Ma" and "Mammy," do not simply signify "Mother." Forcing Tom to say "Mammy" is tantamount to forcing him to recognize his own black identity—or at least the contribution of blackness to his identity—even as he is turned back into a little boy dominated by a powerful woman.

Tom briefly looks at things from the other's point of view, but when he realizes that the other whose view he looks through resides within his own identity, and indeed his own body, he beats a hasty retreat into his early training and former "manner of speech" (*Pudd'nhead Wilson* 45). Confronting this black blood, Tom in effect reverts to infancy, as if crying out "Don't awnt it! don't awnt it!" Instead of acknowledging his ethical responsibility, Tom evades it and, finding himself alienated both from a multicultural imagination and from the monoculturalism of the FFV code, he embarks on his own carnival of crime. This one-man crime wave accompanies Tom's discovery of a protean identity beholden to no one. This is no surprise, because Tom rejects a dialogic conscience due to its association with the other's ability to confer identity. Thus freed, Tom alternately dresses as a young white girl, a young black servant, and an old black woman. These impersonations invert the rules of FFV society, for as Tom grows more insistent in his violation of the race, class, and gender boundaries imposed by society, he becomes more powerful; as he feels the full force of the social definition of black as powerless, of black as woman, he readily adopts those identities, making of them a dynamic power.

When Tom engages in raids on the white townspeople, he might remind us of Frederick Douglass standing up to Covey, or even of Wright's Bigger Thomas, who gains black identity by revenging himself on whites. But Tom's protean identity depends upon a non-recognition by others and an evasion of the power of any group to confer identity. Eschewing insideness, Tom embraces his unitary otherness, but knowledge of one's otherness depends upon an other, and by deciding that no one defines him, Tom becomes no one at all. He is not trying to be someone he's not, but rather trying to be someone who *is* not. In disguising himself to evade his identity and his responsibility, Tom virtually ceases to exist; paraphrasing Roxy, one might suggest, then, that "ain't nobody kin *define* his own self." The other's ability to confer identity, while often pernicious, is felt most awfully in its absence. Like the man in "The Facts Concerning the Recent Carnival of Crime in Connecticut," Tom escapes the purgatory of a dogmatic philosophy to revel in the hell of a relativistic one.

Tom's identity crisis reflects a broader societal identity crisis. His refusal to acknowledge the black blood within himself parallels society's refusal to acknowledge its own black blood—even in the more general form of the contributions of blacks to social and individual identities. Black blood races through all veins of society and through the minds of its citizens. The one-sixteenth or one-thirty-second part of black blood is of minor importance, but the significance society imputes to it is monumental: society's insistence that the boundary between black and white is absolute proves unavailing because attempts to expunge the racial other from consciousness (individual and national) etch the racial other obsessively into consciousness.

The switch in *Pudd'nhead Wilson* looks toward a multicultural society in which a black and white interaction creates identity. In *What Is Man?* Twain contends that one "has only to change his habitat—his associations" to alter consciousness (Twain, *What Is Man?* 163). Twain imagines a personality that would embrace, as he hoped society would, a multicultural ethic. Twain's belief that environment determines and necessarily limits character, in the context of his search for a multicultural ethos, gives rise to his use of doubled or switched characters from different races and classes. For by switching characters and causing them to change environments, Twain gives them the opportunity to achieve an insideness that, if it does not offer a "complete fusion," holds the possibility that each will become "like another conscience" for the other.

It takes no great stretch of the imagination to see Twain reaching out for a fusion that eluded him in childhood, a crossing of race and class boundaries. When Twain's characters switch with each other, they enter the unique, particularized void (linguistic and ethical) created by the other's absence. They enter the context of the other, and experience the life of the other virtually from inside the other's skin. This is Twain's primary aesthetic concern, and one reason he admired Howells's artistry in becoming "like another conscience" inside of his characters. Perpetrating these switches, Twain practices dialogic writing by placing characters of different races and classes with distinct dialects and autonomous voices into situations in which they must interact. In doing so, the characters themselves become "like another conscience" inside each other, and create, to a sometimes surprising degree, consciousness itself. Twain's realism encompasses both the ethical interaction of these voices and the aesthetic attempt to make them "talk as they do talk." By his use of the switch technique, Twain rejects society's attempt to physically segregate, but just as important, he opposes society's attempt to psychologically segregate. As characters are switched, they lead the life of the other, and otherness forms their character. Twain thus not only imagined a truly multicultural society, one in which individual multicultural identities flourish, he also created a multicultural literature to speed its coming.

Bibliography

Bakhtin, Mikhail. "Author and Hero in Aesthetic Activity." In *Art and Answerability: Early Philosophical Essays*, translated by Vadim Liapunov, 4–256. Austin: University of Texas Press, 1990.

———. *Problems of Dostoevsky's Poetics*. Translated by Caryl Emerson. Minneapolis: University of Minnesota Press, 1984.

Bell, Michael Devitt. *The Problem of American Realism: Studies in the Cultural History of a Literary Idea*. Chicago: University of Chicago Press, 1993.

Bellamy, Gladys Carmen. *Mark Twain as a Literary Artist*. Norman: University of Oklahoma Press, 1950.

Booth, Wayne C. *The Company We Keep: An Ethics of Fiction*. Berkeley: University of California Press, 1988.

Borus, Daniel. *Writing Realism: Howells, James, and Norris in the Mass Market*. Chapel Hill: University of North Carolina Press, 1989.

Carton, Evan. "*Pudd'nhead Wilson* and the Fiction of Law and Custom." In *American Realism: New Essays*, ed. Eric Sundquist, 82–94. Baltimore: Johns Hopkins University Press, 1982.

Coburn, Mark D. "'Training Is Everything': Communal Opinion and the Individual in *Pudd'nhead Wilson*." *Modern Language Quarterly* 30 (1970): 209–219.

Cox, James M. *Mark Twain: The Fate of Humor*. Princeton: Princeton University Press, 1966.

Fishkin, Shelley Fisher. *Was Huck Black? Mark Twain and African-American Voices*. New York: Oxford University Press, 1993.

Gillman, Susan. *Dark Twins: Imposture and Identity in Mark Twain's America*. Chicago: University of Chicago Press, 1989.

Howells, William Dean. "Mark Twain." *The Century* 24 (September 1882): 780–783.

Kaplan, Amy. *The Social Construction of American Realism*. Chicago: University of Chicago Press, 1988.

Leavis, F. R. Introduction to *Pudd'nhead Wilson*, by Mark Twain. New York: Grove Press, 1955.

Nielsen, A. L. "Mark Twain's *Pudd'nhead Wilson* and the Novel of the Tragic Mulatto." *Greyfriar* 26 (1985): 14–30.

Paine, Albert Bigelow. *Mark Twain: A Biography*. 4 vols. New York: Gabriel Wells, 1923.

Rowlette, Robert. *Mark Twain's* Pudd'nhead Wilson: *The Development-Design*. Bowling Green, Ohio: Bowling Green University Popular Press, 1971.

Sewell, David. *Mark Twain's Languages: Discourse, Dialogue, and Linguistic Variety*. Berkeley: University of California Press, 1987.

Sundquist, Eric J. "Mark Twain and Homer Plessy." *Representations* 24 (1988): 102–128.

Todorov, Tzvetan. *Mikhail Bakhtin: The Dialogical Principle*. Translated by Wlad Godzich. Manchester: Manchester University Press, 1984.

Twain, Mark. *Adventures of Huckleberry Finn*. Edited by Walter Blair and Victor Fischer. Berkeley and Los Angeles: University of California Press, 1988.

———. *The American Claimant*. New York: Gabriel Wells, 1923.

———. *The Autobiography of Mark Twain*. Edited by Charles Nider. 1959. Reprint, New York: Harper Perennial, 1990.

———. *Mark Twain-Howells Letters: The Correspondence of Samuel L. Clemens and William Dean Howells, 1872–1910*. Edited by Henry Nash Smith and William M. Gibson. 2 vols. Cambridge: Harvard University Press, 1960.

———. *The Prince and the Pauper*. Edited by Victor Fischer and Lin Salamo. Berkeley: University of California Press, 1979.

———. *Pudd'nhead Wilson and Those Extraordinary Twins*. Edited and with a textual introduction by Sidney Berger. New York: Norton, 1980.

———. *What Is Man? and Other Philosophical Writings*. Edited by Paul Baender. Berkeley: University of California Press, 1973.

———. "What Paul Bourget Thinks of Us." In *Literary Essays*, 148–170. New York: Gabriel Wells, 1923.

Wellek, Rene. *Concepts of Criticism*. Edited by Stephen G. Nichols. New Haven: Yale University Press, 1963.

Contributors

Susan Alves currently serves as the Curriculum Coordinator for the English Department at Rockport (Mass.) High School. She is a contributor to and co-editor (with Aleta Cane) of *The Only Efficient Instrument: American Women Writers and the Periodical* (forthcoming).

Barbara J. Ballard is Associate Professor of History at Marymount Manhattan College. She is co-author (with Marcus C. Bruce) of *Debating the Negro: Booker T. Washington, W. E. B. Du Bois, and the Twentieth Century* (forthcoming).

Jeannine DeLombard is Assistant Professor of English at the University of Toronto. She is currently at work on a manuscript titled *"At the Bar of Public Opinion": Black Testimony and White Advocacy in Antebellum Literary Abolitionism*, which examines the use of legal rhetoric in the anti-slavery movement and in antebellum print culture.

Juniper Ellis is Assistant Professor of English at Loyola College in Maryland, where she teaches U.S. literature and world literatures in English, including Maori and South Pacific writing. She is currently Fulbright lecturer in American Literature at the University of Trier, Germany. She has published articles and interviews in journals such as *Massachusetts Review, Arizona Quarterly, Ariel*, and *Journal of Commonwealth Literature*.

Joe B. Fulton is Associate Professor of English at Baylor University in Waco, Texas. He is the author of *Mark Twain's Ethical Realism: The Aesthetics of Race, Class, and Gender* (1997) and *Mark Twain in The Mar-*

gins: The Quarry Farm Marginalia and the Composition of A Connecticut Yankee in King Arthur's Court (2000).

Henry Louis Gates, Jr., is W. E. B. Du Bois Professor of the Humanities, Harvard University, Chair of Afro-American Studies, and Director of the W. E. B. Du Bois Institute for Afro-American Research. He is the author of *Wonders of the African World* (1999), editor of *The Norton Anthology of African American Literature* (1996), and co-editor of the encyclopedia *Encarta Africana* on CD-ROM by Microsoft and in book form by Basic Civitas Books under the title *Africana: The Encyclopedia of the African and African American Experience* (1999).

Richard E. Greene is the former president of St. Thomas University in Florida and Goddard College in Vermont. His research interests include the pre–Civil War era and policy issues in higher education, especially the relationship between college presidents and boards of trustees. He is the author of several articles on history and higher education.

Richard Hardack received his Ph.D. at the University of California at Berkeley, taught as a visiting professor at Haverford College, has published over twenty articles, and is currently finishing his law degree at UC Berkeley.

Julie Husband is Assistant Professor of English at the University of Northern Iowa. She has published articles on Frederick Douglass and on *The Lowell Offering,* a magazine written and edited by women mill workers in the 1840s.

Gillian Johns has been a Ford Foundation Dissertation Fellow and is Assistant Professor of English at Oberlin College. Her interests include African-American humor, rhetoric, and genre theory.

Verner D. Mitchell is Assistant Professor of English at the University of Memphis and writes on American literature and culture. He is the editor of *This Waiting for Love: Helene Johnson, Poet of the Harlem Renaissance* (2000).

Christine Palumbo-DeSimone is Assistant Professor of English at Temple University in Philadelphia. She is the author of *Sharing Secrets: Nineteenth-Century Women's Relations in the Short Story* (2000).

Janet Harrison Shannon is Associate Professor and Chair of the Department of Sociology at Davidson College. Her research interests include the formation and development of urban communities and the sociology of childhood. Her most recent article is an analysis of secrecy in the black community, based on the writings of James Baldwin. She is currently researching the Ganges, a group of Africans captured from a slave ship and indentured in Philadelphia in the 1800s.

C. James Trotman is Professor of English and founding director of the Frederick Douglass Institute at West Chester University in Pennsylvania. He teaches courses in Afro-American and American literature and is the editor of *Langston Hughes: The Man, His Art, and His Continuing Influence* (1995) and *Richard Wright: Myths and Realities* (1988).

Matthew Wilson is Associate Professor of Humanities and Writing at Pennsylvania State University at Harrisburg and has published on a range of contemporary American novelists, as well as on Charles W. Chesnutt. He has also published an edition of Chesnutt's manuscript novel *Paul Marchand, F.M.C.* (1998).

Julie Winch is Professor of History at the University of Massachusetts at Boston. She is author of *Philadelphia's Black Elite: Activism, Accommodation, and the Struggle for Autonomy, 1787–1848* (1998) and editor of Cyprian Clamorgan's *The Colored Aristocracy of St. Louis* (1999) and *"The Elite of Our People": Joseph Willson's Sketches of Black Upper-Class Life in Antebellum Philadelphia* (2000). Her biography of James Forten is scheduled for publication in 2001.

Index

257

Index

Index

263

Index

264